The Good Retirement Guide

28TH EDITION

The Good Retirement Guide

EVERYTHING YOU NEED TO KNOW ABOUT HEALTH, PROPERTY, INVESTMENT, LEISURE, WORK, PENSIONS AND TAX

Edited by Frances Kay

KoganPage

LONDON PHILADELPHIA NEW DELHI

The information contained in this book is for general guidance only and does not constitute professional advice. Users should consult with a professional adviser concerning any specific issues, and their impact on any individual or entity, before making any major financial decision.

This 28th edition published in Great Britain in 2014 by Kogan Page Limited

Kogan Page Limited
2nd Floor, 45 Gee Street
London EC1V 3RS
United Kingdom
www.koganpage.com

© Kogan Page, 2013, 2014

British Library Cataloguing in Publication Data

A CIP record for this book is available from the British Library.

ISBN   978 0 7494 7089 0
E-ISBN   978 0 7494 7090 6

Typeset by Graphicraft Limited, Hong Kong
Printed and bound in India by Replika Press Pvt Ltd

Contents

16   No one is immortal   341

Chapter One
Are you looking forward to retirement?

The trouble with retirement is that you never get a day off.

ABE LEMONS, COLLEGE BASKETBALL COACH

Did you know that retirement can be bad for your health? Apparently it carries a risk of depression and as a life-changing event can be more stressful than continuing to work. These are some of the findings of a report published last year by the London-based Institute of Economic Affairs: their think tank surveyed as many as 9,000 adults aged between 50 and 70 (**www.dailymail.co.uk/news/article-2325258**, dated 15 June 2013). Well, if you've just bought a copy of *The Good Retirement Guide* and were hoping to settle down to a nice encouraging read, you might now be thinking it's better to carry on working...

Of course it isn't true. Retirement is wonderful. It offers a wealth of opportunities we are denied while enduring our daily commute to work. Whether we are dreaming of spending time travelling, trying new hobbies or enjoying our hard-earned leisure with our nearest and dearest, it's all down to sensible planning. For those with an optimistic tendency, as long as you prepare well for a good retirement you are actually likely to live longer (**www.bbc.co.uk/news/magazine-18952037**). So how is your retirement planning coming along? If it needs a bit of help, welcome to the latest edition of *The Good Retirement Guide*: the book that contains everything you need to know about retirement. This year's publication is the 28th edition and contains advice and suggestions on planning your future – from finance, pensions, work, home and health, to leisure activities and holidays.

As the experts tell us that retirement for many can now last 30 years or longer, that's about a third of our life to enjoy after we've ceased working. So it makes a lot of sense to plan well for a good retirement.

One of the new popular words that we frequently come across today is 'enrichment'. Although it may sound like jargon, it means improving an experience, adding value, enhancing or uplifting something. There are lots of enrichment courses in schools, colleges and businesses; many organizations and agencies have adopted the word and offer 'enrichment programmes'. Now it's spreading fast to all areas of life and should certainly be applied to those who want a good retirement. If it's going to last over a quarter of a century, a decent helping of enrichment could be just what we all need. Making the most of those retirement years is a matter of individual choice. Each person's circumstances and expectations will be different, and most of us will go through more than one life stage over this period. Such life stages could include:

- *The active years* – where people have more leisure time and generally enjoy pretty good health, which means their income needs are relatively high.

- *The slow down period* – as we age, our activity level diminishes and leisure time becomes more sedentary. Perhaps we will watch travel programmes on TV rather than going on expensive and adventurous holidays to exotic locations, thus reducing income needs.

- *The later years* – as these arrive, age and health issues can catch up with us. This is when it may be necessary to obtain assistance to maintain quality of life and income needs might again increase.

Retirement is changing dramatically because of our increased life expectancy. Statistics reveal that as many as 11 million people living now will become centenarians: 3.3 million are aged 16 and under; 5.4 million are between 17 and 50; 1.4 million are 51–65, and more than 900,000 are already over 65. The International Longevity Centre describe this as 'a huge societal success', but it comes at a price. Some experts even suggest that increased longevity will generate serious intergenerational tensions, where there is a clash of needs for resources between young and old.

To help cope with the pensions crisis, the most frequently proffered advice is to save more or continue working for longer. One outstanding example of the latter is a chap aged 101 who is still working for a security firm in Essex, having clocked up 86 years of full-time work, including torpedo construction during the Second World War (**www.guardian.co.uk/society/video/2013/feb/01/100-years-old-and-still-working-video**). Perhaps to continue working even after receiving the Queen's telegram is a bit extreme, but it's wise to consider all options when it comes to retirement planning.

Work–life balance is something that is important particularly if you want to consider part-retirement for those first active years. It is a popular solution for a number of people who don't want to give up work completely or a job they enjoy. Others prefer to have a total change and take full retirement so that they can spend their time in whatever way they want. Whatever you feel is right for you, do give the matter serious thought because retirement is a major lifestyle change.

Tips for retirement planning:

- Think about what standard of living you want; how much money you think you'll need; and what sort of social life you wish to enjoy.

- If travel is important to you, make sure your budget allows for this.

- Sign up for a pre-retirement course.

- Work out your finances/pensions/investments with your professional adviser.

- Ask friends or former colleagues who have already retired for their best retirement suggestions.

- Consider where you live – is moving house necessary or desirable?

- Resist the temptation once you've retired to commit yourself to too many new things too early – wait six months to see how you feel.

- And, most important... read your copy of *The Good Retirement Guide*!

This book is vital when planning to retire as it helps you make the most of what you've got. Chapter 2 of the *Guide* deals with money in general and includes a useful budget planner. Chapter 3 is all about pensions and Chapter 4 relates to tax matters. Chapter 5 covers investments and Chapter 6 gives information on financial advisers. Chapter 7 provides tips and suggestions on how to complain and protect yourself from scams.

Chapter 8 is all about your home. Chapter 9 covers leisure. Should you be interested in becoming a mature entrepreneur, Chapter 10, Starting your own business, provides good advice and suggestions to help you. Chapter 11 has a number of suggestions for looking for paid work. Hundreds of over-65s become volunteers and Chapter 12, Voluntary work, has an abundance of suggestions you might like to consider.

Your health is the subject of Chapter 13, which most people agree is the key ingredient to a happy and fulfilling retirement. Chapter 14 is about holidays and gives details of a vast choice of travel options. If you are caring for elderly parents, Chapter 15 will be worth reading. Chapter 16 deals with the final stage of life and suggests how to plan for this.

Retirement today is full of opportunity and choice. The 2014 *Guide* is thoroughly updated to reflect recent changes to tax, pensions and opportunities. Planning for retirement can be hard – this book makes it easier.

Pre-retirement courses

Whatever age you are due to retire, taking advantage of a pre-retirement course will help you plan well for the next stage in your life. When would be the best time to attend such a course? One or two years before retirement, or earlier? Some people like to prepare for retirement in stages. It is important that some financial decisions, such as those affecting company or personal pension planning, are taken as early as possible. Others, like whether or not to move house, could wait till much later on.

Courses are designed to address the main subjects: finances, health, activity, leisure, housing and the implications and adjustments needed to be made when you retire. If your pre-retirement studies stimulate discussion with your partner and others in similar situations, it will have achieved its objective.

Listed below are some useful websites with loads of information and advice for those planning retirement:

- **Laterlife Learning** provides pre-retirement and mid-life planning courses available across the UK: **www.laterlife.com** and **www.retirement-courses.co.uk**.

- **Life Academy** is a charity that enables people to learn about managing the changes in their lives through life and retirement planning and financial education: **www.life-academy.co.uk**.

- **Millstream** helps senior people make the most of new opportunities when they leave their main employment: **www.mill-stream.com**.

- **PRIME** (The Prince's Initiative for Mature Enterprise) helps the over-50s achieve financial, social and personal fulfillment: **www.prime.org.uk.**

- **Retirement Counselling Service** (RCS) helps individuals plan their retirement with courses and seminars: **www.the-retirement-site.co.uk.**

- **Retirement Education Services** hosts one- and two-day retirement planning courses throughout the country: **www.res-ltd.net.**

- **Scottish Pre-Retirement Council** is a charity that provides pre-retirement courses: **www.sprc.org.uk.**

New focus for the retired

As the over-50s are such a large and important section of the population, there are numerous sources of advice and information on all retirement issues. Here are some useful websites:

- **Age UK** is the largest charitable organization providing information, advice, products and services to people to improve later life: **www.ageuk.org.uk.**

- **Gov.UK** is the UK government's website for all issues relating to pensions and retirement planning: **www.gov.uk.**

- **National Pensioners Convention** is the campaigning voice for UK pensioners – for dignity, financial security and fulfilment for all older people: **www.npcuk.org.**

- **Retirement Expert** offers expert advice and information on all issues related to retirement: **www.retirementexpert.co.uk.**

- **Retirement Links** provides users of the site with current, meaningful and relevant retirement- and pensions-related articles and publications: **www.retirementlinks.co.uk.**

- **UK Retirement** (part of LaterLife) focuses on planning, enjoying and making the most of retirement: **www.ukretirement.co.uk.**

An easy way to collect good advice and information about retirement and everything related to it is to visit **The 50 Plus Show.** This is Britain's biggest exhibition for the active over-50s and takes place in four locations annually across the UK: Manchester, Glasgow, Birmingham and London. See website: **www.50plusshow.com.**

Chapter Two
Money in general

> *You have to make a fundamental decision. You have to choose whether you organise your money around your life or your life around your money.*
>
> **J K ROWLING'S ACCOUNTANT, QUOTED IN THE *GUARDIAN***

Do you live to work, or work to live? Have you saved hard for your pension, paid off your mortgage and are now ready to take it easy and spend time doing just whatever you want? Now that retirement beckons (or has already arrived and is at your door), this is the start of the rest of your life.

Not all of us are in the fortunate position (money-wise) of J K Rowling, but that's not essential – it is possible to enjoy your retirement on more modest means. What is important is to know where you are financially and not to allow your money to retire at the same time as you. It must continue to work hard for you, so that you've got the financial flexibility you need. With the many money-related decisions that have to be made once you stop working, it is crucial to get them right. One recent article in *Mature Times* (**www.maturetimes.co.uk**) made sober reading: 'Inequalities between rich and poor pensioners in Britain are substantial and growing ... with the wealthy likely to live disease-free for an extra 17 years, according to experts.'

It is easy to blame falling annuity rates and the rising cost of living having led to a reduction in spending, but this is at the same time as an increase in essential costs. According to research by Aviva in December 2012, the over-55s average monthly spend has fallen from £1,300 at the end of 2011 to £1,241 between October and December 2012. Average spending on eating out, holidays and motoring all reduced in that period while essential spends (debt repayments, food, fuel and light) all increased. As a group, the over-55s seem to be prioritizing day-to-day matters, rather than the leisure activities traditionally associated with retirement.

With increasing longevity, and those of pensionable age desiring the best quality of life for as long as possible, it is not surprising that Aviva (the insurance provider) reports that over three-quarters of pensioners are worried about the rising cost of living and not having enough money to meet their needs. That is why working out how much money you have and what you will actually require is essential at this stage. Whether you are close to giving up work or you are several years away from retirement, the most important thing to do is carry out a serious review of your retirement plans. This will help you work out what options there are for maximizing your future income. The worst thing is to be an ostrich and ignore the situation in the hope that it will never happen.

A very good website with loads of useful advice is 'This is Money' (**www.thisismoney.co.uk**). Here are their top tips for achieving perfect personal finances. This applies generally whatever age you have reached, but is particularly important for those coming up to retirement:

Step 1:   Make a will.
Step 2:   Pay off debts.
Step 3:   Get term life assurance.
Step 4:   Fund your company pension to the maximum.
Step 5:   Buy a house you can afford.
Step 6:   Put six months' worth of outgoings in a cash ISA.
Step 7:   Any money that is left can be invested in more ISAs.
Step 8:   Find yourself a fee-based financial planner.

The first step, however, should be to focus on your personal circumstances and take a look at ways to plan your finances. If, for example, you are coming up to retirement and have a stable job with a strong company, you are fortunate. Should redundancy be a distinct possibility, the right preparation is crucial. Where possible, while still working, everyone should build up a cash emergency fund (provided you have no debts – apart from a mortgage). This means saving roughly enough money for six months of bills (living expenses): you could start an ISA, and save as much as you can.

Should your income be likely to drop, it makes sense to cut debt costs as much as possible. If you have savings, remember that the government guarantees £85,000 per person per UK-regulated financial institution. If you've more than this, you can spread it over multiple accounts. If you have a financial problem that you cannot resolve, there is a free service set up by law with the power to sort out problems between consumers and financial businesses. It is called the Financial Ombudsman Service and there is more information about this in Chapter 6.

To ensure you have a comfortable retirement, you will need to carry out a full financial health check. Its purpose is to give you a clear view of your current financial position. You should get a state pension forecast, then contact the pension trustees of your current and previous employers. Once you've done that, work out how much income you are likely to need in retirement. Be as realistic as you can: remember to factor in holidays and any debts you might have. If you have lost track of investments or previous pensions, it is worth spending some time in tracing these.

The ability to manage your money and know how to budget is important. Don't forget that there are some 'retirement freebies' that are well worth taking advantage of: these include travel concessions, some health benefits and help with fuel bills. It's surprising how much these small things add up to.

The key to managing your retirement well is to know how to make whatever money you have go as far as possible. There are many useful websites brimming with information on retirement issues. It is an excellent investment of your time to do some thorough research in this regard. Details of some of the better ones are listed later in this chapter. Since getting a grip on your finances is vital, depending on the standard of living you want to have, you should do this as early as possible.

Doing the sums

How do you get an objective view of your financial affairs? One sensible way is to draw up a budget showing your income and outgoings. To make a proper assessment, you need to draw up several lists:

- expected sources of income on retirement;
- essential outgoings;
- normal additional spending (such as holidays and other luxuries).

The following should also be considered:

- possible ways to boost your retirement income;
- spending now for saving later.

You should also try to factor in some of the variables and unknowns, which are much more difficult to estimate. The fluctuations in the world's economies do not help, but two of the most important items to consider in retirement planning are tax and inflation. Things like stocks and shares, property prices and energy costs go up as well as down and all these affect retirement finances. Emergency situations can arise, the most likely being illness, so, if possible, special provisions should be made. The big question (which no one can answer) is how long you, your partner or any dependents might live.

If you base your calculations on current commitments and expenditure, remember your lifestyle and spending habits may change considerably. To get the figures into perspective, think how you will live in retirement. You should spend some time working out what items will still represent a significant percentage of your budget, and which will no longer be so important. There will be a number of areas where savings can be made, such as buying a new fuel-efficient car, instead of running two older vehicles. There will be others where extra outgoings need to be included. The most practical way of using the list is to tick off the items that will definitely apply to you and, where possible, write down the expenditure involved. While this will be no more than a draft, the closer you are to retirement the more sensible it is to do this exercise. Repeat it as often as necessary, and certainly update it each time you obtain more facts and information.

If retirement is imminent, then doing the arithmetic in as much detail as possible will not only reassure you but also help you plan your future life with greater confidence. You'll feel better knowing how you stand financially. Don't forget that there are probably a number of options open to you. Examining the figures written down will highlight the areas of greatest flexibility. One tip, offered by one of the retirement magazines, is to start living on your retirement income some six months before you retire. Not only will you see if your budget estimates are broadly correct, but since most people err on the cautious side when they first retire you will have the bonus of all the extra money you will have saved.

If retirement is still some years ahead, there will be more unknowns and more opportunities. When assessing the figures, you should take account of your future earnings. Perhaps you should also consider what steps you might be able to take under the pension rules to maximize your pension fund. You could also consider whether you should be putting money aside now in a savings plan and/or making other investments. Imprecise as they will be, the budget planner estimates you make in the various income and expenditure columns should indicate whether, unless you take action now, you could be at risk of having to make serious adjustments in your standard of living later on. To be on the safe side, assume an increase in inflation. Everyone should, if they possibly can, budget for a nest egg to help cover the cost of any emergencies or special events that may come along.

Possible savings

Once you stop working you could save quite a lot because there will be a number of expenses you no longer have. These include travelling costs to and from work, meals out, business clothes, and other work-related incidentals such as drinks with colleagues, staff collections and entertainment. Other costs, such as National Insurance Contributions cease on retirement, and unless you choose to invest in a private plan, your pension payments will also stop. It is important to check (once you retire) what your tax coding is because you may well move to a lower tax bracket.

Extra outgoings

If you are spending more time at home once you retire, your utility bills will increase. You may also find you spend more on outings, hobbies and short breaks and holidays. There is so much choice in retirement these days that as long as you budget well in advance you should have enough money to do all you want. Looking ahead, home comforts become increasingly important and you may want to think about paying other people to do some of the jobs that you previously managed yourself. Anticipating such areas of additional expenditure is not being pessimistic; actually it is the surest way of avoiding future money worries. Once you've worked out your retirement income and expenditure in detail you should be able, with a bit of adjustment and compromise, to manage well.

TABLE 2.1

Items	Estimated monthly *savings*
National Insurance Contributions	....
Pension payments	....
Travel expenses to work	....
Bought lunches	....
Incidentals at work, eg drinks with colleagues, collections for presents	....
Special work clothes	....
Concessionary travel	....
NHS prescriptions	....
Eye tests	....
Mature drivers insurance policy	....
Retired householders insurance policy	....
Life assurance payments and/or possible endowment policy premiums	....
Other	....
TOTAL	....

NB: You should also take into account reduced running costs if you move to a smaller home; any expenses for dependent children that may cease; other costs such as mortgage payments that may end around the time you retire; and the fact that you may be in a lower tax bracket and may not be liable for National Insurance Contributions.

TABLE 2.2

Items	Estimated monthly *costs*
Extra heating and lighting bills	....
Extra spending on hobbies and other entertainment	....
Replacement of company car	....
Private health care insurance	....
Longer or more frequent holidays	....
Life and permanent health insurance	....
Cost of substituting other perks, eg expense account lunches	....
Out-of-pocket expenses for voluntary work activity	....
Other	....
TOTAL	....

NB: Looking ahead, you will need to make provision for any extra home comforts you might want and also, at some point, for having to pay other people to do some of the jobs that you normally manage yourself. If you intend to make regular donations to a charity or perhaps help with your grandchildren's education, these too should be included in the list. The same applies to any new private pension or savings plan that you might want to invest in to boost your long-term retirement income.

Expected sources of income on retirement

Your list will include at least some of the following. Once you have added up these figures, you will have to deduct income tax to arrive at the net spending amount available to you:

Many people have difficulty understanding the tax system, and you should certainly take professional advice if you are in any doubt at all. However, if you carefully fill in your expected sources of income and likely tax implications in Tables 2.3 and 2.4, it should give you a pretty good idea of your net income after retirement and enable you to make at least provisional plans. Remember too that you may have one or two capital sums to invest, such as:

- the commuted lump sum from your pension;
- money from an endowment policy;
- gains from the sale of company shares (SAYE or other share option scheme);
- profits from the sale of your home or other asset;
- money from an inheritance.

TABLE 2.3

A. Income received *before* tax	
Basic state pension	....
State graduated pension	....
SERPS/State Second Pension	....
Occupational pension(s)	....
Stakeholder or personal pension	....
State benefits	....
Investments and savings plans paid gross, eg gilts, National Savings	....
Other incomes (eg rental income)	....
Casual or other pre-tax earnings	....
TOTAL	....
Less: Personal tax allowance and possibly also Married Couple's Allowance	....
Basic-rate tax	....
TOTAL A	....

TABLE 2.3 *continued*

B. Income received *after* tax	
Dividends (unit trusts, shares, etc)	....
Bank deposit account	....
Building society interest	....
Annuity income	....
Other (including earnings subject to PAYE)	....
TOTAL B	....
Total A + Total B	....
Less: higher-rate tax (if any)	....
Plus: Other tax-free receipts, eg some state benefits, income from an ISA	....
Investment bond withdrawals, etc	....
Other	....
TOTAL NET INCOME	....

Unavoidable outgoings

No one will have the same list as another, since one person's priority is another's luxury. For this reason, the divide between 'unavoidable outgoings' and 'normal additional expenditure' (see page 16) is likely to vary considerably with each individual. Almost everyone will want to juggle some of the items between the two lists or add their own particular requisites or special enthusiasms. Whatever your own essentials, some of the following items will certainly feature on your list of unavoidable expenses:

TABLE 2.4

Unavoidable outgoings	
Items	**Estimated monthly cost**
Food	....
Rent or mortgage repayments	....
Council tax	....
Repair and maintenance costs	....
Heating	....
Lighting and other energy	....
Telephone/mobile/internet	....
Postage (including Christmas cards)	....
TV licence/Sky/digital subscription	....
Household insurance	....
Clothes	....
Laundry, cleaner's bills, shoe repair	....
Domestic cleaning products	....
Miscellaneous services, eg plumber and window cleaner	....
Car (including licence, petrol, etc)	....
Other transport	....
Regular savings and life assurance	....
HP and other loan repayments	....
Outgoings on health	....
Other	....
TOTAL	....

NB: Before adding up the total, you should look at the 'Normal additional expenditure' list, as you may well want to juggle some of the items between the two.

Normal additional expenditure

This could include some of the following:

TABLE 2.5

Normal additional expenditure	
Items	**Estimated monthly cost**
Gifts	....
Holidays	....
Newspapers/books/CDs/DVDs	....
Computer (including broadband)	....
Drink	....
Cigarettes/tobacco	....
Hairdressing/beauty treatments	....
Toiletries/cosmetics	....
Entertainment (hobbies, outings, home entertaining, etc)	....
Miscellaneous subscriptions/membership fees	....
Gifts, charitable donations	....
Expenditure on pets	....
Garden purchases	....
Other	....
TOTAL	....

NB: For some items, such as holidays and gifts, you may tend to think in annual expenditure terms. However, for the purpose of comparing monthly income versus outgoings, it is probably easier if you itemize all the expenditure in the same fashion. Also, if you need to save for a special event such as your holiday, it helps if you get into the habit of putting so much aside every month (or even weekly).

Possible ways of boosting your retirement income

Few people can afford to turn away extra income these days, yet there are really only three possible ways to give your retirement finances a boost: these are from your home, work and investment skill.

Your home

Your home offers several different options: moving somewhere smaller, taking in lodgers or raising money on your home. All the possibilities are explored in greater detail in Chapter 8, Your home.

Work

How about continuing to work? There is plenty of scope here for earning money, even in these difficult times. You could talk to your employer to see what options there are for you to remain with your present organization.

Alternatively, retirement for you may offer the chance of setting up on your own. Becoming self-employed or setting up a business may sound attractive but there are start-up costs to be considered. There is a lot more information on work, and how to get it, in Chapters 10, 11 and 12.

Investment

Everyone can try this but if it is unfamiliar territory, what is most important is to get good advice from a trusted professional to help you find the most suitable investment opportunities for you. Chapter 5 sets out the various forms investment can take.

Money – if you are made redundant

With job losses still continuing, and many people fearing being made redundant, much of the information in the earlier part of this chapter is equally valid whether you become redundant or retire in the normal way. However, there are several key points with regard to redundancy that it could be to your advantage to check.

From your employment

You may be entitled to statutory redundancy pay

Your employer is obliged to pay the legal minimum, which is calculated on your age, length of service and weekly pay. To qualify, you will need to have worked for the organization for at least two years, with no age restriction. Redundancy pay is 1.5 weeks' pay for each year worked if you are over 41 years, up to a maximum of £430 a week.

Ex gratia payments

Many employers are prepared to be more generous. As long as it's not more than £30,000, statutory redundancy pay is not taxable. Any payment over this limit is subject to tax and National Insurance.

Benefits that are not part of your pay

Redundancy may mean the loss of several valuable benefits such as a company car, life assurance and health insurance. Some insurance companies allow preferential rates to individuals who were previously insured with them under a company scheme.

Holiday entitlement

You could be owed holiday entitlement for which you should be paid.

Company pension

Company pension scheme members normally have several choices. See the 'Company pension schemes' section in Chapter 3, Pensions.

Your mortgage

Your mortgage lender should be notified as soon as possible and might agree to a more flexible repayment system. Check whether your mortgage package includes insurance against redundancy. There is help available from the state if you are claiming benefits, such as income support or income-based Jobseeker's Allowance. Those claiming these benefits could have their interest payments covered for two years if their mortgage is below £200,000. However, no help is available to pay off the capital of your mortgage.

Other creditors/debts

Any creditors that you may have difficulty in paying (electricity, gas, a bank overdraft) should be informed as early as possible in the hope of agreeing easier payment terms. There could be an argument for paying off credit card bills immediately, even if this means using some of your redundancy pay.

Jobseeker's Allowance (JSA)

Even if you are hoping to get another job very soon, you should sign on without delay. Your National Insurance Contributions will normally be credited to you. This is important to protect your state pension. To qualify for JSA you need to be under state pension age and must either have paid sufficient Class 1 National Insurance Contributions or have a low income. You must also be both available for and actively seeking work.

Current information about JSA and other possible benefits can be found on the **Gov.uk** website (the gateway for government advice): **www.gov.uk**. **Redundancy Help** can provide answers to queries on all aspects of redundancy; website: **www.redundancyhelp.co.uk**; and another useful agency is **The Citizens Advice Bureau** advice guides; see website: **www.adviceguide.org.uk**.

Money left unclaimed

It is estimated that there are over £15 billion worth of unclaimed assets in the UK. During the course of this year millions of pounds of unclaimed money will be handed over to the Treasury because there are no clues as to who it belongs to. Some funds are in unclaimed benefits and entitlements, others are unclaimed lottery prizes, the remainder is money such as legacies from wills, funds from pensions and insurance policies where there is no next of kin to claim them. More than one in 10 people think they may have forgotten assets and many people do not know how to begin to trace their money.

There are now a number of useful websites to help you. Experian's Unclaimed Assets Register (UAR) has lots of helpful information: **www. uar.co.uk**. For lost building society accounts, see The Building Societies

Association website: **www.bsa.org.uk**. Try **www.mylostaccount.org.uk**, which aims to reunite savers with lost or dormant bank accounts. *Which?* magazine also gives information and advice on how to track down missing accounts and unclaimed money: **www.which.co.uk**. You could also look at **www.findersuk.com**.

Extra income

The number of state benefits and allowances available to help many pensioners that are not claimed is staggering. Many pensioners live on low to middle incomes and have been hit hardest because of falling interest rates, the rising cost of living and public spending cuts. Despite just under half of all pensioners being entitled to pension credit – a top-up for people on low incomes – a third of people don't claim it; 1.8 million pensioners live in poverty yet millions of pounds of pensioner benefits go unclaimed each year. Age UK (Britain's largest charity dedicated to the needs of the elderly) suggests the reasons for this are that many pensioners are unaware of the range of benefits available, or don't realize they are eligible. They also think the process too complicated and intrusive or are simply too proud to claim.

While many of these benefits are 'means tested' some, such as Disability Living Allowance, are not dependent on how poor or how wealthy you are. Moreover, even when means testing is a factor, for some of the benefits income levels are nothing like as low as many people imagine. Because this information is not widely enough known, many individuals – including over a million pensioners – are not claiming help to which they are entitled and for which in many cases they have actually paid through their National Insurance Contributions.

A number of voluntary organizations, benevolent societies and charities also provide assistance to individuals, sometimes in cash or sometimes in the form of facilities, such as special equipment for disabled people. Details are given in the relevant chapters. For further advice and information on benefits check the following websites:

Department for Work and Pensions: **www.dwp.gov.uk**.

Jobcentre Plus: **www.gov.uk** – search 'Benefits'.

Citizens Advice Bureau: **www.citizensadvice.org.uk**.

Age UK: **www.ageuk.org.uk**.

Making your money go further

If you enjoy browsing the internet and this chapter has whetted your appetite for research on the matter of retirement planning, the following websites cover a broad range of topics relating to your finances and retirement:

www.adviceguide.org.uk;

www.everyinvestor.co.uk;

www.financingretirement.co.uk;

www.moneyadviceservice.org.uk;

www.moneyexpertise.co.uk;

www.moneyweek.com;

www.oscaruk.co.uk;

www.thisismoney.co.uk;

www.which.co.uk.

Useful reading

The following publications are especially for those coming up to retirement and the recently retired.

Your Guide to Retirement – Making the Most of Your Money is a comprehensive guide to help you manage the transition from work to retirement. It is published by the Money Advice Service; website: **www.moneyadviceservice.org.uk.**

Wise Guide – Life-improving Advice for the Over-65s is the practical pensioners' handbook to benefits, debt help, discounts and lots more, published by Independent Age; website: **www.independentage.org.**

An excellent book for those wanting detailed information about planning their finances is *Talking about Retirement* by Lyn Ashurst, published by Kogan Page. The author is an authority in her field and gives a comprehensive and detailed study of a careful and planned approach to the retirement process, based on about 50 case studies. For more information and other recommended titles on retirement and associated issues published by Kogan Page, see **www.koganpage.com.**

Chapter Three
Pensions

> *To see what is in front of one's nose needs a constant struggle.*

GEORGE ORWELL QUOTED ON NATIONALREVIEW.COM

The economic downturn is estimated to have cost the over-50s an average of £60,000 during the worst of the recession/credit crunch (call it what you will). This statement comes from a leading think-tank, the Institute for Fiscal Studies (IFS). The loss results from a combination of the drop in property values and investments. A separate report from the NFU Mutual (rural investment specialists) suggests that many older people expect 'never to retire', because they cannot afford to. According to the NFU, this problem has arisen because of a mismatch between expectation and reality. People need to make greater financial provision for their retirement to bridge this gap. The IFS report said millions of people aged between 50 and state pension age have little or no pension and found that 41 per cent will retire on less than two-thirds of their final salary.

The government, in an attempt to solve the pension crisis, introduced auto-enrolment in October 2012. But this won't be enough on its own. Given the demographic reality (by 2025 there will be as many people aged 70+ as there were people aged 65+ in 2010) more and more people will have to find new ways of ensuring a decent standard of living. This is likely to unearth a new socio-economic group: a rising generation of WEARIES – Working, Entrepreneurial and Active Retirees – who may well be forced to continue working into their 70s and beyond due to hardships caused by the looming pension crisis (research carried out by the Future Foundation, article in *Mature Times*: **www.maturetimes.co.uk**).

Gloomy reading, but the pension crisis has been heading towards us for years. As so many of us are living longer, yet not saving enough for our old age, this comes as no surprise. People are inevitably going to get used to working beyond the traditional retirement age if they are to afford a good quality of life in retirement. Many women, for example, are staying on longer in employment because husbands and wives may wish to retire at the same time. State pension age (which is rising for both men and women) is becoming an anchor for decisions about when to retire.

In the recent past there has been much criticism of pension policy with frequent changes and a lack of certainty. But the Coalition government has brought a welcome period of stability. A number of sensible measures have been introduced, such as NEST, the auto-enrolment scheme, and the single-tier state pension. These have been welcomed by the pensions industry. Providing greater clarity at little or no initial extra cost overall will improve the lives of millions and save the government money in the long run.

With auto-enrolment in pensions, greater awareness of the need to save, an expectation and desire to work for longer, coupled with housing assets, a skills shortage and equity release (the medium- or high-value property which pensioner households will use to support their retirement) – all these promise to improve the circumstances of those expecting to retire within the next decade. Alongside employers wanting workers to remain in their posts for longer, and a desire among employees to continue working, it is likely that this group will be better prepared for retirement and ageing than might previously have been thought.

But the antidote to an impoverished old age is obvious: we all must save like mad, and should start doing so as early as possible.

Top tips to improve your retirement living standard from 'This is Money' website is to take things a step at a time, decade by decade (**www.thisismoney.co.uk/pension-plan**):

- *In your 20s* you should focus on clearing your debts, open an ISA and save what you can afford.

- *In your 30s* reassess your debts and outgoings, join your company pension scheme and think long term with your investments.

- *In your 40s* if you haven't started saving, do so now. Keep adding to your ISAs and as your earnings peak, dedicate some to a pension.

- *In your 50s* maximize your contributions, remove risk from your pension investment plan and consider using a SIPP (Self-Invested Personal Pension) for greater control.

- *In your 60s* check that all your debts, including mortgage, are in order. Decide whether you'll buy an annuity immediately or take drawdown and, most important of all, talk to an IFA (Independent Financial Adviser) before you take any action.

The state pension

Those who qualify for a state pension currently start to receive payments in their 60s. The exact age is being equalized for men and women. It is rising to 66 for both sexes by 2020, then to 67 by 2028. People should look at a *state pension calculator* to find the age at which they will receive it.

The Chancellor decided in April 2013 that the flat-rate pension will be effective a year earlier (from 2016 rather than 2017). But for 2013–14 the basic state retirement pension has been increased by 2.5 per cent in line with the minimum increase provisions of the government's 'triple guarantee'. This results in the single rate rising by £2.70 per week (from £107.45 to £110.15 – or £5,728 a year). If you're married and both you and your partner have built up state pension, you'll get double this amount – so £220.10 a week in 2013/14. But if your partner has not built up their own entitlement, they will still be able to claim a state pension based on your record. The maximum is £66 a week.

It then gets more complicated because some people also receive the State Second Pension, or Serps, which is the government's earnings-related additional pension.

If your income is below a certain level, you can boost it by claiming pension credit. This will take your income up to £145.40 a week for a single person and £222.05 a week for a couple (in 2013/14). See further on in this chapter.

Since October 2011 the default retirement age of 65 has been scrapped. Employers are no longer allowed to dismiss staff just because they are 65. But as the state pension comes under increasing pressure, it is important to make private pension savings and not rely on the basic state pension to finance your retirement.

Your right to a state pension

Your state pension depends on how long you have worked and the number of National Insurance qualifying years you have. If you reached the state pension age on or after 6 April 2010, you need to have 30 qualifying years for a full basic state pension. If you reached the pension age before April 2010, then a woman normally needed 39 qualifying years, and a man needed 44 qualifying years during a regular working life to get the full state pension. If you are in a couple and only one person in a couple qualifies for the basic state pension, then you can still receive top-up state pension payments by using one partner's National Insurance record.

Points to note, since 6 April 2010:

- married men and female civil partners will also be entitled to a pension based on their wife's or civil partner's record – but their wife or civil partner must have been born on or after 6 April 1950 and have reached state pension age;

- any pension for a wife, husband or civil partner will be payable whether their spouse or civil partner decides to claim or to defer his or her own state pension;

- the earliest date a male civil partner will be entitled to this is 6 April 2015 because that is the date that a man born on 6 April 1950 reaches pensionable age.

Lived or worked outside Great Britain?

If you have lived in Northern Ireland or the Isle of Man, any contributions paid there will count towards your pension. The same should also apply in most cases if you have lived or worked in an EU country or any country whose social security is linked to Britain's by a reciprocal arrangement. However, there have sometimes been problems with certain countries, so, if you have any doubts, you should enquire what your position is at your pension centre.

Home Responsibilities Protection (HRP)

Since 6 April 2010 Home Responsibilities Protection has been replaced with weekly credits for parents and carers. You can receive these credits for any weeks you are getting Child Benefit for a child under 12, you are an approved foster carer, or you are caring for one or more sick or disabled people for at least 20 hours a week. If you reach state pension age on or after 6 April 2010, any years of HRP you have been awarded before April 2010 will have been converted to qualifying years of credits up to a maximum of 22 years.

For more information about the changes introduced by the Pensions Act 2007, see website: **www.gov.uk** – Working, jobs and pensions.

Other situations

If you have been in any of the following situations you will have been credited with contributions (instead of having to pay them):

- you were sick or unemployed (provided you sent in sick notes to your social security office, signed on at the unemployment benefit office or were in receipt of Jobseeker's Allowance);
- you were a man aged 60–64 and not working;
- you were entitled to maternity allowance, invalid care allowance or unemployability supplement;
- you were taking an approved course of training;
- you had left education but had not yet started working;
- since April 2000, your earnings had fallen between what are known as the lower earnings limit and the primary threshold, ie between £109 and £149 a week (2013/14).

Married women and widows

Married women and widows who do not qualify for a basic pension in their own right may be entitled to a basic pension on their husband's contributions at about 60 per cent of the level to which he is entitled.

Husband and wife are assessed separately for tax and a married woman is entitled to have her section of the joint pension offset against her own personal allowance, instead of being counted as part of her husband's taxable income. For many pensioner couples, this should mean a reduction in their tax liability.

Reduced-rate contributions note: many women retiring today may have paid a reduced-rate contribution under a scheme that was abolished in 1978. Women who were already paying a reduced-rate contribution were, however, allowed to continue doing so. These reduced-rate contributions *do not count* towards your pension and you will not have had any contributions credited to you. If you are still some years away from retirement, it could be to your advantage to cancel the reduced-rate option, as by doing so you may be able to build up a wider range of benefits without paying anything extra. This applies if you are currently (2013/14) earning between £109 and £149 a week. If you are earning above the primary threshold (£149), to get the same extra benefits you would have to start paying extra contributions. For advice, contact your local tax office or see the website: **www.hmrc.gov.uk**.

How your state pension is worked out

Anyone trying to decide whether they can afford to retire should get their state pension forecast from the Pension Service (**www.dwp.gov.uk**). It is worth getting an early estimate of what your pension will be, as it may be possible to improve your NIC record by making additional Class 3 voluntary contributions. See website: **www.gov.uk** – Working, jobs and pensions.

Since April 2011, the basic pension is increased annually by the highest of price inflation, earnings or 2.5 per cent. But if you retire abroad, you only get these increases if you live in a European Economic Area (EEA) country, Switzerland or a country with which the UK has a reciprocal agreement that includes state pensions. Due to improvements in service arrangements, you only need to claim a state pension two months before your state pension birthday date. You can check your state pension age using the calculator on the Gov.uk website: **www.gov.uk** – State pension.

If you do not qualify for a full basic state pension you may be able to pay Class 3 NIC if you have gaps in your National Insurance record. Paying them would mean that years that would not normally be qualifying years would count towards your basic state pension. Your forecast letter will tell you whether or not you can do this. There are time limits for paying Class 3 NIC and you must normally pay them within six years of the end of the tax year for which you are paying.

If you need help deciding whether you need to pay extra contributions, you can obtain help from the National Insurance Contributions Office (**www.hmrc.gov.uk/nic**) or The Pensions Advisory

Service (**www.pensionsadvisoryservice.org.uk**). To find out how much pension you are entitled to, you can apply for an online forecast (**www.thepensionservice.gov.uk**).

Additional state pension

If you are (or have been) in employment, you may have been building up an additional state pension, known as the State Second Pension. The amount you receive depends on your earnings and your NIC record. There are other means of entitlement to some S2P: for example, if you earn below a certain amount set by the government, if you cannot work through long-term illness or disability, or if you are a carer.

The S2P is not available to the self-employed, for whom the alternative pension choices are either a personal pension or a stakeholder pension. If you are an employee, you are automatically included in S2P unless you decide to contract out, or you are a member of an employer's occupational pension scheme that is contracted out. If you decide to contract out, you stop building up your S2P entitlement and build up a replacement for it in your own pension. You will continue to be contracted out of S2P unless you decide to contract back in.

The end of S2P in 2016 will hit highest earners the hardest. Currently self-employed workers receive only the basic state pension, as they do not qualify for S2P. However, from 2016 they will be treated the same as employees for the purposes of state pension entitlement. Under the flat-rate pension, anyone with 35 qualifying years of NICs will be eligible for the full £144 a week, and means testing will be abolished.

For more information about contracting out, or if you have any queries regarding the S2P scheme, you can obtain help from this website: **www.gov.uk** – Working, jobs and pensions.

Deferring your pension

When you reach the state pension age, you decide whether or not to start drawing the state pension. Many people prefer to stop working gradually by reducing hours or shifting to part-time work, so you might not need your entire pension straight away. By deferring your state pension, you can have a bigger pension when it does start, or alternatively a lump sum. Your state pension is increased by 1 per cent for each five weeks you defer it, ie an increase of 10.4 per cent a year for each year you defer. But this is only worth considering if you can live without the pension for now. You can continue deferring your pension for as long as you like. The extra money will be paid to you when you eventually decide to claim your pension. The lump sum is worked out as if your deferred pension had been invested and earned a return of 2 per cent more than the Bank of England base rate. If you plan to defer your pension, you should also defer any graduated pension to which you may be entitled – or you risk losing the increases you would otherwise obtain. More information can be found on the Pension Service website: **www.gov.uk** – Working, jobs and pensions.

Adult Dependency Increase

This is an increase in the state pension for a husband, wife or someone who is looking after your children, as long as certain conditions are met. Since 6 April 2010, you are no longer entitled to claim an Adult Dependency Increase. If you were already entitled to this increase on 5 April 2010 you will be able to keep it until you no longer meet the conditions for the increase, or 5 April 2020, whichever is the first.

Income Support

If you have an inadequate income, you may qualify for Income Support. There are special premiums (ie additions) for lone parents, disabled people, carers and pensioners. A condition of entitlement is that you should not have capital, including savings, of more than £16,000. A big advantage is that people entitled to Income Support receive full help with their rent and should also not have any Council Tax to pay. See 'Housing Benefit' and 'Council Tax Benefit' in Chapter 8.

Pension Credit

Pension Credit is an income-related benefit for those who have reached the minimum qualifying age and live in Great Britain. You do not need to have paid NIC to get it. There are two parts to Pension Credit.

Guarantee Credit may be paid to you if you have reached the minimum qualifying age. It tops up your income to a guaranteed minimum level (for the year 2013/14 it is £145.40 if you are single, or £222.05 if you have a partner).

Savings Credit is for those who have saved money towards their retirement. You may be able to get it if you are aged 65 or over. You may be able to get Savings Credit as well as Guarantee Credit. You may still get Pension Credit if you live with your grown-up family or own your own home.

If you wish to apply for Pension Credit, you can do so up to four months before the date from which you want to start getting Pension Credit. The longest Pension Credit claims can be backdated is three months. You do not have to pay tax on Pension Credit. If entitled to it, you may get Savings Credit (for the year 2013/14) of £18.06 a week if you are single or £22.89 a week if you have a partner.

The age from which you may get Pension Credit – the qualifying age – is gradually going up to 66 in line with the increase in the state pension age for women to 65 and the further increase to 66 for men and women. To find out when you reach the qualifying age for Pension Credit, visit **www.gov.uk** – State pension.

If you apply for Pension Credit, you may also apply for Council Tax Benefit and Housing Benefit at the same time. The age at which people can get Housing Benefit and Council Benefit for pensioners is also increasing from 60 to 65 between April 2010 and 2020. *Housing Benefit* is to help people on a low income pay some or all of their rent. *Council Tax Benefit* is to help people on a low income pay some or all of their council tax. You do not have to pay tax on either of them.

Visit the **Gov.uk** website to find out more information: **www.gov.uk** – Heating and housing benefits.

Other sources of help

Don't be ashamed to claim.

An estimated 1.5 million people could claim benefits but the means test puts some people off claiming the top-ups they are entitled to. Every year as much as £5.5 billion of benefits that older people are entitled to go unclaimed, despite many of them struggling to make ends meet. According to leading charities – AgeUK and Elisabeth Finn – much needs to be done in terms of raising awareness of welfare benefits available and reducing some of the negative perceptions against claiming when times are tough.

For help relating to benefits, **Turn2Us** (website: **www.turn2us.org.uk**) is a charity set up specifically to identify potential sources of funding for those facing financial difficulty. Individuals can log on to this website for free and in confidence. Also look at **AgeUK**'s website, Britain's leading charity for older people: **www.ageuk.co.uk**.

Community Care Grants, Budgeting Loans and Crisis Loans can all help with exceptional expenses if you are facing financial difficulties. These are all dealt with through the **Gov.uk** website. See **www.gov.uk** – Jobseeker's Allowance and low income benefits for the widest range of online government information for the public, covering benefits, financial support, rights, employment, independent living and much more. For information for disabled people, see **www.gov.uk** – Disability benefits.

Early retirement and your state pension

Because some people retire early, they can mistakenly assume it is possible to get an early pension. While the information is correct as regards many employers' occupational pension schemes, as well as for stakeholder and personal pensions, it does not apply to the basic state pension. If you take early retirement before the age of 60, it may be necessary for you to pay voluntary Class 3 NIC to protect your contributions record for state pension purposes. Your local tax office can advise you about NICs.

Other situations

Pensions can be paid to an overseas address, if you are going abroad for six months or more. See website: **www.gov.uk** – Working, jobs and pensions (see section 'State pension if you retire abroad').

If you are in hospital, your pension can still be paid to you and you will receive your pension in full for the duration of your stay, regardless of how long you have to remain in hospital. For advice, contact either the Pension Service or the Citizens Advice Bureau.

Christmas bonus

This is paid shortly before Christmas to pensioners who are entitled to a qualifying benefit. For many years the sum has been £10. The bonus is combined with your normal pension payment for the first week in December.

Advice

The Pension Service provides information to current and future pensioners so that making informed decisions about pension arrangements is straightforward. If you need help with your retirement plans it can assist you. It will explain what the state will provide when you retire and let you know what pension-related benefits you may be entitled to.

If you have any queries or think you may not be obtaining your full pension entitlement, you should contact the Pension Service as soon as possible. If you think a mistake has been made, you have the right to appeal and can insist on your claim being heard by an independent tribunal. Before doing so, you would be strongly advised to consult a solicitor at the Citizens Advice Bureau or the Welfare Advice Unit of your social security office. For further information about pensions, there is a booklet full of advice entitled *Pensioners' Guide* obtainable from the Pension Service, part of the Department for Work and Pensions: **www.directgov.uk/en/PensionsandRetirementPlanning**.

Other useful sources of information include:

The Pensions Advisory Service: **www.pensionsadvisoryservice.org.uk**.

The Service Personnel and Veterans Agency: **www.veterans-uk.info**.

Citizens Advice: **www.citizensadvice.org.uk**.

Private pensions

You can save as much as you like towards your pension but there is a limit on the amount of tax relief you can get. The lifetime allowance is the maximum amount of pension savings you can build up over your life that benefits from tax relief. If you build up pension savings worth more than the lifetime allowance you'll pay a tax charge on the excess. The annual allowance now stands at £50,000 a year for everyone until April 2014 when it reduces to £40,000 a year. This reduction of 20 per cent was introduced by the Chancellor in his April 2013 budget, at the same time he reduced the lifetime allowance from currently £1.5 million to £1.25 million with effect from April 2014. This yearly contribution should still be more than adequate for most people. For those who have taken a break from contributions, there will be the useful option to potentially carry forward up to three years' annual allowance. Those who are in final salary schemes or those with employer, employee and individual pension contributions over two consecutive tax years which combine to over £50,000 will need to be particularly aware of the limits. It would be wise to check with your pension provider when your current 'pension input period' (the accounting period for your pension scheme) ends.

Wealthier investors can build up their defined contribution pension funds to £1.5 million until April 2014, at which point the changes come into effect. After that time there will be an 'individual protection' regime provided to honour those funds. While these changes do set a cap on the amount of pensions tax relief individuals can obtain, they still permit significant tax-free savings into a pension and are far simpler than the restrictive regime they replaced. It is important to bear in mind that tax rules and tax reliefs can and do change and their exact value depends on each individual's circumstances.

Despite a certain amount of apprehension, pension savings are still one of the most tax-effective investments available because you receive income tax relief on contributions at your highest tax rate and the growth in your pension fund is totally exempt from income tax and capital gains tax. Another advantage is that part of the pension can be taken as a tax-free cash lump sum when you retire. For further information, see **www.hmrc/pensionschemes**.

NB: Many part-timers who were previously excluded can now join their employer's occupational pension scheme as of right.

Company pension schemes

Types of company pension schemes

The pension that your employer offers may be 'contributory' (you and your employer pay into it) or 'non-contributory' which means that only your employer does. If the scheme offered is a group stakeholder pension scheme, your employer doesn't have to contribute, so you alone may be putting money in. There are four main types of company pension:

Final salary

These are known as a type of defined benefit scheme. You build up a pension at a certain rate – 1/60th is quite common – so for each year you've been a scheme member, you receive 1/60th of your final salary.

Final salary schemes are costly for employers to run and have all but disappeared. In the private sector only 1.3 million workers are in a final salary scheme and few schemes are open to new employees. More public sector workers (such as teachers, police, NHS and local government workers) pay into a final salary scheme, but this is still only 5.3 million out of 29 million employed people in the UK. If you work for one of the few remaining employers with a final salary scheme, you should join it.

Career average

These are another type of defined-benefit scheme, because the benefit (your pension) is worked out using your salary and the length of time you have been a member of the pension scheme. The pension you receive will be based on an average of your earnings in the time that you're a member of the scheme (often averaged over the last three years before retirement). What you receive will depend on the proportion of those earnings that you get as pension for each year of membership. The most common are 1/60th or 1/80th of your earnings for each year of membership.

The benefits of such schemes are that the pension is based on your length of membership and salary, so you have a fair idea of how much your pension will be before retirement. Also, your employer should ensure there is enough money at the time you retire to pay you a pension, and you get tax relief on your contributions. Scheme investments grow generally free of income tax and capital gains tax. Your pension benefits are linked to your salary while you are working, so they automatically increase as your pay rises. Your pension income from the scheme will normally increase each year in line with CPI instead of RPI.

Is there a risk? If a salary-related occupational scheme or the sponsoring employer gets into financial trouble, the Pension Protection Fund can provide some protection. You can normally get a pension of up to 90 per cent of your expected pension, subject to a cap. (See the Pension Protection Fund website for more information: **www.pensionprotectionfund.gov.uk**.)

Money purchase

These are also known as defined-contribution schemes. The money paid in by you and your employer is invested and builds up a fund that buys you an income when you retire. Most schemes offer a choice of investment funds. The amount paid in varies, but the average employer contribution in 2010 to money-purchase schemes was 8 per cent of salary.

It helps to think of money-purchase pensions as having two stages:

Stage 1. The fund is invested, usually in stocks and shares and other investments, with the aim of growing it over the years before you retire. You can usually choose from a range of funds to invest in. The **Pensions Advisory Service** (TPAS) has an online investment choices planner to help you decide how to invest your contributions (see **www.pensionsadvisoryservice.org.uk/online-planners**).

Stage 2. When you retire, you can take a tax-free lump sum from your fund and use the rest to secure an income – usually in the form of a lifetime annuity. The amount of pension you'll get at retirement will depend on: how much you pay into the fund; how much your employer pays in (if anything); how well your invested contributions perform; the charges taken out of your fund by your pension provider; how much you take out as a tax-free lump sum; annuity rates at the time you retire – and, the type of annuity you choose.

The benefits of money-purchase schemes are that you get tax relief on your contributions; your fund grows generally free of income tax and capital gains tax; you may be able to choose the funds to invest in; and your employer may contribute, if it's a work-based pension.

Group personal/stakeholder

If you've decided on a private pension, you can shop around for either of the above. These are also money-purchase schemes, ie the pension you get is not linked to your salary. Your employer offers access to either a personal or stakeholder plan, which you own, and can take with you if you get a new job. Your employer will choose the scheme provider, deduct the contributions you make from your salary and pay these to the provider, along with employer contributions. There are some differences between them.

Stakeholder pensions must have certain features. Some of these include limited charges; low minimum contributions; flexible contributions; penalty-free transfers; and a default investment fund – ie a fund your money will be invested in if you don't want to choose one yourself. If your employer offers a *group stakeholder* pension, it doesn't have to pay into it.

Personal pensions: these are similar to stakeholder pensions, but they usually offer a wider range of investment choices. If your employer offers a *group personal* pension scheme, it must contribute at least 3 per cent on your behalf. Personal pension charges may be similar to stakeholder pension charges but some are higher. You can compare stakeholder and personal pensions from different providers on the website **www. moneyadviceservice.org.uk.**

Auto-enrolment

The government has recently developed its own system to encourage low- to middle-wage earners to contribute to a personal pension plan. This is the National Employment Savings Trust, the not-for-profit, low-cost workplace pension scheme into which employees can be entered.

From October 2012 about 8 million employees up to state pension age began saving into this company pension scheme for the first time. This auto-enrolment scheme was introduced for all companies who employ more than 50,000 people and has been extended to all companies since 2013. This scheme promises to provide some income for several million people who previously would have had nothing beyond the state pension. As encouragement, employers are given tax breaks if they do not opt out.

Automatic enrolment, the government hopes, will start a savings revolution, but first people will need to understand the value of saving for their future. If too many exercise their right to opt out, the government will be forced to consider compulsory membership – and there will be no need for tax breaks to encourage saving into a pension. The government will review the position in 2017. The aim of pension tax relief is to encourage people to contribute into a private pension arrangement. If it became compulsory there would be no need to provide that incentive and therefore it could be withdrawn. In which case the amount of money being saved into pension plans might go down not up (see **www.nestpensions.org.uk**).

Self-Invested Personal Pensions (SIPPs)

If you want to use a pension to save for your retirement, you don't have to give your money to a fund manager. You can manage your own retirement fund with a self-invested personal pension (SIPP). Most stock-brokers offer Sipp accounts and the good news is that the government is so eager for you to save via a SIPP it will even give you tax back. You can either pay a lump sum to a pension provider or drip feed in monthly amounts. The latter can be made via a scheme into which both you and your employer pay. But instead of your employer directing where your money goes, you get free rein over where it's invested. You can buy a range of asset classes, from stocks to bonds to gold bullion (though you can't buy fine wines). Monthly contributions can be as low as £50. You can pay in amounts equal to 100 per cent of your annual salary up to a current ceiling of £50,000 per year. You can access your SIPP from age 55 and you can normally take up to 25 per cent as a tax-free cash sum with the balance being used to buy an annuity. SIPPs are not suitable for everyone; broadly they are for people with larger pension pots. As SIPPs are fee-based arrangements, the smaller the fund the more expensive they are. If you are someone who finds the idea of investing your own money daunting, a SIPP may not be for you.

Until now residential property has not been permitted in SIPPS, but the government is currently exploring whether SIPP investors may be able to convert unused commercial property to residential use by amending Investment Regulated Pensions Schemes rules. This should reduce unnecessary red tape which plagues such projects at the moment. This could be good for the property and pension sector, though professional advice beforehand would be essential. For advice talk to your financial adviser or look at the website **www.moneymadeclear.gov.uk**.

Flexible drawdown

The introduction of 'flexible drawdown', effective since 6 April 2011, allows pension investors to take money from their pension as and when they want it. By taking money out of your pension you would, however, be removing it from a tax-free environment, so you would probably leave funds in the pension until you needed them, at which point you could draw out however much you needed. Leaving funds in the pension makes tax-efficient sense because the fund growth is free from UK income and capital gains tax (tax deducted from dividends at source cannot be reclaimed). You will still normally be able to draw up to 25 per cent of your pension tax free when you take retirement benefits.

Some of the requirements you will have to meet to be eligible for flexible drawdown include being over 55 to start drawing a pension; also receiving a secure pension of at least £20,000 per annum. This can include the state pension, final salary pensions and pension annuities. The reason for this requirement is so that even if you draw your entire pension out and spend it, you are unlikely to fall back on means-tested state benefits.

Other requirements are if either you or your employer makes contributions to a pension scheme; this could mean that you are prohibited from using flexible drawdown until the start of the tax year after those contributions are made. After you have moved into flexible drawdown, you will be effectively prevented from accruing any more pension benefits, so it is only worth it once you have finished building up pension benefits.

Family pensions

Another change to pension rules is that you now have greater scope to pass your pension on to your heirs. You can now pass your pension on to beneficiaries of your choice as a lump sum, even if you are older than 75 when you die. This will be subject to a 55 per cent tax charge. The tax charge is designed to claw back the tax relief already provided. The government is keeping the current provision which generally allows you to pass your pension on to a beneficiary as a tax-free lump sum if you die before 75, provided you have not started drawing retirement benefits.

If you have a small pension pot

If the value of your pension rights is below a certain level, it may be possible to give up those rights in exchange for a cash sum. From 6 April 2012 the link to the Lifetime Allowance has been removed. The threshold is announced each year by the government: for the year 2013/14 the limit is £18,000. An important point, if you have more than one pension plan, is that the 'exempt' amount of £18,000 does not apply to each of them but is the total aggregate value of all your plans.

Minimum retirement age

The minimum age at which you are allowed to take early retirement and draw your pension has been 55 since 6 April 2010. It may be possible to draw retirement benefits earlier if you are in poor health and unable to work.

Becoming self-employed

If, as opposed to switching jobs, you leave paid employment to start your own enterprise, you are allowed to transfer your accumulated pension rights into a new fund. There are two main choices. The most obvious solution is to invest your money with an insurance company, or to take either a personal or a stakeholder pension. An alternative course of action, which might be more attractive if you are fairly close to normal retirement age, is to leave your pension in your former employer's scheme. Before making a decision, take professional advice from your Independent Financial Adviser.

Questions on your pension scheme

If you have a query or if you are concerned in some way about your pension, you should approach whoever is responsible for the scheme in your organization. The sort of questions you might ask will vary according to circumstance, such as before you join the scheme, if you are thinking of changing jobs, if you are hoping to retire early and so on. The questions listed here are simply an indication of some of the key information you may require to plan sensibly ahead.

If you want to leave the organization to change jobs

- Could you have a refund of contributions if you were to leave shortly after joining?
- How much will your deferred pension be worth?
- Should you want to move the transfer value to another scheme, how long would you have to wait from the date of your request? (This should normally be within three to six months.)

If you leave for other reasons

- What happens if you become ill – or die – before pension age?
- What are the arrangements if you want to retire early? Most schemes allow you to do this if you are within about 10 years of normal retirement age, but your pension may be reduced

accordingly. Many schemes operate a sliding scale of benefits, with more generous terms offered to those who retire later rather than earlier.

If you stay until normal retirement age

- What will your pension be on your present salary? And what would it be assuming your salary increases by, say, 5 or 10 per cent before you eventually retire?

- What spouse's pension will be paid? Can a pension be paid to other dependants?

- Similarly, can a pension be paid to a partner, male or female?

- What happens if you continue working with the organization after retirement age?

- What are the arrangements if you retire from the organization as a salaried employee but become a retained consultant or contractor?

If you just want information

- Are any changes envisaged to the scheme? For example, if it is a final salary one, is there any chance that it might be wound up and a money-purchase one offered instead?

- If there were a new money-purchase scheme, would the company be making the same contributions as before or would these be lower in future?

- Is there any risk that benefits – either members' own or those for dependants – could be reduced?

- Is there a possibility that members might be required to pay higher contributions than at present?

Should I transfer my long-lost fund?

- Are there any benefits to transferring old pensions into one new scheme? One benefit is the saving on fees. However, you should assess the performance and fees for the new scheme into which you want to transfer the funds. Watch out for transfer charges. These are punitive fees that act as a sneaky deterrent for savers trying to integrate their pensions and keep matters simple.

Other help and advice

Previous schemes

In addition to understanding your current pension scheme, you may also need to chase up any previous schemes of which you were a member. According to the 'This is Money' financial website, an amazing £1.4 billion is estimated to be forgotten and hidden away in accounts worth less than £5,000. At the moment around 70,000 people get in touch with the DWP for help in finding a lost pension. Hundreds more queries are fielded by the Pensions Advisory Service.

For free help tracking down a pension, contact the Pension Tracing Service, which assists individuals who need help in tracing their pension rights: **www.gov.uk** – Working, jobs and pensions. Choose the link to 'Workplace and personal pensions'. If you have any queries or problems to do with your pension, there are three main sources of help available to you. These are the trustees of your pension scheme, the Pensions Advisory Service and the Pensions Ombudsman.

Trustees or managers

These are the first people to contact if you do not properly understand your benefit entitlements or if you are unhappy about some point to do with your pension. Pensions managers (or other people responsible for pensions) should give you their names and tell you how they can be reached.

The Pensions Advisory Service

The Pensions Advisory Service provides members of the public with general information and guidance on pension matters and assists individuals with disputes with personal, company and stakeholder pensions. See the Pensions Advisory Service website: **www.pensionsadvisoryservice.org.uk**.

Pensions Ombudsman

You would normally approach the Ombudsman *only* if neither the pension scheme manager (or trustees) nor the Pensions Advisory Service is able to solve your problem. The Ombudsman can investigate: 1) complaints of maladministration by the trustees, managers or administrators of a pension scheme or by an employer; 2) disputes of fact or law with the trustees, managers or an employer. The Ombudsman does not, however, investigate complaints about mis-selling of pension schemes, a complaint that is already subject to court proceedings, or those that are about a state social security benefit, or disputes that are more appropriate for investigation by another regulatory body. There is also a time limit for lodging complaints, which is normally within three years of the act, or failure to act, about which you are complaining.

There is no charge for the Ombudsman's service. The Pensions Ombudsman has now also taken on the role of Pension Protection Fund Ombudsman and will be dealing with complaints about, and appeals from, the Pension Protection Fund. He will also be dealing with appeals from the Financial Assistance Scheme (see below) and the Pensions Ombudsman website: **www.pensions-ombudsman.org.uk**.

If you have a personal pension, the Financial Ombudsman Service (FOS) could help you. Since last year, the maximum award that the Financial Ombudsman can make has increased from £100,000 to £150,000. See website: **www.financial-ombudsman.org.uk**. It is possible you may be referred to the Pensions Ombudsman, but if so you will be informed very quickly.

Protection for pension scheme members

New rules have been introduced to protect pension scheme members in the event of a company takeover or proposed bulk transfer arrangement. There is now also a Pension Protection Fund (PPF) to help final salary pension scheme members who are at risk of losing their pension benefits owing to their employer's insolvency. Members below the scheme's normal retirement age will receive 90 per cent of the Pension Protection Fund level of compensation plus annual increases, subject to a cap and the standard fund rules. See website: **www.pensionprotectionfund.org.uk**.

There is more help too for members who lost pension savings in a company scheme before the introduction of the Pension Protection Fund. The Financial Assistance Scheme (FAS) offers help to some people who have lost out on their pension. It makes payments to top up scheme benefits to eligible members of schemes that are winding up or have wound up. Assistance is also payable to the survivor of a pension scheme member. It is payable from normal retirement age (subject to a lower age limit of 60 and an upper age limit of 65). See website: **www.pensionprotectionfund.org.uk**.

Pension rights if you continue to work after retirement age

When you reach normal retirement age you will usually stop making contributions into your company pension scheme even if you decide to carry on working. If your employer wants you to leave, they will have to give you at least six months' notice in writing. If you are facing such a decision, here are some points to bear in mind:

- You can continue working, draw your company pension and put some (or possibly all) of your earnings into a separate scheme.
- You can leave your pension in the fund, where it will continue to earn interest until you retire. In most private schemes you could expect to receive in the region of an extra 8 per cent for every year that you delay retirement.
- You can leave your pension in the fund, as described above, and additionally contribute to a personal or stakeholder pension, provided your contributions do not exceed the annual allowance (2014) of £50,000.
- Provided your scheme rules allow, you can continue working for your existing employer and draw your pension benefits, as opposed to – as previously – having to defer them until you left the organization.

Equal pension age

Employers are required to treat men and women equally with regard to retirement and pension issues. They must have a common pension age, and pension schemes must offer the same benefits to their male and female members.

Divorce, separation and bereavement

Divorce

Pension sharing became legally available in respect of divorce or annulment proceedings commenced on or after 1 December 2000. Although women usually benefit most from pension sharing, recent legislative changes equally allow an ex-husband to have a share in his former wife's pension rights. The question of pension sharing is a subject to raise with your solicitor if you are in the process of divorce proceedings. But however much in favour your legal adviser may be, in the final analysis it is up to the court to decide on what it sees as the fairest arrangement – and pension sharing is only one of several options available.

Divorced wives

If you have a full basic pension in your own right, this will not be affected by divorce. However, if, as applies to many women, despite having worked for a good number of years you have made insufficient contributions to qualify for a full pension, you should contact your pension centre, quoting your pension number and NI number. It is possible that you may be able to obtain the full single person's pension, based on your ex-husband's contributions. Your right to use your ex-husband's contributions to improve or provide you with a pension depends on your age and/or whether you remarry before the age of 60. If you are over 60 when you divorce, then whether you remarry or not you can rely on your ex-husband's contributions. If you remarry before the age of 60, then you cease absolutely being dependent on your former husband and instead your pension will be based on your new husband's contribution record. The same rules apply in reverse.

Pension sharing

Provisions to enable the court to share occupational or personal pension rights at the time of divorce or annulment came into law on 1 December 2000. The legislation now equally applies to the additional state pension. Sharing, however, is only one option for dealing with pension rights and would not necessarily apply in all cases.

Separated wives

Even if you have not lived together for several years, from an NI point of view you are still considered to be married. The normal pension rules apply including, of course, the fact that, if you have to depend on your husband's contributions, you will not be able to get a pension until he is both 65 and in receipt of his own pension. If you are not entitled to a state pension in your own right, you will receive the dependant's rate of benefit, which is about 60 per cent of the full rate (or less if your husband is not entitled to a full pension). In such a case, you can apply for Income Support to top up your income. Once you are 60, you can personally draw the wife's pension without reference to your husband.

If your husband dies, you may be entitled to bereavement benefits in the same way as other widows. If there is a possibility that he may have died but that you have not been informed, you can check by contacting the General Register Office website: **www.gro.gov.uk**. The indexes to all birth, marriage and death entries in England and Wales are available from the National Archives website: **www.nationalarchives.gov.uk**.

Widows

There are three important benefits to which widows may be entitled: Bereavement Payment, Bereavement Allowance and Widowed Parent's Allowance. These are all now equally applicable to widowed men or those who have entered a civil partnership. Widows who were already in receipt of the Widow's Pension before it was replaced are not affected by the change and will continue to receive their pension as normal.

Bereavement Payment

This is a tax-free, lump-sum payment of £2,000 to help you when your husband, wife or civil partner has died. To get Bereavement Payment you must usually be under state pension age (currently 65 for men and 60 for women). Even if you are over state pension age, you may be able to get one, if your husband, wife or civil partner was not getting a state pension. The time limit for claiming a Bereavement Payment is 12 months after the person's death. You can fill in a claim form, obtainable from the Pension Service: **www.gov.uk**.

Bereavement Allowance

Bereavement Allowance is paid to widows and widowers between the ages of 55 and 59 inclusive. The standard weekly amount (2013/14) is £105.95. It is normally paid automatically once you have sent off your completed form BB1. In the event of your being ineligible, owing to insufficient NIC having been paid, you may still be entitled to receive Income Support, housing benefit or a grant or loan from the social fund. As applies to Widow's Pension, widows who remarry or live with a man as his wife cease to receive Bereavement Allowance. See website: **www.direct.gov.uk/benefits**.

Widowed Parent's Allowance

This is a taxable benefit for widows or widowers who are under state pension age and who have at least one child for whom they are entitled, or treated as entitled, to Child Benefit. The current value (2013/14) is £105.95 a week plus a share of any additional state pension you have built up. The share of additional pension payable will be between 50 and 100 per cent depending on your date of birth. The allowance is usually paid automatically. If for some reason, although eligible, you do not receive the money, you should inform your social security or Jobcentre Plus office. See website: **www.direct.gov.uk**.

Retirement pension

Once a widow reaches 60, she will normally receive a state pension based on her own and/or her late husband's contributions. If at the time of death the couple were already receiving the state retirement pension, the widow will continue to receive her share. An important point to remember is that a widow may be able to use her late husband's NIC to boost the amount she receives. Separate from the basic pension, a widow may also receive money from her late husband's occupational pension, whether contracted in or out of the state scheme. She may also get half of any of his graduated pension.

War widows and widowers

War Widow's or Widower's Pension is a tax-free pension for surviving widows, widowers or civil partners of veterans who died as a result of serving in HM armed forces before 6 April 2005. You may also be able to get extra money or help with funeral costs. The Service Personnel and Veterans Agency will pay War Widow's or Widower's Pension if any of the following applied before 6 April 2005:

- Your husband, wife or partner died as a result of a war injury, or because of a war-risk injury as a merchant seaman.
- Your husband, wife or partner was getting a War Disablement Pension at the 80 per cent rate or higher and was getting Unemployability Supplement.
- Your husband's, wife's or partner's death was due to, or happened sooner because of, their service with the Polish Forces under British command in the Second World War, or their service with the Polish Resettlement Forces.

- Your husband, wife or partner received, or was entitled to, Constant Attendance Allowance under the War Pension Scheme at the time they died.

- Your husband, wife or partner was a civil defence volunteer or a civilian and their death was due to, or happened sooner because of, a war injury or war service injury they suffered while serving in the Second World War.

If you are a widow, widower or surviving civil partner whose husband, wife or partner left service before 31 March 1973, you can keep your pension if you remarry, form a civil partnership or live with a new partner after 6 April 2005. Otherwise this pension may stop.

If you think you may be entitled to claim a War Widow's or Widower's Pension, visit the Service Personnel and Veterans Agency website: **www.veterans-uk.info**.

Chapter Four
Tax

If you can't explain it to a six-year-old, you don't understand it yourself.

ALBERT EINSTEIN, QUOTED IN *THE CHICAGO TRIBUNE*

No one likes paying tax. For the year 2014–15, the personal tax allowance is rising to £10,000. This is the first slice of income that all but the highest paid can earn before income tax kicks in. The good news is that there are many perfectly legitimate ways to ensure that you don't pay more tax than you have to. Here are a few tips on how to minimize your tax bill – most are dealt with in more detail later in the chapter.

- Interest on savings has been low over the last few years but whatever you earn from your savings is usually taxed at 20 per cent. If you have a partner who does not work then transferring savings into their name is one way of saving tax.

- ISAs are another good way to shelter some of your savings. For those paying higher rate tax, holding dividend paying shares in an ISA makes sense.

- With regard to bonds, it makes sense for all taxpayers to put these in ISAs. The income from government bonds (gilts) and corporate bonds is paid gross and is treated in the same way as bank interest. Do remember that bonds must have at least five years remaining to maturity before you can put them in an ISA.

- NS&I also have some savings products that are particularly helpful to higher-rate taxpayers.

- If you work for a company that is listed on the stock exchange, it may have a SAYE scheme. This is where you save money every month for a set period of time and at the end have the option of buying shares at a predetermined price. In the meantime all the interest received on the savings is tax free.

- Paying into a pension is another way to invest tax efficiently.

- Giving to charity. If you are a higher-rate taxpayer and donate to a charity using gift aid, you can claim the difference between the basic and higher rate of income tax as a tax refund. (You can do this on your self-assessment form.)

- Don't forget you can minimize CGT (Capital Gains Tax) by splitting assets with a partner in order to make use of two CGT allowances, but you can't carry any unused allowance forward.

- With Inheritance tax (IHT) everyone has a personal allowance of £325,000. Legal couples can have their partner's allowance transferred to them if they die, giving a potential allowance of £650,000. You can minimize IHT in a number of ways (see later in this chapter).

- Finally, VCTs (Venture capital trusts): if you are prepared to take the risk, you can put money into a fund that invests in unquoted companies. You get tax relief on the money you invest providing you hold the intestment for at least five years.

(Source: *The Week: PROSPER* **www.theweek.co.uk**)

Prudent tax planning is essential but take heed: the government is aiming to raise nearly £11 billion by clamping down on tax avoidance by savers, homeowners and business partners. These changes introduced in the April 2013 Budget (and due to come into force in April 2014) focus on avoidance, combined with a new general anti-abuse rule, could lead to traditional tax-planning measures being outlawed, experts have warned. Areas likely to come under the spotlight include partnerships: groups of highly paid employees who have been removed from the payroll by their employers and set up in a partnership. Another area of concern is the introduction of a third-party company or corporation into an otherwise legitimate partnership. Another area to watch is offshore accounts. A new agreement with the Isle of Man, Guernsey and Jersey will allow for 'automatic information exchange' and cover a wider range of accounts. Double trust arrangements were used to mitigate inheritance tax (IHT) until the practice was abolished in 2006. Existing schemes were allowed to continue but a clampdown has been announced. Anyone with these arrangements should now seek advice.

If HMRC is unhappy with any aspect of your tax planning arrangements, it can refer the matter to a panel to decide whether the measures are 'reasonable'. Advisers are concerned that there is no precedent for how the panel will work, or the decisions it may take. Make sure your arrangements are sound.

Understanding the broad principles of taxation helps you save money. While you were employed you may have been contributing many thousands of pounds to HM Revenue & Customs (HMRC), but in practice you may have had very little direct contact with the tax system. The accounts department would have automatically deducted – and accounted for – the PAYE on your earnings as a salaried employee. If you were self-employed, or had other money unconnected with your job, you may have had more dealings with your tax office.

The most common types of tax are income tax, National Insurance Contributions, capital gains tax and inheritance tax. On reaching retirement you should be able to calculate how much money (after deduction of tax) you will have available to spend: the equivalent, if you like, of your take-home pay. Your tax adviser should be fully conversant with your financial affairs so that he or she can advise in the light of your own circumstances. The following information is based on our understanding of current taxation, legislation and HMRC practice following the 2013 Budget statement. The impact of taxation (and any tax relief) depends on individual circumstances.

Income tax

This is calculated on all (or nearly all) of your income, after deduction of your personal allowance and, in the case of older married people, of the Married Couple's Allowance. The reason for saying 'nearly all' is that some income you may receive is tax free; types of income on which you do not have to pay tax are listed a little further on.

Most income counts, however. You will be assessed for income tax on your pension, interest you receive from most types of savings, dividends from investments, any earnings (even if these are only from casual work), plus rent from any lodgers, should the amount you receive exceed £4,250 a year. Many social security benefits are also taxable. The tax year runs from 6 April to the following 5 April, so the amount of tax you pay in any one year is calculated on the income you receive (or are deemed to have received) between these two dates. The four different rates of income tax for 2013/14 are:

- The 10 per cent starting rate for savings, which applies to the first £2,790 of any savings income. If an individual's taxable non-savings income exceeds the starting rate limit, then the 10 per cent starting rate for savings will not be available for savings income.

- The 20 per cent basic-rate tax for income up to £32,010. But in 2014/15, the basic rate will apply to a narrower band of income – £31,865.

- The 40 per cent higher-rate tax, which is levied on all taxable income from £32,011 up to £150,000. In 2014/15 the higher rate will kick in at £41,865 of income.

- The top rate of 45 per cent is levied on incomes in excess of £150,000.

NB: 300,000 more people have been drawn into the higher rate (40 per cent) tax band from 2013/14 as the threshold has been reduced from £42,475 to £41,450. (The rates available for dividends for 2013/14 tax year are the 10 per cent dividend ordinary rate, 32.5 per cent dividend upper rate and the 37.5 per cent dividend additional rate.)

Tax allowances

Personal allowance

Your personal allowance is the amount of money you are allowed to retain before income tax becomes applicable. When calculating how much tax you will have to pay in any one year, first deduct from your total income the amount represented by your personal allowance. You should add any other tax allowance to which you may be entitled – see further on. You will not have to pay any income tax if your income does not exceed your personal allowance (or total of your allowances), and you may be able to claim a refund for any tax you have paid, or that has been deducted from payments made to you, during the year.

Calculating your personal allowance since the introduction of independent taxation has become easier. Everyone receives the same basic personal allowance regardless of whether they are male, female, married or single. It does not matter where the income comes from, whether from earnings, an investment, a pension or another source.

The figures for the tax year 2013/14 are as follows:

- Personal allowance for people born after 5 April 1948 is £9,440. It will rise again to £10,000 in 2014/15.

- Personal allowance for people born between 6 April 1938 and 5 April 1948 is £10,500.

- Personal allowance for people born before 6 April 1938 is £10,660.

- From 6 April 2013 those allowances for anyone already aged 65 have been frozen, and the extra personal allowance scrapped for anyone who turned 65 after 5 April 2013. (This was dubbed the 'granny tax'.)

Married Couple's Allowance

Married Couple's Allowance (for those aged under 75) is no longer applicable. Age-related Married Couple's Allowance (aged 75 and over) for 2013/14 is £7,915. The minimum amount of Married Couple's Allowance is £3,040.

Some important points you should know:

- Married Couple's Allowance is available to people born before 6 April 1935. Tax relief for this allowance is restricted to 10 per cent.

- A widowed partner, where the couple at the time of death were entitled to Married Couple's Allowance, can claim any unused portion of the allowance in the year he or she became widowed.

- Registered blind people can claim an allowance of £2,160 a year. If both husband and wife are registered as blind, they can each claim the allowance. It is called the Blind Person's Allowance. If you think you would be eligible, you should contact your local tax office with relevant details of your situation. If you were entitled to receive the allowance earlier but for some reason missed out on doing so, you may be able to obtain a tax rebate.

Useful reading

For more detailed information about tax allowances, see HMRC website: **www.hmrc.gov.uk**. The Inland Revenue booklet, IR 121, *Approaching Retirement (A Guide to Tax and National Insurance Contributions)* is also useful.

Same-sex partners

Same-sex couples are treated the same as married couples for tax purposes. The most important thing to note is that only one property can qualify as their principal home for exemption from capital gains tax (CGT). Against this, there is no CGT to pay on transfer of assets between the couple, and similarly any assets left in a will to each other are free of inheritance tax.

Tax relief

Separate from any personal allowances, you can obtain tax relief on the following:

- a covenant for the benefit of a charity, or a donation under the Gift Aid scheme;
- contributions to occupational pensions, self-employed pension plans and other personal pensions;
- some maintenance payments, if you are divorced or separated and were aged 65 or older at 5 April 2000.

Mortgage interest relief

Mortgage interest relief was abolished on 6 April 2000. The only purpose for which relief is still available is in respect of loans secured on an older person's home to purchase a life annuity. However, to qualify, the loan must have been taken out (or at least processed and confirmed in writing) by 9 March 1999. Borrowers in this situation can continue to benefit from the relief for the duration of their loan. As before, the relief remains at 10 per cent on the first £30,000 of the loan.

Maintenance payments

Tax relief for maintenance payments was also withdrawn on 6 April 2000. Individuals in receipt of maintenance payments are not affected and will continue to receive their money free of income tax. Those who had to pay tax under the pre-March 1988 rules now also receive their payments free of tax. Most individuals paying maintenance, however, face higher tax bills. This applies especially to those who set up arrangements before the March 1988 Budget. While previously they got tax relief at their highest rate, from 6 April 2000 when maintenance relief was withdrawn they no longer get any relief at all. An exception has been made in cases where one (or both) of the divorced or separated spouses was aged 65 or over at 5 April 2000. Those paying maintenance are still able to claim tax relief – but only at the 1999/2000 standard rate of 10 per cent.

Pension contributions

HMRC sets limits on the contributions that individuals can invest in their pension plan and on the pension benefits they can receive. All company and personal pensions are now set under a single tax regime and new rules have been implemented (see Chapter 3, Pensions, for more information).

For further information on Pension Credit, see Chapter 3, Pensions, or look under 'Pension Credit' on the website: **www.gov.uk**.

Tax-free income

Some income you may receive is entirely free of tax. It is important to know what income is non-taxable and what can be ignored for tax purposes. If you receive any of the following, you can forget about the tax aspect altogether (for a full list see Citizens Advice Bureau website: **www.adviceguide.org.uk** – taxable and non-taxable income):

- Attendance Allowances;
- Back to Work Bonus;
- Bereavement Payment;
- Child Benefit; NB: Child Benefit cuts have been introduced for families with at least one parent earning £50,000, and axed for those on £60,000;

- Child dependency additions;
- Council Tax Benefit;
- Disability Living Allowance;
- Housing Benefit;
- Industrial Injuries disablement pension;
- Income-related Employment and Support Allowance;
- Income Support (in some circumstances, such as when the recipient is also getting Jobseeker's Allowance, Income Support benefit will be taxable);
- Social Fund payments;
- Pension Credit;
- all pensions paid to war widows (plus any additions for children);
- pensions paid to victims of Nazism;
- certain disablement pensions from the armed forces, police, fire brigade and merchant navy;
- annuities paid to the holders of certain gallantry awards;
- the £10 Christmas bonus (paid to pensioners);
- the Winter Fuel Payment (paid to pensioners);
- the extra £400 Winter Fuel Payment paid to households with a resident aged 80 and over;
- National Savings Premium Bond prizes;
- winnings on the National Lottery and other forms of betting;
- rental income of up to £4,250 a year from letting out rooms in your home;
- income received from certain insurance policies (mortgage payment protection, permanent health insurance, creditor insurance for loans and utility bills, various approved long-term care policies) if the recipient is sick, disabled or unemployed at the time the benefits become payable;
- SAYE bonuses;
- all income and dividends received from savings in an Individual Savings Account (ISA);
- all dividend income from investments in venture capital trusts (VCTs).

The following are not income, in the sense that they are more likely to be one-off rather than regular payments. However, as with the above list they are tax free:

- virtually all gifts (in certain circumstances you could have to pay tax if the gift is above £3,000 or if, as may occasionally be the case, the money from the donor has not been previously taxed);
- a redundancy payment, or a golden handshake in lieu of notice, up to the value of £30,000;
- a lump sum commuted from a pension;
- a matured endowment policy;
- accumulated interest from a Tax Exempt Special Savings Account (TESSA) held for five years;
- dividends on investments held in a Personal Equity Plan (PEP);
- compensation money paid to people who were mis-sold personal pensions;
- compensation paid to those who were mis-sold free-standing AVCs (FSAVCs). To qualify for exemption from tax, the money must be paid as a lump sum as opposed to annual payments.

Income tax on savings and investments

Savings

For the tax year 2013/14 the 10 per cent starting rate applies to savings income up to £2,790.

Investments

For most investments on which you are likely to receive dividends, basic-rate tax will have been deducted before the money is paid to you. If you are a basic-rate taxpayer, the money you receive will be yours in its entirety. If you pay tax at the higher rate, you will have to pay some additional tax and should allow for this in your budgeting.

Exceptionally, there are one or two types of investment where the money is paid to you gross – without the basic-rate tax deducted. These include NS&I income bonds, capital bonds, the NS&I Investment

Account and all gilt interest. (People who prefer to receive gilt interest net can opt to do so.) As with higher-rate taxpayers, you will need to save sufficient money to pay the tax on the due date.

Avoiding paying excess tax on savings income

Banks and building societies automatically deduct the normal 20 per cent rate of tax from interest before it is paid to savers. As a result, most working people, except higher-rate taxpayers, can keep all their savings without having to worry about paying additional tax. While convenient for the majority, a problem is that some 4 million people on low incomes – including in particular many women and pensioners – are unwittingly paying more tax than they need. Those most affected are non-taxpayers (anyone whose taxable income is less than their allowances) who, although not liable for tax, are having it taken from their income before they receive the money.

Non-taxpayers can stop this happening quite simply by requesting their bank and/or building society to pay any interest owing to them gross, without deduction of tax at source. If applicable, all you need do is request form R85 from the institution in question or HMRC Enquiry Centre, which you will then need to complete. If you have more than one bank or building society account, you will need a separate form for each account. People who have filled in an R85 should automatically receive their interest gross. If your form was not completed in time for this to happen, you can reclaim the tax from your tax office after the end of the tax year in April.

Reclaiming tax overpaid

If you are a non-taxpayer and have not yet completed an R85 form (or forms), you are very likely to be eligible to claim a tax rebate. To obtain a claim form and, if relevant, copies of form R85 for you to complete and give to your bank or building society, see website: **www.hmrc.gov.uk**.

Mistakes by HMRC

HMRC does sometimes make mistakes. Normally, if it has charged you insufficient tax and later discovers the error, it will send you a supplementary demand requesting the balance owing. However, under a provision known as the 'Official Error Concession', if the mistake was due to HMRC's failure 'to make proper and timely use' of information it received, it is possible that you may be excused the arrears.

Undercharging is not the only type of error. It is equally possible that you may have been overcharged and either do not owe as much as has been stated or, not having spotted the mistake, have paid more than you needed to previously. So if you have reason to think your tax bill looks wrong, check it carefully. If you think there has been a mistake, write to your tax office explaining why you think the amount is too high. If a large sum is involved it could well be worth asking an accountant to help you.

As part of the Citizen's Charter, HMRC has appointed an independent Adjudicator to examine taxpayers' complaints about their dealings with HMRC and, if considered valid, to determine what action would be fair. Complaints appropriate to the Adjudicator are mainly limited to the way HMRC has handled someone's tax affairs. Before approaching the Adjudicator, taxpayers are expected to have tried to resolve the matter either with their local tax office or, should that fail, with the regional office.

Genuine mistakes are excused by HMRC but individuals may need to convince officials that they had not been careless in completing their returns, otherwise they could be at risk of incurring a penalty of 30 to 100 per cent of the tax involved, plus the tax owed itself and interest, and potentially HMRC widening its focus on you and your tax affairs.

Important dates to remember: The deadline for filing paper self-assessment forms for the 2013/14 tax year is 31 October 2014. For those filing online will have until 31 January 2015.

Further information

For further information, see HMRC booklet *Code of Practice 1, Putting Things Right: How to complain*, available from tax offices. Contact the Adjudicator's Office for information about referring a complaint. The Adjudicator acts as a fair and unbiased referee looking into complaints about HMRC, including the Tax Credit Office, the Valuation Office and the Office of the Public Guardian and the Insolvency Service. See website: **www.adjudicatorsoffice.gov.uk**.

The TaxPayers' Alliance campaigns towards achieving a low-tax society: **www.taxpayersalliance.com**.

TaxHelp for Older People (TOP) is an independent, free tax advice service for over-60s whose household income is less than £17,000 a year: **www.taxvol.org.uk**.

Useful tax forms that can help you pay less tax

- R40 – If you want to claim back tax paid on savings and investments, you need to complete this form.

- R85 – Getting your interest paid without tax being taken off. Not a taxpayer? This form will save you having to claim tax back each year.

- P161 – Are you going to be 65 (61 for a woman) in this tax year? Or is your income changing, for example, state pension and private pensions are due to start? If yes, this form will inform HMRC of your age and income, allowing it to give you your age allowance and your new tax codes.

- R27 – This form helps you to settle the tax affairs of someone who has died. It is worth completing because it often creates a repayment and helps to sort out any final transfer of Married Couples' Allowance. Your solicitor, if you have one, will usually deal with it for you.

- P53 – If you have recently taken a lump sum rather than buying an annuity (pension), an enormous amount of tax was deducted before you received it. To claim this back immediately you should complete a P53.

- P45 – You should receive one of these when you finish work with an employer. If you start a new job in the same tax year it is important that you give it to your new employer. It will ensure you are given the correct tax code and the right tax is deducted.

- P46 – As important as the P45. If you start a new job and you do not have a P45 you must complete a P46. Your employer should prompt you to do this. If not, ask for one. This form also sorts out your tax codes.

- Forms 575 and 18 – If you are thinking of transferring some of your Married Couples' Allowance, Form 575 allows you to transfer the excess at the end of the tax year. Form 18 allows you to transfer the minimum amount.

Most forms can be obtained via the HMRC website: **www.hmrc.gov.uk**.

NB: HMRC is closing all of its 281 Enquiry Centres which gave face-to-face help to 2.5 million people with tax queries. This move starts in 2014 with the centres being replaced by a telephone service and home visits. The aim is to save HMRC £13 million a year. One of the reasons given by HMRC for introducing this change is that the number of people using the Enquiry Centres across the UK had halved from 5 million in 2005/06 to 2.5 million in 2011/12. The five-month pilot scheme started in June 2013. In future if you have a query you will have to use the HMRC telephone helpline or go online to get your tax query answered. (**www.bbc.co.uk/news/business-21789759**)

Tax credits

The amount of tax credits you get depends on how many children you have living with you, whether you work and how many hours you work, if you pay for childcare, if you or any child living with you has a disability, or if you are coming off benefits.

Working Tax Credit

This is an earnings top-up given to low-income workers, including the self-employed. Eligibility is normally restricted to couples and single parents with a low income. HMRC advises that the easiest way to check whether you are eligible is to complete the form listed under 'Tax credits' on its website: **www.hmrc.gov.uk**.

Child Tax Credit

This is a cash payment given to all families with a low household income that have at least one child under 16, or under 20 if in full-time education, and is paid in addition to a basic tax credit payment.

Need to claim

Payment is not automatic. In both cases – Working Tax Credit and Child Tax Credit – you need to complete an application form, obtainable from any Tax Enquiry Centre or via the website: **www.gov.uk** – Tax Credits.

Post-war credits

Post-war credits are extra tax that people had to pay in addition to their income tax between April 1941 and April 1946. The extra tax was treated as a credit to be repaid after the war. People who paid credits were given certificates showing the amount actually paid. In 1972 people who could produce at least one of their post-war credit certificates were invited to claim. In cases where the original credit holder has died without claiming repayment and the post-war credit certificate is still available, repayment can be made to the next of kin or personal representative of the estate. Interest is payable on all claims at a composite rate of 38 per cent. The interest is exempt from income tax. All claims should be sent to the Special Post-War Credit Claim Centre at HM Revenue & Customs, HM Inspector of Taxes, PWC Centre V, Ty Glas, Llanishen, Cardiff CF4 5TX.

Tax rebates

When you retire, you may be due for a tax rebate. If you are, this would normally be paid automatically, especially if you are getting a pension from your last employer. You should ask for a P45 form. Then either send it – care of your earlier employer – to the pension fund trustees or, in the event of your receiving only a state pension, to the tax office together with details of your age and the date you retired. Ask your employer for the address of the tax office to which you should write. If the repayment is made to you more than a year after the end of the year for which the repayment is due – and is more than £25 – HMRC will automatically pay you (tax-free) interest. HMRC calls this a 'repayment supplement'.

NB: HMRC says it never sends notifications of a tax rebate by e-mail, or asks you to disclose personal or payment information by e-mail. For more advice and suggestions to protect yourself from phishing scams, see Chapter 7 – How to complain and cautionary advice.

Mis-sold PPI

Millions of borrowers have been receiving refunds after being mis-sold payment protection insurance (PPI) with credit cards and personal loans.

This is good news as many are receiving cheques for thousands of pounds. Even better, they are being paid 8 per cent interest on the refunds, to compensate for being without their money all that time. *But* while there is no tax to pay on the refund element, which simply returns their own money to them, they have to pay tax on the interest, just as they do on earned interest in a savings account. Some lenders are deducting basic tax at 20 per cent, which non-taxpayers can reclaim, and higher-rate payers must report to the Revenue. The longer someone has been without their money, the higher the interest proportion of it will be.

Capital gains tax (CGT)

You may have to pay capital gains tax if you make a profit (or, to use the proper term, 'gain') on the sale of a capital asset. CGT applies only to the actual gain you make, so if you buy shares to the value of £100,000 and sell them later for £125,000, the tax office will be interested only in the £25,000 profit you have made. There is an exemption limit of currently £10,600 a year. For married couples, from 6 April 2014 each partner enjoys his or her own annual exemption of £11,000 and from 6 April 2015 this rises by 1 per cent to £11,100. This means a couple can make gains of £22,000 free of CGT in 2014. However, it is not possible to use the losses of one spouse to cover the gains of the other. Transfers between husband and wife remain tax free, although any income arising from such a gift will of course be taxed.

Any gains you make are taxed at 18 per cent for basic-rate taxpayers and 28 per cent for higher-rate and additional-rate taxpayers. Company owners benefit from a doubling of the lifetime limit on 'entrepreneurs' relief' to £10 million since 6 April 2011. The relief limits CGT to 10 per cent on the sale of business assets under certain conditions.

Free of capital gains tax

The following assets are not subject to CGT and do not count towards the gains you are allowed to make:

- your main home (but see the note below);
- your car;

- personal belongings up to the value of £6,000 each;
- proceeds of a life assurance policy (in most circumstances);
- profits on UK government stocks;
- National Savings certificates;
- SAYE contracts;
- building society mortgage cashbacks;
- futures and options in gilts and qualifying corporate bonds;
- Personal Equity Plan (PEP) schemes (now automatically ISAs);
- gains from assets held in an Individual Savings Account (ISA);
- Premium Bond winnings;
- betting and lottery winnings and life insurance policies if you are the original owner;
- gifts to registered charities;
- small part-disposals of land (limited to 5 per cent of the total holding, with a maximum value of £20,000);
- gains on the disposal of qualifying shares in a Venture Capital Trust (VCT) or within the Enterprise Investment Scheme (EIS), provided these have been held for the necessary holding period (see below).

Enterprise Investment Scheme (EIS)

Changes to investment limits and qualifying criteria allow more companies to attract up to £10 million a year of equity investment through the Enterprise Investment Scheme (EIS) and Venture Capital Trusts (VCTs) – both tax-efficient investment schemes – since April 2012.

The effect of the rules enacted in the Finance Act 2012 was that 'if an investor re-invests a capital gain arising in 2012/13 in SEIS shares either in 2012/13, or in 2013/14 subject to an election [under ITA 2007 s 257AB], then that gain is exempt from capital gains tax'. However, the legislation 'does not permit the amount of a 2013/14 gain to be invested in 2013/14 and become exempt from capital gains tax'.

Mitigating CGT by means of EIS or SEIS reinvestment is a complex area and expert advice is recommended. See HMRC website: **www.hmrc.gov.uk**.

Your home

Your main home is usually exempt from CGT. However, if you convert part of your home into an office or into self-contained accommodation on which you charge rent, the part of your home that is deemed to be a 'business' may be separately assessed and CGT may be payable when you come to sell it. (CGT would not apply if you simply take in a lodger who is treated as family, in the sense of sharing your kitchen or bathroom.)

If you leave your home to someone else who later decides to sell it, then he or she may be liable for CGT when the property is sold (although only on the gain since the date of death). There may also be inheritance tax implications, so you are strongly advised to consult a solicitor or accountant. If you own two homes, only one of them is exempt from CGT, namely the one you designate as your 'main residence'.

Selling a family business

CGT is payable if you are selling a family business and is 28 per cent for higher-rate and additional-rate taxpayers, but the reduced level of 18 per cent for basic-rate taxpayers. One possible option is the CGT deferral relief allowable to investors in an EIS. The key changes that potential investors should note are:

- the amount that can be invested is now £500,000 (previously £400,000);
- the amount an individual may invest in shares issued in the first half of the tax year and qualifying for income tax relief for the previous year is now £50,000 (previously £25,000);
- qualifying companies are limited to £7 million of gross assets before an investment (£8 million after an investment); and
- companies with property-backed assets, such as farming and nursing homes, no longer qualify as eligible trading companies.

This is a complex area, so before either retiring or selling shares you should seek professional advice.

Useful reading

For further information about capital gains tax, see booklet CGT1, *Capital Gains Tax: An Introduction*, available from any tax office. There are also a number of useful help sheets downloadable from the HMRC website: **www.hmrc.gov.uk**.

Inheritance tax (IHT)

Inheritance tax (IHT) is the tax that is paid on your 'estate'. The tax threshold (the level at which you'll need to pay tax) has been set at £325,000 and frozen at this rate until 2019 at the earliest. The threshold amount for married couples and civil partners is £650,000. The value of estates over and above this sum is taxed at 40 per cent.

There is no immediate tax on lifetime gifts between individuals. The gifts become wholly exempt if the donor survives for seven years. When the donor dies, any gifts made within the previous seven years become chargeable and their value is added to that of the estate. The total is then taxed on the excess over £325,000. Chargeable gifts benefit first towards the £325,000 exemption, starting with the earliest gifts and continuing in the order in which they were given. Any unused balance of the £325,000 threshold goes towards the remaining estate.

The £325,000 threshold allows married couples or civil partners to transfer the unused element of their IHT-free allowance to their spouse or civil partner when they die. IHT will, however, still be levied at 40 per cent above £325,000 on the estate of anyone who is single or divorced when they die.

The government changed the tax law in April 2012 to encourage donating to charities, and reduced the inheritance tax payable on estates that give at least 10 per cent to charity. The remainder is taxed at 36 per cent against the usual 40 per cent inheritance tax rate. Existing wills can be amended by codicil to include this 10 per cent provision. There is no such benefit to those whose estate falls below the current IHT threshold.

Gifts or money up to the value of £3,000 can be given annually free of tax, regardless of the particular date they were given. Additionally, it is possible to make small gifts to any number of individuals free of tax, provided the amount to each does not exceed £250.

An important consideration relating to IHT is the need to make a will. For further information, see 'Wills', in Chapter 16. If you have already written a will, have it checked by a professional adviser to ensure that you do not give money unnecessarily to HMRC. In view of the recent changes to IHT, check with your professional adviser or HMRC. For assistance see website: **www.gov.uk** – Probate and Inheritance Tax Helpline.

Tax treatment of trusts

There may be inheritance tax to pay when assets – such as money, land or buildings – are transferred into or out of trusts when they reach a 10-year anniversary. There are complex rules that determine whether a trust needs to pay IHT in such situations. New rules came into effect on 22 March 2006 for new trusts, additions of new assets to existing trusts, and other IHT-relevant events in relation to existing trusts. Transitional rules provided for a period of adjustment for certain existing trusts to 6 April 2008.

This is a particularly complex area, and professional advice is recommended. Further information is available on the website: **www.hmrc.gov.uk** – Inheritance tax and trusts.

Independent taxation

Both husband and wife are taxed independently on their own income. Each has his or her own personal allowance and rate band, and both independently pay their own tax and receive their own tax rebates. Couples should note that independent taxation applies equally to both capital gains tax and inheritance tax. Property left to a surviving spouse is, as before, free of inheritance tax.

Self-assessment

Tax return forms are sent out in April, and the details you need to enter on the form you receive in April 2014 are those relating to the 2013/14 tax year. All taxpayers now have a legal obligation to keep records of all their different sources of income and capital gains. These include:

- details of earnings plus any bonus, expenses and benefits in kind received;
- bank and building society interest;
- dividend vouchers and/or other documentation showing gains from investments;
- pension payments, eg both state and occupational or private pensions;

- miscellaneous income, such as freelance earnings, maintenance payments and taxable social security benefits;
- payments against which tax relief can be claimed (eg charitable donations or contributions to a personal pension).

HMRC advises that taxpayers are obliged to keep these records for 22 months after the end of the tax year to which they relate. If you are self-employed or a partner in a business, as well as the above list, you also need to keep records of all your business earnings and expenses, together with sales invoices and receipts. All records (both personal and business) need to be kept for five years after the fixed filing date.

Those most likely to be affected by the self-assessment system include anyone who normally receives a tax return, higher-rate taxpayers, company directors, the self-employed and partners in a business. If your only income is your salary from which tax is deducted at source, you will not have to worry about self-assessment. If, however, you have other income that is not fully taxed under PAYE (eg possibly benefits in kind or expenses payments) or that is not fully taxed at source, you need to notify HMRC within six months of the end of the tax year, and you may need to fill in a tax return.

If your financial affairs change, as they sometimes do on retirement (eg if you become self-employed or receive income that has not already been fully taxed), it is your responsibility to inform HMRC and, depending on the amount of money involved, you may need to complete a tax return. The government has recently revised the guidelines, and higher-rate taxpayers will no longer automatically receive a self-assessment form if their affairs can be handled through the PAYE system.

Please note that *self-calculation is optional*. HMRC will continue as before to do the sums for you if you think you are at risk of making a mistake. If you submit a paper return this must be filed by 31 October each year; the deadline for online filing is 31 January the following year.

Further information

See booklets SA/BK4, *Self-Assessment – A General Guide to Keeping Records*; SA/BK6, *Self-Assessment – Penalties for Late Tax Returns*; SA/BK7, *Self-Assessment – Surcharges for Late Payment of Tax* and SA/BK8, *Self-Assessment – Your Guide*, all obtainable free from any tax office. See website: **www.gov.uk** or HMRC website: **www.hmrc.gov.uk**.

Retiring abroad

There are many examples of people who retired abroad in the expectation of being able to afford a higher standard of living and who returned
home a few years later, thoroughly disillusioned. A vital question that
is often overlooked is the taxation effects of living overseas. If you are
thinking of retiring abroad, do thoroughly investigate the potential
effects this will have on your finances to avoid unpleasant surprises.

Taxation abroad

Tax rates vary from one country to another: a prime example is VAT,
which varies considerably in Europe. Additionally, many countries levy
taxes that don't apply in the UK. Wealth tax exists in quite a few parts
of the world. Estate duty on property left by one spouse to another is
also fairly widespread. There are all sorts of property taxes, different
from those in the UK, which – however described – are variously assess-
able as income or capital. Sometimes a special tax is imposed on foreign
residents. Some countries charge income tax on an individual's worldwide income, without the exemptions that apply in the UK.

Apart from the essential of getting first-class legal advice when buying
property overseas, if you are thinking of retiring abroad the golden
rule must be to investigate the situation thoroughly before you take an
irrevocable step, such as selling your home in the UK.

Your UK tax position if you retire overseas

Many intending emigrants cheerfully imagine that, once they have
settled themselves in a dream villa overseas, they are safely out of the
clutches of the UK tax office. This is not so. You first have to acquire
non-resident status. If you have severed all your ties, including selling
your home, to take up a permanent job overseas, this is normally granted
fairly quickly. But for most retirees, acquiring unconditional non-
resident status can take up to three years. The purpose is to check that
you are not just having a prolonged holiday but are actually living as
a resident abroad. During the check period, HMRC may allow you
conditional non-resident status and, if it is satisfied, full status will be
granted retrospectively.

Rules

The rules for non-residency are pretty stringent. You are not allowed to spend more than 182 days in the UK in any one tax year, or to spend more than an average of 90 days per year in the UK over a maximum of four tax years. Even if you are not resident in the UK, some of your income may still be liable for UK taxation.

UK income tax

All overseas income (provided it is not remitted to the UK) is exempt from UK tax liability. Income deriving from a UK source is, however, normally liable for UK tax. This includes any director's or consultant's fees you may still be receiving, as well as more obvious income such as rent from a property you still own.

An exception may be made if the country in which you have taken up residency has a double tax agreement with the UK (see below). If this is the case, you may be taxed on the income in your new residence – and not in the UK.

Additionally, interest paid on certain British government securities is not subject to tax. Non-residents may be able to arrange for their interest on a British bank deposit or building society account to be paid gross. Some former colonial pensions are also exempt.

Double tax agreement

A person who is a resident of a country with which the UK has a double taxation agreement may be entitled to exemption or partial relief from UK income tax on certain kinds of income from UK sources and may also be exempt from UK tax on the disposal of assets. The conditions of exemption or relief vary from agreement to agreement. It may be a condition of the relief that the income is subject to tax in the other country.

NB: if, as sometimes happens, the foreign tax authority later makes an adjustment and the income ceases to be taxed in that country, you have an obligation under the self-assessment rules to notify HMRC.

Capital gains tax

This is only charged if you are resident or ordinarily resident in the UK; so if you are in the position of being able to realize a gain, it is advisable to wait until you acquire non-resident status. However, to escape CGT you must wait to dispose of any assets until after the tax year of your departure and must remain non-resident (and not ordinarily resident) in the UK for five full tax years after your departure. Different rules apply to gains made from the disposal of assets in a UK company; these are subject to normal CGT.

Inheritance tax

You escape IHT only if:

- you were domiciled overseas for all of the immediate three years prior to death;
- you were resident overseas for more than three tax years in your final 20 years of life; and all your assets were overseas.

Even if you have been resident overseas for many years, if you do not have an overseas domicile you will have to pay IHT at the same rates as if you lived in the UK.

Domicile

You are domiciled in the country in which you have your permanent home. Domicile is distinct from nationality or residence. A person may be resident in more than one country, but at any given time he or she can be domiciled in only one. If you are resident in a country and intend to spend the rest of your days there, it could be sensible to decide to change your domicile. If, however, you are resident but there is a chance that you might move, the country where you are living would not qualify as your domicile. This is a complicated area, where professional advice is recommended if you are contemplating a change.

UK pensions paid abroad

If your state pension is your only source of UK income, tax is unlikely to be charged. If you have an occupational pension, UK tax will normally be charged on the total of the two amounts. Both state and occupational pensions may be paid to you in any country. If you are planning to retire to Australia, Canada, New Zealand or South Africa, it would be advisable to check on the up-to-date position regarding any annual increases you would expect to receive to your pension. Some people have found the level of their pension frozen at the date they left the UK, while others have been liable for unexpected tax overseas.

If the country where you are living has a double tax agreement with the UK, as previously explained, your income may be taxed there and not in the UK. The UK now has a double tax agreement with most countries. For further information, check the position with your local tax office. If your pension is taxed in the UK, you will be able to claim your personal allowance as an offset.

Any queries about your pension should be addressed to the International Payments Office, **International Pensions Centre**. For contact details see website: **www.gov.uk** – International Pensions Centre. See Chapter 3 (Pensions) for more information.

Health care overseas

People retiring to another EU country before state retirement age can apply for a form E106, which will entitle them to state health care in that country on the same basis as for local people. This is valid only for a maximum of two and a half years, after which it is usually necessary to take out private insurance cover until state retirement age is reached. More information and advice can be obtained from the website: **www.gov.uk** – Britons living abroad. Thereafter, UK pensioners can request the International Pensions Centre at Newcastle (see under 'UK pensions paid abroad' above) for a form E121, entitling them and their dependants to state health care as provided by the country in which they are living.

Useful reading

The Daily Telegraph Tax Guide by David Genders, published annually by Kogan Page; see website: **www.koganpage.com**. *Residents and Non Residents – Liability to Tax in the UK* (IR20) is available from any tax office. Leaflet SA29, *Your Social Security Insurance, Benefits and Health Care Rights in the European Community*, contains essential information about what to do if you retire to another EU country, available from any social security or Jobcentre Plus office or website: **www.jobcentreplus.gov.uk**.

Chapter Five
Investment

Successful investing has never been easy but since the financial crisis began, it's been a bit like journeying into the unknown. Bond yields are at record lows, central banks have never printed quite so much money (quantitative easing) nor have governments been quite so persistently in debt in all of recorded history (Britain has run a deficit for 51 of the last 60 years). With the likelihood of inflation rearing its ugly head again in the future and the markets as uncertain as ever, there's not much to cheer the average investor. If you're a short-term trader it's important to be aware of events around the globe that might move markets, since our world has never been more interconnected. But for those who are more interested in saving for retirement and for the long term, the principles of successful investing remain the same. Keep the costs down, shelter as much money from the taxman as you can, and buy assets when they are cheap and sell when they are expensive.

One thing investors know for certain is that getting (and paying for) good advice is essential if you are to avoid nasty surprises. The Retail Distribution Review (known as the RDR) was introduced in January 2013 for the benefit of everyone who invests and it is one of the few bits of good news that could make your retirement more pleasant than it might have been. RDR has been a fantastic thing for transparency and it is shaking up the industry. But the financial industry doesn't take threats to its profitability lying down – it always has a cunning plan. What can you do to avoid the issue? Put your money in investment trusts rather than unit trusts, buy individual shares (if you don't mind doing the research) or buy clean funds via a cheap transparent adviser. (More on this in Chapter 6 – Financial advisers.)

But back to basics: there's a big difference between 'saving' and 'investing'. Investing is for the long term. It's money you can put away for your retirement, and in the long run it should grow more rapidly than in a savings account. If you are saving for a shorter-term goal, say you're going to need it in less than five years, then you're looking to get the most interest paid on your money. This chapter does not attempt the impossible but where saving and investing is concerned it highlights things to look out for and what to avoid.

Here are some tips for starters:

- *Don't let your emotions ruin you.* Approach investing calmly and never panic. If the market crashes don't rush to dump everything. At the other end of the spectrum, overconfidence is also a threat.

- *Don't invest and forget.* Regularly reviewing your portfolio is essential. A six-monthly check should suffice and being disciplined increases the chance of improved investment performance.

- *Don't invest without understanding the risks.* Beware of investing by label: funds don't always do what they say on the tin.

- *It's risky to take no risk.* To grow your money you need to beat inflation and add a bit on top. Diversify: spread your risk, don't overinvest in one firm or sector and invest globally not just in your home market.

- *Be contrarian.* Have confidence to buy unpopular assets. Buy at a point of maximum pessimism, when prices are low and when volumes are low. Boom and bust have never been abolished, the same goes for stock market cycles.

- *Don't invest in myths.* That when times are tough you should avoid smaller domestic companies because they suffer more than larger global businesses. Being overcautious could mean missing out on some decent gains.

- *Be critical.* A critical, sceptical mind is key to investing skill. Form your own opinion and never go along with something just because 'an expert says so'.

- *Don't risk investing money you can't afford to lose.* When told by a friend that he was being kept awake at night because of his investments, JP Morgan, the founder of the investment bank, reportedly advised him 'to sell down to the sleeping point'.

- *Pick a strategy and stick with it.* Find a strategy that you are comfortable with and don't chop and change.

- *Start small then scale up.* The small investor can invest in any sector they like. Aim to find good firms at low prices. Study your target firms and understand why they are successful. Once you're comfortable with your strategy then gradually increase the amounts traded.

Thanks to the internet, investors have unprecedented opportunity to access information and advice. Here are some useful websites you could look at:

- *The Motley Fool.* Offers stock market news and analysis, plus some colourful discussion boards: **www.fool.co.uk**.

- *Henry Tapper.* An actuary who provides insightful views on all things pension and retirement-related: **www.henrytapper.com**.

- Ethical Money: **www.ethicalmoney.org**.

- Money Advice Service: **www.moneyadviceservice.org.uk**.

- Money Facts: **www.moneyfacts.co.uk**.

- Money Supermarket: **www.moneysupermarket.com**.

- This is Money: **www.thisismoney.co.uk**.

- Which?: **www.which.co.uk**.

Since everyone has different financial aims, there is no one-size-fits-all approach to investing. In very simple terms, there are four different types of investment you could consider:

- *Cash investments* – made into a bank account or cash ISA. These are generally short term and offer easy access to your money, and lower risk so the potential returns are much less than other types of investment. Your money is secure, but it could lose value due to tax and inflation.

- *Bonds and gilts* – effectively, an IOU from the government or big companies. When you buy one you are lending money that earns an agreed fixed rate of interest. Government bonds (called gilts) are backed by the state and are as good as guaranteed. Corporate bonds carry greater risk but offer the possibility of improved returns.

- *Investing in property* – directly as a buy-to-let investor or indirectly through certain investment funds carries more risk. Property prices go down as well as up, and it can take time to sell property. Be sure to seek advice beforehand.

- *Shares* – sometimes referred to as 'equities', basically means putting money on the stock market. You can do this by buying shares in individual companies or by investing through a professionally managed investment fund, such as a unit trust.

While you were working, you probably had an emergency fund equal to at least three months' take-home pay. In retirement you may not need such a big fund. Work out what you need to have put away for a rainy day; once you have this sum set aside, you could consider investing for higher potential returns.

Sources of investable funds

If you are looking at investment options from your resources, possible sums of quite significant capital include:

- *Commuted lump sum from your pension.* There is now one set of rules for all types of pension scheme, with members allowed a maximum of 25 per cent of their pension fund or 25 per cent of their lifetime limit, whichever is lower. There is no tax to pay when you receive the money.

- *Insurance policies* designed to mature on or near your date of retirement. These are normally tax free.

- *Profits on your home*, if you sell it and move to smaller, less expensive accommodation. Provided this is your main home, there is no capital gains tax to pay.

- *Redundancy money*, golden handshake or other farewell gift from your employer. You are allowed £30,000 redundancy money free of tax. The same is usually true of other severance pay up to £30,000. But there can be tax to pay if, however worded, your employment contract indicates that these are deferred earnings.

- *Sale of SAYE* and other share option schemes. The tax rules vary according to the type of scheme and since the rules are liable to change with each Budget statement, further information should be sought on the HMRC website: **www.hmrc.gov.uk**.

General investment strategy

Investments differ in their aims, their tax treatment and the amount of risk involved. If you are taking the idea of investing seriously, the aim for most people is to acquire a balanced portfolio. This could comprise a mix of investments variously designed to provide some income to supplement your pension and also some capital appreciation to maintain your standard of living in the long term. Except for annuities and National Savings and Investments, which have sections to themselves, the different types of investment are listed by groups, as follows: variable interest accounts, fixed interest securities, equities and long-term lock-ups. As a general strategy, mix and match your investments so they are spread across several groups.

Annuities

This is one of the biggest decisions that most people approaching retirement have to make: cashing in their pension and buying an annuity. When you buy an annuity, you hand over a lump sum (usually your pension fund, although you can withdraw up to 25 per cent of it as a tax-free lump sum first) to an insurance company in return for a regular, guaranteed income for the rest of your life. Under the current rules the earliest age you can do this is 55. This income is taxable if it exceeds your personal allowance. If you are retiring today, low annuity rates probably make you wince. That doesn't mean you should necessarily ignore them. Once you have bought your annuity, the income you receive is effectively free of investment risk. That has been transferred to your provider. There is little danger of running out of money as your provider has to pay you for as long as you live.

When you approach retirement your pension company will contact you about purchasing an annuity. They will provide you with a quotation, which will tell you the amount of money you have in your 'pension pot', the amount of tax free lump sum you are entitled to take, and the level of income you will receive each month (should you convert your pension fund to an annuity with them). Check you are getting the correct allowance and that you have the right tax code. This tells the pension company how much tax to deduct but there is no guarantee that it will be right. For more information, see **www.incometaxcalculator.com**. Specialist help for older people is available from **www.taxvol.org.uk**.

You need to do some research to make sure which type of annuity is best for you. You only get one chance to purchase an annuity, and once you have done so there is no going back. The benefit of shopping around is that you could very well receive more money by doing so. Each annuity provider will have different rates dependent on its own underwriting criteria and your own position. Research shows that by shopping around you may be able to increase the amount of income you receive by up to 20 per cent. Choosing an annuity is a decision that should not be taken without the help of a specialist financial adviser, who has experience in this field.

The gender gap closed in December 2012, from which point insurers are no longer allowed to take gender into account when fixing annuity rates. Rates for men will get worse and won't improve much for women either.

Types of annuities

There are several different kinds of annuities.

The most basic is a *level annuity*. This pays you a fixed income for the rest of your life. If you die, the income usually stops. And – crucially – it will not change if prices rise. So in an inflationary world, your purchasing power will fall every year. For example, if inflation averages 4 per cent a year, the purchasing power of your annuity income will halve in 18 years.

To avoid this you could buy an *increasing annuity*. Here the amount of income you receive will rise in line with inflation each year, or by a set percentage. And if you are worried about your insurance company keeping a large chunk of your pension fund should you die after only a few years of retirement, you could buy a *guaranteed annuity*. So if you bought a five-year guarantee, and you died after two years, your nominated beneficiary (your spouse perhaps) would receive annuity income for another three years.

Another option is a *joint-life annuity* where your partner can receive some or all of your pension income if you die before them. If you want to take a bit more of a risk, you could choose an *investment-linked annuity*. Here you start with an initial level of income while your fund is invested in an insurance company's with-profits-fund. If the fund makes a profit, your income goes up. If it loses money, however, your income goes down.

Your health can also have a significant impact. If you are a smoker or have an illness, you may be eligible for an *enhanced annuity* or *impaired life annuity*. These pay a higher annual income than a standard annuity. In short, the annuity provider is betting that you won't live as long, so it can afford to pay you more.

It pays to shop around

There are a wide range of annuities available and everyone is entitled to shop around for the best one for their circumstances. This is known as the OMO (Open Market Option). In other words you don't have to take the offer from your existing pension provider – you are free to go to any provider. Figures show that less than half of people shop around. Failing to do so is a huge mistake, particularly since annuity rates have fallen in recent years. The reasons for the fall in rates are due to people living longer. Insurance companies have to keep paying incomes for longer. Second, falling interest rates make it harder to generate a source of funds to pay annuity income. Currently there is a gap of around 20 per cent between the best and the worst annuity rates – so don't just take the first offer that comes your way.

Other options

If you don't want to buy an annuity because of low rates, there are a number of strategies you can use. One is known as *phased retirement*. This is where you set up a series of annuities and drawdowns with 25 per cent tax-free lump sums. You will get a lower starting income but if you think annuity rates are going to rise it might be worth considering.

Another possible option is *fixed-term annuities*. Here you set up an annuity for a fixed period (say 5 or 10 years). You get paid an income for the fixed term but at the end of the period, you have a guaranteed pot of money to reinvest again. As with phased retirement, your income will be lower than from a standard annuity.

Alternatives to annuities

Income drawdown is an alternative to buying an annuity at retirement. Instead of purchasing a guaranteed income from an insurance company, pension savings remain invested and a percentage can be 'drawn down' each year. There are two types: 'capped' imposes limits on how much you can withdraw; the other – 'flexible' – puts no limits on withdrawals. These products came into force in April 2011, replacing an unsecured pension or an alternatively secured pension, at the same time the government removed the requirement to buy an annuity by age 75. The catch is that you need at least £20,000 in other sources of guaranteed income, such as state pension and annuities, to qualify. Before making a decision financial advice is essential as there are certain risks. One good piece of news is that the income drawdown rules were changed in the April 2013 Budget. The limit has been restored to 120 per cent (previously limited to 100 per cent) of what you would get from the equivalent annuity. This change will attract more pensions to drawdown, experts predict, as one of the advantages is that drawdown can be used to minimize your tax bill in several ways (see 'How To Choose an Annuity' by Phil Oakley and Tim Bennett, *The Week PROSPER* – **www.theweek.co.uk**).

Tax

It is important in all of the above plans to consider carefully the tax implications. Income tax on optional annuities is relatively low, as part of the income is allowed as a return on capital that is not taxable. Pension-linked annuities are fully taxable.

How to obtain an annuity

The annuity market is large and there is a vast choice of products. A helpful free booklet is Martin Lewis's Money Saving Expert.com *Guide to Annuities* sponsored by Annuity Direct Limited (published March 2013). See: Martin Lewis's website: **www.moneysavingexpert.com** or Annuity Direct: **www.annuitydirect.co.uk**.

Other useful websites include:

Annuity Advisor: **www.annuity-advisor.co.uk**.

Annuity Bureau: **www.annuity-bureau.co.uk**.

Hargreaves Lansdown: **www.h-l.co.uk/pensions**.

Origen Annuities: **www.origenfsannuities.co.uk**.

William Burrows: **www.williamburrows.com**.

You can also buy an annuity direct from an insurance company or via an intermediary, such as an Independent Financial Adviser (IFA). See Chapter 6, Financial advisers, or consult these professional advice websites:

Unbiased.co.uk: **www.unbiased.co.uk**.

The Institute of Financial Planning: **www.financialplanning.org.uk**.

Personal Finance Society (PFS): **www.findanadviser.org**.

Telegraph Retirement Service: **www.telegraph.co.uk/retire**.

National Savings & Investments (NS&I)

NS&I Savings Certificates, of which there are two types (fixed interest and index linked), are free of tax. They do not pay much interest but any tax-free investment is worth considering. For non-taxpayers who invest in NS&I products there is no need to complete an HM Revenue & Customs (HMRC) form to receive money in full, as this is automatic. **www.nsandi.com**.

The main NS&I investments are:

- *Easy Access Savings Accounts*. This is an easy way to build up your savings, with instant access to your money and the option to save regularly by standing order.

- *Income Bonds*. A safe and simple way of earning additional income every month. They pay fairly attractive, variable, tiered rates of interest, increasing with larger investments. Interest is taxable, but paid in full without deduction of tax at source. There is no set term for the investment.

- *Fixed Interest Savings Certificates* are lump-sum investments that earn guaranteed rates of interest over set terms. There are two terms: two years and five years. For maximum benefit, you must hold the certificates for five years.

- *Index-linked Savings Certificates*. Inflation-beating tax-free returns guarantee that your investment will grow in spending power each year whatever happens to the cost of living. Certificates must be retained for either three or five years. Interest is tax free.

- *Children's Bonus Bonds* allow you to invest for a child's future in their own name – and there's no tax to pay on the interest or bonuses. Interest rates are fixed for five years at a time plus a guaranteed bonus. These are tax free for parents and children and need not be declared to HMRC.

NB The April 2013 Budget revealed that the Treasury will not relaunch index-linked savings certificates, the accounts run by NS&I that pay interest matching inflation, plus a bonus on top, tax-free, for at least a year.

Complaints

If you have a complaint about any NS&I product, you should raise this with the Director of Savings. Should the matter not be resolved to your satisfaction it can be referred to the **Financial Ombudsman Service;** see website: **www.financial-ombudsman.org.uk.**

Variable interest accounts

You can save in a wide range of savings accounts with banks, building societies, credit unions and National Savings & Investments (NS&I) – already mentioned. With around 54 million current accounts in the UK, banks and building societies frequently introduce new accounts with introductory bonuses, to attract new customers. Although keeping track may be time consuming, all advertisements for savings products must now quote the annual equivalent rate (AER). AER provides a true comparison taking into account the frequency of interest payments and whether or not interest is compounded.

NB: The over-50s are being advised to show added caution when signing up to a savings account, particularly if it is tailored to their age. By looking only at over-50s products, savers would be ignoring over 93 per cent of the market. There are around 43 different variable-rate bank accounts available for the over-50s in the UK, offered by 22 different providers (*The Mature Times* – **www.maturetimes.co.uk**).

Definition

Other than the interest-bearing current accounts described above, these are all 'deposit'-based savings accounts of one form or another, arranged with banks, building societies, the National Savings & Investments Bank, and some financial institutions that operate such accounts jointly with banks. The accounts include instant-access accounts, high-interest accounts and fixed-term savings accounts. Some institutions pay interest annually; others – on some or all of their accounts – will pay it monthly. Although you may get a poor return on your money when interest rates drop, your savings will nearly always be safe. Should the bank or building society get into serious financial difficulty, up to £85,000 of your money will be 100 per cent protected under the **Financial Services Compensation Scheme**. See website: **www.fscs.org.uk**.

Access

Access to your money depends on the type of account you choose: you may have an ATM card and withdraw your money when you want; you may have to give a week's notice or slightly longer. If you enter into a term account, you will have to leave your money deposited for the agreed specified period. In general, the longer the period of notice required the better the rate of interest earned.

Sum deposited

You can open a savings account with as little as £1. For certain types of account, the minimum investment could be anything from £500 to about £5,000. The terms tend to vary depending on how keen the institutions are to attract small investors.

Tax

With the exception of tax-free cash ISAs and of the National Savings and Investments Bank, where interest is paid gross, tax is deducted at source. However, you must enter the interest on your tax return and, if you are a higher-rate taxpayer, you will have additional liability. Basic-rate taxpayers pay 20 per cent on their bank and building society interest. Higher-rate taxpayers pay 40 per cent. Non-taxpayers can arrange to have their interest paid in full by completing a certificate (R85, available from HMRC or the bank) that enables the financial institution to pay the interest gross. If you largely rely on your savings income and believe you are or have been paying excess tax, you can reclaim this from HMRC. For further information, see 'Income tax on savings and investments' in Chapter 4.

Choosing a savings account

There are two main areas of choice: the type of savings account and where to invest your money.

Instant-access savings account

This attracts a relatively low rate of interest, but it is both easy to set up and very flexible, as you can add small or large savings when you like and can usually withdraw your money without any notice. It is an excellent temporary home for your cash if you are saving short term. However, it is not recommended as a long-term savings plan.

High-interest savings account

Your money earns a higher rate of interest than it would in an ordinary savings account. However, to open a high-interest account you will need to deposit a minimum sum, which could be £500 to £1,000. Although you can always add to this amount, if your balance drops below the required minimum your money will immediately stop earning the higher interest rate. Terms vary between providers. Usually interest is only paid yearly, and you can only withdraw yearly.

Fixed-term savings account

You deposit your money for an agreed period of time, which can vary from a few months to over a year. In return for this commitment, you will normally be paid a superior rate of interest. As with high-interest accounts, there is a minimum investment: roughly £1,500 to £10,000. If you need to withdraw your money before the end of the agreed term, there are usually hefty penalties. If interest rates are still low, your money may be better invested elsewhere.

Equity-linked savings account

This offers a potentially better rate of return, as the interest is calculated in line with the growth in the stock market. Should the market fall, you may lose the interest, but your capital should normally remain protected. The minimum investment varies from about £500 to £5,000 and, depending on the institution; the money may need to remain deposited for perhaps as much as five years.

ISA savings

See later in this chapter, page 93.

Information

For banks, enquire direct at your nearest high street branch. You can also investigate other banks and building societies to see whether they offer better terms. Look at as many as you can since the terms and conditions may vary quite widely. The **Building Societies Association** offers information and advice on savings and types of accounts and much more. See its website: **www.bsa.org.uk**.

The safety of your investment

Investors are protected by the legislative framework in which societies operate and, in common with bank customers, their money (up to a stated maximum) is protected under the **Financial Services Compensation Scheme**. See website: **www.fscs.org.uk**.

Complaints

If you have a complaint against a bank or building society, you can appeal to the **Financial Ombudsman Service** (FOS) to investigate the matter, provided the complaint has already been taken through the particular institution's own internal disputes procedure – or after eight weeks if the problem has not been resolved – and provided the matter is within the scope of the Ombudsman Scheme. Generally speaking, the FOS can investigate complaints about the way a bank or building society has handled some matter relating to its services to customers. See website: **www.financial-ombudsman.org.uk**.

Fixed interest securities

Fixed interest securities pay interest at a rate that does not change with any external variable. The coupon payments are known in advance. Coupons are almost always all for the same amount and paid at regular intervals, regardless of what happens to interest rates generally. There are two risks with fixed income securities: credit risk and interest rate risk.

Credit risk is one of the main determinants of the price of a bond. The price of a debt security can be explained as the present value of the payments (of interest and repayment of principal) that will be made. Credit risk is an issue for lenders such as banks, ie losses to the bank. So correlation with the bank's other lending is what matters, not correlation with debt available in the market.

Interest rate risk is simply the risk to which a portfolio or institution is exposed because future interest rates are uncertain. Bond prices are interest rate sensitive so if rates rise, the present value of a bond will fall sharply. This can also be thought of in terms of market rates: if interest rates rise, then the price of a bond will have to fall for the yield to match the new market rates. The longer the duration of a bond, the more sensitive it will be to movements in interest rates.

If you buy when the fixed rate is high and interest rates fall, you will nevertheless continue to be paid interest at the high rate specified in the contract note. However, if interest rates rise above the level when you bought, you will not benefit from the increase. Generally these securities give high income but only modest, if any, capital appreciation. The securities include high interest gilts, permanent interest-bearing shares, local authority bonds and stock exchange loans, debentures and preference shares.

Gilt-edged securities

Definition

Gilts, or gilt-edged securities, are bonds issued by the UK government that offer the investor a fixed interest rate for a predetermined, set time, rather than one that goes up or down with inflation. But the gilt market isn't what it used to be. The Bank of England used to own no gilts at all. Now, via quantitative easing, it owns £375 billion, more than a quarter of the market. More importantly, it's nearly half of the £800 billion the government has issued since December 2007. The 10-year gilt yield is now around 2.0 per cent and seemed to bottom out around August 2012. If thinking of buying gilts, diversify your portfolio.

Buying gilts is best done when interest rates are high and look likely to fall. When general interest rates fall, the value of the stock will rise and can be sold profitably. When buying or selling, consideration must be given to the accrued interest that will have to be added to or subtracted from the price quoted. Gilts are complicated by the fact that you can either retain them until their maturity date, in which case the government will return the capital in full, or sell them on the London Stock Exchange at market value.

Yields are low and while bank interest rates remain at current levels things are not likely to improve.

Index-linked gilts

Index-linked gilts are government-issued bonds – glorified IOUs – that you can buy to obtain a guaranteed rate of return over inflation. In previous years they have performed well, but if you are buying them now you will be doing so at a premium and it is likely you will suffer capital losses as their value falls back, even while your income remains above inflation. However, if you are less worried about preserving your capital and require inflation-linked income, then these can still be useful in a balanced portfolio.

Tax

Gilt interest from whatever source is paid gross. Gross payment means that you must allow for a future tax bill before spending the money. Recipients who prefer to receive the money net of tax can ask for this to be arranged. A particular attraction of gilts is that no capital gains tax is charged on any profit you may have made, but equally no relief is allowed for any loss.

How to buy

You can buy gilts through banks, building societies, a stockbroker or a financial intermediary, or you can purchase them through **Computershare Investor Services**; see website: **www.computershare.com**. In all cases, you will be charged commission.

Assessment

Gilts normally pay reasonably good interest and offer excellent security, in that they are backed by the government. You can sell at very short notice, and the stock is normally accepted by banks as security for loans, if you want to run an overdraft. Index-linked gilts, which overcome the inflation problem, are generally speaking a better investment for higher-rate taxpayers – not least because the interest paid is very low.

Gilt plans

This is a technique for linking the purchase of gilt-edged securities and with-profit life insurance policies to provide security of capital and income over a 10- to 20-year period. It is a popular investment for the commuted lump sum taken on retirement. These plans are normally obtainable from financial intermediaries.

Permanent interest-bearing shares (PIBS)

These are a form of investment offered by some building societies to financial institutions and private investors as a means of raising share capital. They have several features in common with gilts: they pay a fixed rate of interest that is set at the date of issue; this is likely to be on the high side when interest rates generally are low and on the low side when interest rates are high. The interest is usually paid twice yearly, there is no stamp duty to pay or capital gains tax on profits. Despite the fact that PIBS are issued by building societies, they are very different from normal building society investments. They are generally rated as being in the medium- to high-risk category, so professional advice should be taken first.

Equities

These are all stocks and shares, purchased in different ways and involving varying degrees of risk. They are designed to achieve capital appreciation as well as give you some regular income. Most allow you to get your money out within a week. Millions of people in the UK invest in shares. Equity securities usually provide steady income as dividends but they fluctuate with the ups and downs in the economic cycle. Investing has never been easier with the growing number of internet-based trading facilities. Equities include ordinary shares, unit trusts, OEICs (see below), investment trusts and REITs.

Equities probably provide the greatest potential for income that can beat inflation over the medium to long term. Dividend yields on many equity funds are currently in excess of 3–4 per cent per annum, due to the corporate world's finances being in a healthier state than those of governments. Most businesses are well placed to continue to pay decent levels of dividends unless there is a protracted period of economic recession.

Unit trusts and OEICs

Definition

Unit trusts and OEICs (Open-Ended Investment Companies, a modern equivalent of unit trusts) are forms of shared investments, or funds, which allow you to pool your money with thousands of other people and invest in world stock markets. The advantages are that it is simple to understand, you get professional management and there are no day-to-day decisions to make. Additionally, every fund is required by law to have a trustee (called a 'depository' in the case of OEICs) to protect investors' interests.

Unit trusts have proved incredibly popular because your money is invested in a broad spread of shares and your risk is reduced, but they are rapidly being replaced by the OEIC (pronounced 'oik'). The minimum investment in some of the more popular funds can be as little as £25 a month or a £500 lump sum. Investors' contributions to the fund are divided into units (shares in OEICs) in proportion to the amount they have invested. Unit trusts and OEICs are both open-ended investments. As with ordinary shares, you can sell all or some of your investment by telling the fund manager that you wish to do so. The value of the shares you own in an OEIC, or units in a unit trust, always reflects the value of the fund's assets. The key differences between the two are:

- *Pricing*: when investing in unit trusts, you buy units at the offer price and sell at the lower bid price. The difference in the two prices is known as the spread. To make a return the bid price must rise above the offer before you sell the units. An OEIC fund contrastingly has a single price, directly linked to the value of the fund's underlying investments. All shares are bought and sold at this single price. An OEIC is sometimes described as a 'what you see is what you get' product.

- *Flexibility*: an OEIC fund offers different types of share or sub-fund to suit different types of investor. The expertise of different fund management teams can be combined to benefit both large and small investors. There is less paperwork as each OEIC will produce one report and accounts for all sub-funds.

- *Complexity*: unit trusts are, legally, much more complex, which is one of the reasons for their rapid conversion to OEICs. Unit trusts allow an investor to participate in the assets of the trust without actually owning any. Investors in an OEIC buy shares in that investment company.

- *Management*: with unit trusts, the fund's assets are protected by an independent trustee and managed by a fund manager. OEICs are protected by an independent depository and managed by an authorized corporate director.

- *Charges*: unit trusts and OEICs usually have an upfront buying charge, typically 3–5 per cent, and an annual management fee of between 0.5 and 1.5 per cent. It is possible to reduce these charges by investing through a discount broker or fund supermarket, but this means acting without financial advice. Charges on OEICs are relatively transparent, shown as a separate item on your transaction statement.

Investment trusts

Over the past decade investment trusts beat unit trusts in eight of nine key sectors. One of the biggest benefits investment trusts offer is to income investors. While open-ended funds must pay out all the income they receive, investment trusts can hold some back in reserve. This allows them to offer a smoother and more certain return. There are four major advantages an investment trust has over a unit trust:

- *Cost*. The initial charges on unit trusts typically range from 4 to 6 per cent but there is also the annual fee costing in the region of 1.5 to 2 per cent. An investment trust also levies annual fees, but on average they are lower because most investment trusts don't pay commission to financial advisers.

- *Gearing*. Like other companies, investment trusts are fairly free to borrow for investment purposes. Unit trusts, however, are usually restricted by regulation. But when markets are rising and the trust is run well, gearing will deliver superior returns.

- *Size*. Investment trusts tend to be smaller than unit trusts on average, and so are less unwieldy and more focused on their investment objectives. To grow beyond their initial remit, they need permission from shareholders. Many also have a fixed life expectancy. Conversely, unit trusts are called 'open ended' because they can expand and contract to meet demand. (Big is not always beautiful.)

- *Discounts.* Because their shares are listed and traded freely (unlike a unit trust), investment trusts can end up with a market capitalization that is greater than (at a 'premium'), or lower than (at a 'discount') its assets under management (the 'net asset value', or NAV). If the discount narrows after you buy, you'll make a small gain on top of any increase in the trust's NAV.

How to obtain

Units and shares can be purchased from banks, building societies, insurance companies, stockbrokers, specialist investment fund providers and Independent Financial Advisers, directly from the management group and via the internet. Many of the larger firms may use all these methods. For a list of unit trusts, investment trusts and OEICs the **Investment Management Association** (IMA) website gives information: **www.investmentfunds.org.uk**. Or you can look at the following:

www.thisismoney.co.uk/investing;

www.moneyweek.com;

www.moneysupermarket.com;

www.investment-advice.org.uk;

www.investorschronicle.co.uk.

For further information on investment advice, see Chapter 6, Financial advisers.

Tax

Units and shares invested through an ISA have special advantages (see 'Individual Savings Account', below). Otherwise, the tax treatment is identical to that of ordinary shares.

Assessment

Unit trusts and OEICs are an ideal method for smaller investors to buy stocks and shares: less risky and easier. This applies especially to tracker funds, which have the added advantage that charges are normally very low. Some of the more specialist funds are also suitable for those with a significant investment portfolio.

Complaints

Complaints about unit trusts and OEICs are handled by the **Financial Ombudsman Service** (FOS). It has the power to order awards of up to £100,000. Before approaching the FOS, you must first try to resolve the problem with the management company direct via its internal complaints procedure. If you remain dissatisfied, the company should advise you of your right to refer the matter to the FOS; see website: **www.financial-ombudsman.org.uk**.

The safety of your investment

Investors are protected by the legislative framework and, in common with bank customers, their money (up to a stated maximum) is protected under the **Financial Services Compensation Scheme** (FSCS); see website: **www.fscs.org.uk**.

Ordinary shares listed on the London Stock Exchange

Definition

Public companies issue shares as a way of raising money. When you buy shares and become a shareholder in a company, you own a small part of the business and are entitled to participate in its profits through a dividend, which is normally paid six monthly. It is possible that in a bad year no dividends at all will be paid. However, in good years, dividends can increase very substantially. The money you invest is unsecured. This means that, quite apart from any dividends, your capital could be reduced in value – or if the company goes bankrupt you could lose the lot. The value of a company's shares is decided by the stock market. The price of a share can fluctuate daily, and this will affect both how much you have to pay if you want to buy and how much you will make (or lose) if you want to sell.

See the **London Stock Exchange** website: **www.londonstockexchange. com**, to find a list of brokers in your area that would be willing to deal for you. The securities department of your bank or one of the authorized share shops will place the order for you, or you can do it online. Whichever method you use, you will be charged both commission and stamp duty, which is currently 0.5 per cent. Unless you use a nominee account (see below), you will be issued with a share certificate that you or your financial adviser must keep, as you will have to produce it when you wish to sell all or part of your holding. It is likely, when approaching a stockbroker or other share-dealing service, that you will be asked to deposit money for your investment upfront or advised that you should use a nominee account. This is because of the introduction of several new systems, designed to speed up and streamline the share-dealing process.

There are three types of shares that are potentially suitable for small investors:

- *Investment companies* invest in the shares of other companies. They pool investors' money and so enable those with quite small amounts to spread the risk by gaining exposure to a wide portfolio of shares, run by a professional fund manager. See the **Association of Investment Companies** website: **www.theaic.co.uk**.

- *Real estate investment trusts (REITs)* pool investors' money and invest it for them collectively in commercial and residential property. They offer individuals a cheap, simple and potentially less risky way of buying shares in a spread of properties, with the added attraction that the funds themselves are more tax efficient, as both rental income and profits from sales are tax free within the fund. Also, if wanted, REITs can be held within an ISA or Self-Invested Personal Pension (SIPP). It is recommended that professional advice is taken before investing.

- *Convertible loan stocks* give you a fixed guaranteed income for a certain length of time and offer you the opportunity to convert them into ordinary shares. While capital appreciation prospects are lower, the advantage of convertible loans is that they usually provide significantly higher income than ordinary dividends. They are also allowable for ISAs.

Tax

All UK shares pay dividends net of 10 per cent corporation tax. Basic-rate and non-taxpayers have no further liability to income tax. Higher-rate taxpayers must pay further income tax at 22 per cent. Quite apart from income tax, if during the year you make profits by selling shares that in total exceed £10,600 (the annual exempt amount for an individual in 2012/13) you will be liable for capital gains tax, which is now calculated at a flat rate of 28 per cent.

NB: From April 2014 investors in London's Alternative Investment Market (AIM) will no longer pay 0.5 per cent stamp duty on transactions. In the past AIM shares were deemed risky but there is now a proposal to allow them to be included in a shares ISA, making them free of income and capital gains tax. But investors are advised to be cautious, possibly opting for a professionally managed fund.

Assessment

Although dividend payments generally start low, in good companies they are likely to increase over the years and so provide a first-class hedge against inflation. Good advice is critical, as this is a high-risk, high-reward market.

Individual Savings Account (ISA)

Definition

Despite low interest rates, savers who use cash ISAs can build up their nest eggs three times faster than those who put them in instant access accounts. If you're looking to get the most interest paid on your savings, a cash ISA is about the best bet. ISAs are very popular forms of investment as all income and gains generated in the account are tax free, and they stay tax free, year after year. It is important to shop around for the best rates and take full advantage of your annual allowance. There are two types of ISA: cash ISAs and stocks and shares ISAs. The ISA allowance is the amount you are allowed to invest in each financial year, set by the Chancellor of the Exchequer in the annual Budget. At 6 April 2013 the limit is £5,760 per year in a cash ISA and up to £11,520 in a stocks and shares ISA. The cash ISA limit is half the value of the stocks and shares ISA limit. The 2013 Budget ignored calls to change the rules on ISAs and let the full £11,580 allowance be held in cash.

It's up to you to choose the best home for your money. Instant access cash ISAs are perfect for money you may need in the short term. However, if you don't need it for a long time, notice cash ISAs and fixed-rate cash ISAs offer better interest rates. New ISAs are often introduced with attractive bonus rates, then after 12 months this is quietly removed and your savings are left earning very little. The only way to avoid this is to check your old accounts and then switch.

Self-select stocks and share ISAs are growing in popularity. Rather than opting to buy a fund for your ISA, these let you pick from a wide range of individual investments. First you'll have to find the best one. Most brokers offer some sort of self-select ISA. Self-select ISAs usually come with an annual management fee. This will be either a fixed amount (normally between £20 and £50 per year) or a percentage of the total investment. There are two types of brokers (execution-only and full service). Execution-only brokers simply provide you with the internet trading platform and charge the lowest fees. Full service or advisory brokers give advice on what to put into your ISA and are consequently more expensive. Given that the whole point of a self-select ISA is to avoid paying too many fees, think carefully before choosing.

The Junior ISA (JISA) replaced the short-lived Child Trust Fund (CTF) scheme. New junior ISAs are a tax-efficient wrapper for your investments. There is no capital gains tax or income tax to be paid but the annual allowance is smaller – £3,720 (2013/2014) and they are available to all children born on or after 3 January 2011, or born before September 2002, or are under 18 and do not have a Child Trust Fund (see below). The fund is locked until the child is 18 when they get control of the money.

Tax

ISAs are completely free of all income tax and capital gains tax. You should be aware that a 20 per cent charge is levied on all interest accruing from non-invested money held in an ISA that is not specifically a cash ISA.

Assessment

ISAs offer a simple, flexible way of starting, or improving, a savings plan. While cash ISAs remain useful, there are fewer advantages to basic-rate taxpayers as a result of the charges and the removal of the dividend tax credit. For further information on the various forms of ISAs, see these websites:

www.thisismoney.co.uk/investing;

www.moneyweek.com;

www.moneyadviceservice.org.uk;

www.moneysavingexpert.com;

www.moneysupermarket.com;

www.investment-advice.org.uk;

www.investorschronicle.co.uk;

www.investmentfunds.org.uk.

www.telegraph.co.uk/isas

NB: The banks are set to agree a new ISA transfer system which should reduce the time (up to three weeks) it can currently take to move from one ISA to another. Bear in mind that you can transfer a cash ISA into a shares ISA but not the other way round. While the current year's cash ISA must be moved between providers, whole, allowances from previous years can be split between different providers. Remember that once you take money out of any ISA, you can't put it back in.

Child Trust Funds

Children born after December 2010 are not eligible for a Child Trust Fund. However, accounts set up for eligible children will continue to benefit from tax-free investment growth. Withdrawals will not be possible until the child reaches 18. The child, friends and family will be able to contribute £1,200 per year. It was announced in the April 2013 Budget that for these children there are now moves afoot to enable them to transfer their funds. See website: **www.childtrustfund.gov.uk**.

Useful reading

How the Stock Market Works by Michael Becket of the *Daily Telegraph*, published by Kogan Page; see website: **www.koganpage.com**.

Long-term lock-ups

Certain types of investment, mostly offered by insurance companies, provide fairly high guaranteed growth in exchange for your under-taking to leave a lump sum with them or to pay regular premiums for a fixed period, usually five years or longer. The list includes life assurance policies, investment bonds and some types of National Savings Certificates.

Life assurance policies

Definition

Life assurance can provide you with one of two main benefits: it can either provide your successors with money when you die or it can be used as a savings plan to provide you with a lump sum (or income) on a fixed date. There are three basic types of life assurance: whole-life policies, term policies and endowment policies.

- *Whole-life policies* are designed to pay out on your death: you pay a premium every year and, when you die, your beneficiaries receive the money. The insurance holds good only if you continue the payments. If one year you did not pay and were to die, the policy could be void and your successors would receive nothing.

- *Term policies* involve a definite commitment. As opposed to paying premiums every year, you elect to make regular payments for an agreed period, for example until such time as your children have completed their education, say eight years. If you die during this period, your family will be paid the agreed sum in full. If you die after the end of the term (when you have stopped making payments), your family will normally receive nothing.

- *Endowment policies* are essentially savings plans. You sign a contract to pay regular premiums over a number of years and in exchange receive a lump sum on a specific date, this could be from 10 to 25 years. Once you have committed yourself, you have to go on paying every year (as with term assurance). There are heavy penalties if you decide that you no longer wish to continue.

An important feature of endowment policies is that they are linked to death cover. If you die before the policy matures, the remaining payments are excused and your successors will be paid a lump sum on your death. The amount of money you stand to receive, however, can vary hugely, depending on the charges and how generous a bonus the insurance company feels it can afford on the policy's maturity. Over the past few years, payouts have been considerably lower than their earlier projections might have suggested. Aim to compare at least three policies before choosing.

Both whole-life policies and endowment policies offer two basic options: with profits or without profits:

- *Without profits* – sometimes known as 'guaranteed sum assured'. The insurance company guarantees you a specific fixed sum, you know the amount in advance and this is the sum you – or your successors – will be paid.

- *With profits* – you are paid a guaranteed fixed sum plus an addition, based on the profits that the insurance company has made by investing your annual or monthly payments. The basic premiums are higher and the profits element is not known in advance.

- *Unit linked* is a refinement of the 'with profits' policy, in that the investment element of the policy is linked in with a unit trust.

Premiums can normally be paid monthly or annually, as you prefer. The size of premium varies enormously, depending on the type of policy you choose and the amount of cover you want. As a generalization, higher premiums tend to give better value, as relatively less of your contribution is swallowed up in administrative costs. You may be required to have a medical check if large sums are involved. More usually, you fill in and sign a declaration of health. If you make a claim on your policy and it is subsequently discovered that you gave misleading information, your policy could be declared void and the insurance company could refuse to pay. Many insurance companies offer a better deal if you are a non-smoker. Some also offer more generous terms if you are teetotal. Women generally pay less than men of the same age because of their longer life expectancy.

How to obtain

Policies are usually available through banks, insurance companies, Independent Financial Advisers and building societies. Be careful with the small print: terms and conditions that sound very similar may obscure important differences that could affect your benefit. To be sure of choosing the policy best suited to your requirements, consult an IFA. For help in finding an IFA in your area, see websites: **www.unbiased.co.uk**; **www.financialplanning.org.uk**; **www.findanadviser.org**. See also Chapter 6, Financial advisers.

Disclosure rules

Advisers selling financial products have to abide by a set of disclosure rules, requiring them to give clients certain essential information before a contract is signed. They present potential clients two 'key facts' documents: 'About our services', describing the range of services and the type of advice on offer; and 'About the cost of our services'. IFAs must offer clients the choice of paying fees or paying by commission. For further information consult the **Association of British Insurers** (ABI) website: **www.abi.org.uk**. See also Chapter 6, Financial advisers.

Tax

Under current legislation, the proceeds of a qualifying policy – whether taken as a lump sum or in regular income payments are free of all tax. If, as applies to many people, you have a life insurance policy written into a trust, there is a possibility that it could be hit by inheritance tax rules affecting trusts if the sum it is expected to pay out is above the (2013/14) £325,000 IHT threshold. The best advice is to check with a solicitor.

Assessment

Life assurance is a sensible investment, whether the aim is to provide death cover or the benefits of a lump sum to boost your retirement income. It has the merit of being very attractive from a tax angle, though you are locked into a long-term commitment. So choosing the right policy is very important. Shop around, take advice and, above all, do not sign anything unless you are absolutely certain that you understand the small print.

Complaints

Complaints about life assurance products, including alleged mis-selling, are handled by the **Financial Ombudsman Service** (FOS). Before approaching the FOS, you first need to try to resolve a dispute with the company direct. See website: **www.financial-ombudsman.org.uk**.

The **Financial Services Compensation Scheme** (FSCS) is the compensation fund of last resort for customers of authorized financial services firms. If a firm becomes insolvent or ceases trading, the FSCS may be able to pay compensation to its customers. See website: **www.fscs.org.uk**.

Alternatives to surrendering a policy

If you wish to terminate an endowment policy before the date of the agreement and avoid the punitive costs, you could sell the policy for a sum that is higher than its surrender value. See the **Association of Policy**

Market Makers website: **www.apmm.org**. For those looking for investment possibilities, second-hand policies could be worth investigating. Known as traded endowment policies (TEPs), they offer the combination of a low-risk investment with a good potential return. A full list of appropriate financial institutions and authorized dealers that buy and sell mid-term policies is obtainable from the Association of Policy Market Makers. It can also arrange for suitable policies to be valued by member firms, free of charge.

Bonds

Until recently, it was fairly difficult for small investors to access the corporate bond market. But a couple of years ago the London Stock Exchange established a retail bond platform designed to make trading corporate bonds as easy as trading listed shares. It has proved very popular and yields have been quite respectable. Since March 2011 nearly £1.7 billion has been raised by companies in the market. Bonds generally offer less opportunity for capital growth; they tend to be lower risk as they are less exposed to stock market volatility; but they have the advantage of producing a regular guaranteed income. The three main types of bonds are:

- *Gilts* (government bonds) explained earlier in this chapter, are the least risky. They are secured by the government, which guarantees both the interest payable and the return of your capital in full if you hold the stocks until their maturity.

- *Corporate bonds* are fairly similar except that you are lending it to a large company, rather than owning a piece of it, as you do with an equity. The company has to repay the loan at some point, known as the bond's redemption date. It will pay out the 'face value' of the bond and the company also has to pay interest on the loan, known as the 'coupon'. After they are issued, bonds trade in the secondary market, just like shares. Bond prices are driven by two main factors: interest rates and credit risk. Most bonds have a fixed income; the longer the time to maturity, the more sensitive the bond is to changes in interest rates.

  One reason to hold bonds is for income. Should corporate profits stall, companies might have to cut dividends. But unlike dividends, bond coupons can't be suspended, so your income is more predictable. The main risks to bonds are rising interest rates and credit risk. With market interest rates at rock-bottom levels, they can only go up over time. If this happens then fixed-income investments like bonds will look very unattractive. To hedge against these you should diversify: buy a portfolio of different maturity date bonds and spread your corporate bond companies across different industry sectors. In general, the higher the guaranteed interest payments, the less totally secure the company in question.

- *Investment bonds* are different in that they offer potentially much higher rewards but also carry a much higher degree of risk. If you are thinking of buying bonds, expert advice is very strongly recommended.

Investment bonds

Definition

This is the method of investing a lump sum with an insurance company, in the hope of receiving a much larger sum back at a specific date – normally a few years later. All bonds offer life assurance cover as part of the deal. A particular feature of some bonds is that the managers have wide discretion to invest your money in almost any type of security. The risk/reward ratio is, therefore, very high. They can produce long-term capital growth but can also be used to generate income.

While bonds can achieve significant capital appreciation, you can also lose a high percentage of your investment. An exception is guaranteed equity bonds, which, while linked to the performance of the FTSE 100 or other stock market index, will protect your capital if shares fall. However, while your capital should be returned in full at the end of the fixed term (usually five years), a point not always appreciated is that, should markets fall, far from making any return on your investment you will have lost money in real terms. Your capital will have fallen in value, once inflation is taken into account; and you will have lost out on any interest that your money could have earned had it been on deposit.

All bond proceeds are free of basic rate tax, but higher rate tax is payable. However, higher-rate taxpayers can withdraw up to 5 per cent of their initial investment each year and defer the higher-rate tax liability for 20 years or until the bond is cashed in full, whichever is earlier. Although there is no capital gains tax on redemption of a bond (or on switching between funds), some corporation tax may be payable by the fund itself, which could affect its investment performance. Companies normally charge a front-end fee of around 5 per cent plus a small annual management fee, usually not related to performance.

Tax

Tax treatment is complicated, as it is influenced by your marginal income tax rate in the year of encashment. For this reason, it is generally best to buy a bond when you are working and plan to cash it after retirement.

Offshore bonds

It has been suggested that offshore bonds are the new pensions with a recent surge of interest in offshore bonds from high earners looking for an alternative to pensions for their retirement savings. These can provide significant tax savings for investors because up to 5 per cent of capital can be withdrawn while deferring higher-rate tax for up to 20 years with no immediate tax to pay.

Offshore bonds are an insurance 'wrapper' around a portfolio of investments, which receive tax advantages by allowing you to defer the tax on the growth of the investments. Capital growth in an onshore bond is taxed at 20 per cent, whereas offshore bond capital grows tax free. While basic-rate taxpayers have no more tax to pay when they cash in an onshore investment bond, higher-rate taxpayers must pay a further 20 per cent and top-rate taxpayers must pay 30 per cent. With offshore bonds there is no tax to pay until you encash the bond, when higher-rate taxpayers will pay the entire 40 per cent and the top-rate payers will be liable for 50 per cent.

Charges for offshore bonds are high: typically 0.3 to 1 per cent upfront plus £400 to 0.25 per cent a year, depending on how much is invested. Adviser commission on top means the bonds are generally best for investments greater than £100,000 and held for more than five years. In comparison with pensions, these schemes are being increasingly recommended for retirement savings for higher-rate taxpayers who use their ISA and capital gains allowance, and no longer benefit from higher-rate tax relief.

Investor protection

The Financial Services Authority (FSA) the UK's banking regulator was set up in 1997 as part of the so-called tripartite structure whereby banks, insurers, building societies and other such firms were regulated by the FSA, the Treasury and the Bank of England. The FSA has been abolished and replaced with two successor organizations. The changes mark the end of the system set up by the previous Labour government. Since 1 April 2013, the Prudential Regulation Authority (PRA) ensures the stability of financial services firms and is part of the Bank of England. It regulates around 1,700 financial firms. The Financial Conduct Authority (FCA) is now the City's behavioural watchdog. The Bank of England has also gained direct supervision for the whole of the banking system through its powerful Financial Policy Committee (FPC), which can instruct the two new regulators. These changes were announced by the Chancellor, George Osborne, back in 2010, aiming to make it clear who is in charge over supervising the financial services sector and avoid a recurrence of failing banks and enormous state-backed bailouts. The regulator changes see the Bank of England gain much more control over the functioning of the financial system and are the biggest changes to the central bank since it was given independence in 1997.

Since January 2012 when the Retail Distribution Review (RDR) came into effect, all financial advisers have to set out their charges explicitly, so you will know how much they cost you (see Chapter 6 Financial advisers).

Investment businesses must adhere to a proper complaints procedure, with provision for customers to receive fair redress, where appropriate. Unsolicited visits and telephone calls to sell investments are for the most part banned. Where these are allowed for packaged products (such as unit trusts and life assurance), should a sale result the customer will have a 14-day cooling-off period (or a seven-day 'right to withdraw' period if the packaged product is held within an ISA and the sale follows advice from the firm). The cooling-off period is to give the customer time to explore other options before deciding whether to cancel the contract or not.

A single Ombudsman scheme

The single statutory Financial Ombudsman Service (FOS) provides a 'one-stop shop' for dissatisfied consumers and covers complaints across almost the entire range of financial services and products – from banking services, endowment mortgages and personal pensions to household insurance and stocks and shares. The list equally includes unit trusts and OEICs, life assurance, FSAVCs and equity release schemes. A further advantage is that the FOS applies a single set of rules to all complaints. Since April 2007 the Financial Ombudsman Service has also covered – for the first time – the consumer-credit activities of businesses with a consumer-credit licence issued by the Office of Fair Trading. Consumer-credit activities now covered by the Ombudsman range from debt consolidation and consumer hire to debt collecting and pawnbrokers.

For further information on Complaints, scams and how to protect yourself, see Chapter 7.

Chapter Six
Financial advisers

I always advise people never to give advice.

PG WODEHOUSE

L ast year might not have been a great year for investment returns – but it was a great year for investors. Why? Because of the Retail Distribution Review (RDR). This new set of regulations came into effect on 1 January 2013 and, among other things, it stopped independent financial advisers (IFAs) from taking (and financial companies from paying) commissions when you invest in financial products. The result being that every time you buy a product, open an individual savings account or set up a pension, you will know exactly what you have paid your IFA to help you do so. So is there such a big difference? Yes: it's all about transparency – instead of the money to be paid to your IFA being taken from your investment by the fund manager, it is now paid by you to your IFA directly.

Top tips: Why RDR is important

- It has improved the integrity of investment advice. If your adviser can't take commission, he can't indulge in commission bias.

- It has pushed prices down across the board. Many big fund managers have come out with what they call 'clean' prices (prices with the old adviser payment cut out) and they are a lot cheaper. However, trading fees and broker commissions are not included in either the calculations of the annual management charge (AMC) or the wider total expense ratio (TER). This matters, as both can be very high.

- It is good for transparency. You can buy investment trusts rather than unit trusts. You can buy individual shares (if you can face doing the necessary research). You can buy clean funds via a cheap transparent adviser.

- Keep asking questions. Customers need to know what they are paying for. The more often you ask about how much your investments are costing, and the extent to which you are getting value from them (and the manager looking after them), the better.

- Your adviser is now better than he was, since all advisers have to meet a basic standard of education and new-style advisers will understand what is going on in the investment world.

- Your financial adviser is going to be classified as independent or restricted. If he is independent, he will be looking at the entire market for you. If he is restricted he will just be looking at products offered by a limited number of providers.

(Source: **www.theweek.co.uk**)

Another change over the last couple of years is face-to-face financial advisory services. A number of companies have reduced or completely withdrawn this service, abandoning their clients at a time when they most need assistance. It's all an indirect result of the new regulations regarding the FSA and the RDR. Many leading high street banks only offer online service and with other companies there is only limited advice available. So if you wish to continue obtaining face-to-face advice, you will need to research where this can be found. One source where you can find information is the Telegraph Investment and Savings Service: **www.telegraph.co.uk/invest**.

Choosing an adviser

When choosing an adviser, there are usually four main considerations: respectability, suitability, price and convenience. Establishing that an individual is a member of a recognized institution is a basic safeguard. If you are thinking of using a particular adviser, do you already know him or her in a professional capacity? If not, you should certainly check on the adviser's reputation, ideally talking to some of his or her existing clients. Do not be afraid to ask for references. Most reputable professionals will be delighted to assist, as it means that the relationship will be founded on a basis of greater trust and confidence.

In April 2013 the UK's banking regulator, the Financial Services Authority (FSA) was abolished and replaced with two successor organizations. **The Prudential Regulation Authority** (PRA) ensures the stability of financial services firms and is part of the Bank of England (see **www.bankofengland.co.uk**). **The Financial Conduct Authority** (FCA) is now the City's behavioural watchdog (see **www.fca.org.uk**). It will police firms' conduct to ensure consumers are protected. It ensures that your financial adviser meets certain standards regarding how they give you advice on types of insurance, mortgages and investments (such as personal pensions, life insurance and annuities).

A simple definition of financial advice is that which takes into account your particular circumstances. If you buy a financial product without professional advice, you will have fewer grounds for complaint if the product turns out to be unsuitable. But if you do take advice and then find that the product wasn't suitable, you may have grounds to make a complaint and receive compensation for any loss. You can help prepare yourself for a meeting with a financial adviser by thinking carefully about your needs and priorities.

For your protection

The **Financial Services Compensation Scheme** (FSCS) is the body that can pay you compensation if your financial services provider goes bust. FSCS is independent. It was set up by the government under the Financial Services and Markets Act 2000. The financial services industry funds FSCS and the compensation it pays. It does not charge anyone for using its services. There are limits to how much compensation it pays, and these are different for different types of financial products. To be eligible for compensation, the financial service firm must have been authorized by the Financial Services Authority (FSA). See website: **www.fscs.org.uk**.

Despite the safeguards of the Financial Services Act, when it comes to investment – or to financial advisers – there are no cast-iron guarantees. Under the investor protection legislation, all practitioners and/or the businesses they represent offering investment or similar services must be authorized by the FCA or, in certain cases, by a small number of designated professional bodies that themselves are answerable to the FCA. A basic question, therefore, to ask anyone offering investment advice or products is: are you registered and by whom? Information is easily checked via the Financial Conduct Authority website: **www.fca.org.uk**.

Accountants

Accountants are specialists in matters concerning taxation. Many accountants can also help with raising finance and offer support with the preparation of business plans. Additionally, they may be able to advise in a general way about pensions and your proposed investment strategy. Most accountants, however, do not claim to be experts in these fields. They may refer their clients to stockbrokers or other financial advisers for such specialized services. If you need help in locating a suitable accountant, any of the following should be able to advise:

Association of Chartered Certified Accountants (ACCA): website: **www.accaglobal.com**.

Institute of Chartered Accountants in England and Wales (ICAEW): website: **www.icaew.com**.

Institute of Chartered Accountants of Scotland (ICAS): website: **www.icaew.com**.

Complaints

Anyone with a complaint against an accountancy firm should contact the company's relevant professional body for advice and assistance – see ACCA, ICAEW or ICAS, above.

Banks

Banks provide comprehensive services, in addition to the normal account facilities. These include investment, insurance and tax-planning services, as well as how to draw up a will. Other more specialized banks such as Hoare's, Coutts and overseas banks are all part of the UK clearing system and can offer a very good service.

The main banks are listed below with their websites. If you prefer to call into your local branch, a specialist adviser should be able to assist you.

Barclays Bank plc: **www.barclays.co.uk**.

Co-operative Bank: **www.co-operativebank.co.uk**.

HSBC: **www.hsbc.co.uk**.

Lloyds TSB: **www.lloydstsb.com**.

NatWest (part of the RBS Group): **www.natwest.com**.

RBS (Royal Bank of Scotland): **www.rbs.co.uk**.

Santander Group (formerly Abbey and now including Alliance & Leicester): **www.santander.co.uk**.

Complaints

The FSA regulates the way banks and building societies do business with you. If you have a complaint about a banking matter, you must first try to resolve the issue with the bank or building society concerned. If you remain dissatisfied, you can contact the **Financial Ombudsman Service;** see website: **www.financial-ombudsman.org.uk**.

Independent Financial Advisers (IFAs)

The role of IFAs has become more important since the number of investment, mortgage, pension protection and insurance products has multiplied and financial decision making has become increasingly complicated. An IFA is the only type of adviser who is able to select from all the investment policies and products on offer in the marketplace. It is his or her responsibility to make sure you get the right product for your individual needs.

IFAs must assess whether customers are at risk of over-committing themselves or taking some other risk that might jeopardize their security. This means they have to gain a full understanding of your circumstances and requirements before helping to choose any financial products. You should ask your adviser a number of questions including – most important – by whom they are regulated. All IFAs must be authorized and regulated by the Financial Conduct Authority and are obliged to offer what is termed 'suitable advice'. To check whether your IFA is registered, see the **FCA's Central Register** website: **www.fca.org.uk**.

Or to find an IFA, see the following websites:

Ethical Investment Research Service (EIRIS): **www.yourethicalmoney.org**.

Institute of Financial Planning: **www.financialplanning.org.uk**.

MyLocalAdviser: **www.mylocaladviser.co.uk**.

The Personal Finance Society (PFS): **www.thepfs.org**.

Unbiased.co.uk: **www.unbiased.co.uk**.

Insurance brokers

The insurance business covers a very wide area, from straightforward policies – such as motor or household insurance – to rather more complex areas, including life assurance and pensions. Whereas IFAs specialize in advising on products and policies with some investment content, brokers primarily deal with the more straightforward type of insurance, such as motor, medical, household and holiday insurance. Some brokers are also authorized to give investment advice. A broker will help you choose the policies best suited to you, assist with any claims, remind you when renewals are due and advise you on keeping your cover up to date. An essential point to check before proceeding is that the firm the broker represents is regulated by the FCA. A condition of registration is that a broker must deal with a multiplicity of insurers and therefore be in a position to offer a comprehensive choice of policies. Generally speaking, you are safer using a larger brokerage with an established reputation. Also, before you take out a policy, it is advisable to consult several brokers in order to get a better feel for the market.

The British Insurance Brokers' Association represents nearly 2,200 insurance broking businesses and will help you find an insurance broker: see website: **www.biba.org.uk**.

Complaints

The Association of British Insurers (ABI) represents some 400 companies providing all types of insurance from life assurance and pensions to household, motor and other forms of general insurance. About 90 per cent of the worldwide business done by British insurance companies is handled by members of the ABI. For information on insurance products see website: **www.abi.org.uk**.

Occupational pension advice

If you are (or have been) in salaried employment and are a member of an occupational pension scheme, the normal person to ask is your company's personnel manager or pensions adviser or, via him or her, the pension fund trustees. Alternatively, if you have a problem with your pension you could approach your trade union, since this is an area where most unions are particularly active and well informed. If you are in need of specific help, a source to try could be **The Pensions Advisory Service**. For information on state, company, personal and stakeholder pensions, and for help with problems or complaints about pensions, see website: **www.pensionsadvisoryservice.org.uk**.

As with most other financial sectors, there is also a **Pensions Ombudsman**. You would normally approach the Ombudsman if neither the pension scheme trustees nor the Pensions Advisory Service are able to solve your problem. Also, as with all Ombudsmen, the Pensions Ombudsman can only investigate matters that come within his orbit. These are: complaints of maladministration by the trustees, managers or administrators of a pension scheme or by an employer; and disputes of fact or law with the trustees, managers or an employer. The Pension Ombudsman is also the Pension Protection Fund Ombudsman. See website: **www.pensions-ombudsman.org.uk**.

Another source of help is the **Pension Tracing Service**, which can provide individuals with contact details for a pension scheme with which they have lost touch. There is no charge for the service. See website: **www.direct.gov.uk/pensions**.

Two other organizations that are interested in matters of principle and broader issues affecting pensions, are the **National Association of Pension Funds**, which is committed to ensuring that there is a sustainable environment for workplace pensions, website: **www.napf.co.uk**; and **The Pensions Regulator**, for information about work-based pensions, website: **www.thepensionsregulator.gov.uk**.

Solicitors

Solicitors are professional advisers on subjects to do with the law or on matters that could have legal implications. Their advice can be invaluable in vetting any important document before you sign it. Often the best way of finding a suitable lawyer (if you do not already have one) is through the recommendation of a friend or other professional adviser, such as an accountant. If you need a solicitor specifically for a business or professional matter, organizations such as local Chambers of Commerce, small business associations, your professional institute or trade union may be able to put you in touch with someone in your area who has relevant experience.

Two organizations to contact for help are **The Law Society**, website: **www.lawsociety.org.uk**; and **Solicitors for Independent Financial Advice** (SIFA), which is the trade body for solicitor financial advisers: **www.sifa.co.uk**.

Complaints

If you are unhappy about the service you have received from your solicitor, you should first try to resolve the matter with the firm through its complaints-handling partner. If you still feel aggrieved you can approach the **Solicitors Regulation Authority** (**www.sra.org.uk**).

For practical assistance if you are having problems with your solicitor, you can approach the Legal Services Ombudsman. This must be done within three months or your complaint will risk being out of time and the Ombudsman will not be able to help you. See the **Legal Services Ombudsman** website: **www.legalombudsman.org.uk**.

General queries

For queries of a more general nature, you should approach the **Law Society**: see website: **www.lawsociety.org.uk**. For those living in Scotland or Northern Ireland, see **The Law Society of Scotland**: website: **www.lawscot.org.uk** or **The Law Society of Northern Ireland**: website: **www.lawsoc-ni.org**, respectively.

Stockbrokers

A stockbroker is a regulated professional broker who buys and sells shares and other securities through market makers or agency-only firms on behalf of investors. A broker may be employed by a brokerage firm. A transaction on the stock exchange must be made between two members of the exchange.

There are three types of stockbroking service:

- *Execution only* which means the broker will carry out only the client's instructions to buy or sell.
- *Advisory dealing* where the broker advises the client on which shares to buy and sell, but leaves the financial decision to the investor.
- *Discretionary dealing* where the stockbroker ascertains the client's investment objectives and then makes all the dealing decisions on the client's behalf.

Roles similar to that of stockbroker include investment adviser and financial adviser. A stockbroker may or may not be an investment adviser.

While some stockbrokers now charge fees in the same way as a solicitor, generally stockbrokers make their living by charging commission on every transaction. You will need to establish what the terms and conditions are before committing yourself, as these can vary quite considerably between one firm and another. Nearly all major stockbrokers now run unit trusts.

To find a stockbroker: you can approach an individual through recommendation or visit the **London Stock Exchange** website: **www.londonstockexchange.com,** or the **Association of Private Client Investment Managers and Stockbrokers** (APCIMS) website: **www.apcims.co.uk**.

Complaints

If you need to make a complaint about a financial product or service, these tips are worth noting:

- What are you unhappy about?
- Try to stay calm. This can help you get your points across more clearly and effectively.
- Contact the business you think is responsible and explain what has gone wrong. Try to have any relevant information to hand, such as statements or policy documents.
- Put your complaint in writing – and keep a copy of your letter.
- The business will have a complaints procedure. If the business doesn't settle the matter to your satisfaction, the Financial Ombudsman Service may be able to help.

Financial Ombudsman Service (FOS)

This is a free service, set up by law with the power to sort out problems between consumers and financial businesses. Follow the steps outlined above, then contact the FOS, which will investigate your complaint. If the Ombudsman considers the complaint justified, it can award compensation. See **Financial Ombudsman Service** website: **www.financial-ombudsman.org.uk**.

The FOS is the single contact point for dissatisfied customers, as it covers complaints across almost the entire range of financial services, including consumer credit activities (such as store cards, credit cards and hire purchase transactions). The service is free; however, before contacting the FOS you must first try to resolve your complaint with the organization concerned (see above). Also, the Ombudsman is powerless to act if legal proceedings have been started. See the **Financial Ombudsman Service** website: **www.financial-ombudsman.org.uk**.

Other useful websites are:

www.ukinvestmentadvice.co.uk;

www.thisismoney.co.uk;

www.moneyweek.com;

www.wwfp.net;

www.best-advice.co.uk;

www.investment-advice.org.uk.

Chapter Seven
Scams and complaints

ALLAN ESLER SMITH

Allan is a Fellow of the Institute of Chartered Accountants and now specializes in helping people start up in business as you will read in Chapter 10. Previously Allan managed the Investigations and Recoveries Team at Investors Compensation Scheme (the predecessor of our current Financial Services Compensation Scheme). Allan's work paved the way for millions of pounds of compensation to be paid to victims of endowment, pension and other financial mis-selling. Allan knows a thing or two about scams pulled in the past through this and other senior investigation roles and shares advice on how to safeguard your wealth.

Intelligent, honest people don't fall victim to scammers, do they? Read on and save yourself, friends or elderly neighbours money, time and effort.

I first came across the scammers in 1984 on the Magic Bus returning from a backpacking holiday around the Greek Islands. The bus stopped somewhere in the mountains of Yugoslavia for a lunch break. Within minutes the local lads were out with three shells and a pea and launched into their game. All you had to do was watch them place the pea under the shell and spot it after they shuffled the three shells. Winners doubled their stake. My friend and I had no money at this stage of our holiday but we watched the locals take apart our fellow students, which included future doctors, lawyers and accountants. It enlightened me to a whole new world. Shills pretend to play the game to entice new entrants; lightning-fast sleight of hand then ensures novice players lose as the stakes get higher. Muscle then trails any unlikely big winner to retrieve the money through intimidation or theft. The concept has been alive and well for thousands of years. In simple terms, scammers have employed sleight of hand and a few back-up techniques such as vanity and knowing that folk never want to admit to being stupid. Many scammers are so good you will never spot what they have done in the same way as a good magician really will leave you believing that they made someone 'float' on stage. Smoke, mirrors, sleight of hand and anything can be made to look possible.

So how can we protect ourselves? First of all forget the 'it could never happen to me' line. I've lost count of how many times I've read a story and thought the victim should have known better and deserved what they got. The old saying that 'a fool and their money are easily parted' comes to mind. All those people who receive a cold call, for instance a telephone call or letter from someone they have never heard of, and then go on to invest in some wholly useless investment. However, quite often the victims are just like you and me but have encountered very professional scammers who have employed all their tricks, and before you know it a payment has been made. If it was as little as a few pounds you might write it off to bad luck and experience but what if it was a few hundred pounds, a few thousand, or even more?

My four 'tests' could help protect you.

The duck test

A respected Detective Superintendent summed up the duck test for me. The test flows from cutting short a debate over the identification of a duck and, out of pure frustration, is drawn to a close by 'It looks like a duck, it walks like a duck, it quacks like a duck it is a (expletive deleted) duck!'. It's a simple common sense approach – ignore the smoke and mirrors and sleight of hand – anything that is used to distract you from the real issue. Does it look, feel, and 'smell' like a scam? If so walk away, put the letter in the bin or put down the phone.

The Granny test

For many years I headed up the Investigations Teams in a major bank dealing with a financial adviser sales' force of over 1,000. I remember walking into a sales force conference soon after I was appointed and meeting the advisers and their managers for the first time. Many I wouldn't have let anywhere near my grandmother as they were commission driven and, in my mind, were likely to place the next sale (and commission) above the best needs of the client. My initial instincts proved true as we gradually had to oversee major programmes of redress and compensation especially around personal pension and endowment mis-selling. The message here is to trust your instincts, especially after you ask yourself the rather telling question about whether you would let the character you are dealing with anywhere near your mother or grandmother on the subject of financial advice. Instincts have been honed in the human species over thousands of years – if they have served you well in the past, trust them.

Actions speak louder than words

Scammers, generally, are all talk (unsurprisingly they very good at it) and no action. Delivering against what is said for any reasonable person should be easy to achieve. If the actions don't happen just walk away and don't give them a second chance to take advantage of you.

Too good to be true?

Scammers know that greed can get the better of many people and employ it to their purposes. If it sounds too good to be true, it is probably a scam.

Some common scams

Advance fee fraud

This is the scammer's favourite and has been dressed up in a hundred different guises. The spine is remarkably simple. A payment is made by you with the promise of a bigger pay-out in return. Perhaps it is cloaked in terms of funds left for you by a mystery relative where you pay a processing fee of £50; then maybe you are asked to pay another release fee of £150 and on it goes with a promise of a £10,000 sucking you in (which, of course, you will never actually receive).

The surprise prize ballot win

There is usually a premium rate number to claim the prize and the ultimate actual prize is probably worthless or trivial. File anything like this under B for bin.

Romance scams

The new lover or someone showing you interest or attention who, and unremarkably, shows you the attention you crave just when you need it or are at a low point. Maybe then they need some money for a sick mother or child. Scammers can be very clever and know how to manipulate you to get the response they want. They usually want you to keep things 'secret' as they know any friend you confide in will tell you to run a mile. Sadly emotional involvement and shame prevent folk from acting rationally and the scammers know this. Smoke, mirrors, sleight of hand and, just like a magician, your money is gone before you know it.

Credit and bank card cloning

This can be the jackpot for the scammers but how can they actually get your credit or bank card? The cloning devices that they attach to a bank's cash machine are not so farfetched these days – we had an incident in a nearby village only last month. But it need not be so far-fetched. How about the scammer who takes a temporary job in a holiday resort and clones the cards when their tipsy customer give over their credit card at the end of the night to pay for a nice meal out? You should never let your card out of your sight – restaurants will always bring the credit card machine to you (or you go to it). The end of this story? The holiday season finishes and the scammer moves on to activate and plunder their season of cloned cards.

If you spot a scam or have been scammed, report it and get help. Contact the **Police's Action Fraud** team on **0300 123 2040** or online at **www.actionfraud.police.uk** or the Police in your area.

Keeping safe from telephone cold calls and e-mail scammers

The above examples are just some of the higher profile and potentially higher value scams but there are many more. Some you may encounter over the phone and internet on a weekly basis.

Cold callers on the telephone can be irritating at best and sometimes downright scary as they may not take no for an answer. My own phone rings again and there is a temporary silence then a click and then the buzz of chatter in the background. It's yet another cold call from some overseas country that I really don't want to receive. The way these calls are intruding into our life is becoming a real problem. I therefore kept a log of the most irritating calls over a fortnight to try and understand what these people are after and what you, in turn, can do about it.

'*Good afternoon it's John from UK Lifestyle Survey.*' I ask where he is calling from. 'I'm calling from India,' John says and cheerfully explains that he is representing UK leading energy suppliers and wants to know who my energy supplier is. I say that I am not prepared to say and he puts down the phone. These calls are just seeking to gather marketing data from you. Who you buy from and where you live and the data is usually sold on and you will be bombarded with more calls and literature after you are put on their 'suckers list'.

'Good morning we are opening a home improvement shop in the local area and we would like to send you a £1,000 voucher. Would you like to spend it on improving a kitchen or bedroom?' I have to admit this is a great opening line and I'm intrigued but then sanity prevails as the 'voucher' will be no different to the discount I could negotiate when someone comes out to measure up and quote for a new kitchen, bedroom bathroom etc. Again these calls are just seeking to gather more marketing data and replying will just cause more and more calls. Interestingly this call is from the UK and I use the magic words 'I am signed up for the Telephone Preference Service and you should not be calling this number'. However the answer came back that they had a note that I had agreed to receive such calls and they now wanted to send me my voucher. I explained that they could keep their voucher and for the avoidance of any doubt they were to record that the telephone number they were calling was registered with the Telephone Preference Service and any previous authority was withdrawn.

The Telephone Preference Service (TPS) is a free service. It is the official central opt-out register on which you can record your preference not to receive unsolicited sales or marketing calls. It is a legal requirement that all organizations (including charities, voluntary organizations and political parties) do not make such calls to numbers registered on the TPS unless they have your consent to do so. You can register your phone number with the telephone preference service by calling 0845 070 0707 or you can do this online at **www.tpsonline.org.uk**.

I was waiting for one of these types of calls and in it came. Possibly the most sinister of the lot. 'Good morning, your computer has reported a fault to Microsoft', and they went to explain that they were calling to help me fix it. Apparently they had 'received an error report from Windows' and in a fanfare they championed 'we are Microsoft certified'.

'Please turn on your computer and check...'. I had to intervene at this point as a good friend who works in IT had warned me about this lot. 'They are after access to your computer and it is like walking up to a stranger in the street and handing them your wallet' was his simple and straightforward advice. After a moment's reflection he added 'No, it's actually worse than that'.

Basically these guys are scammers and they take you through a very basic procedure that reveals an error code and they use your non-knowledge of IT to make you feel vulnerable. At best they then get you to sign up for a maintenance package which, they say, will improve the performance of your computer. At worse they will gain access to your computer and leave spyware/software on it to collect data such as bank and other passwords and the like and you can imagine where this story will lead.

'So where are you based?' I asked the plausible but foreign sounding lady. 'I'm based in London at Buckingham Palace Road,' came the reply. 'And what tube line did you use to get to work this morning?' I enquired. But this caller was determined and dodged my cheeky question and requested 'Can you turn on your computer and check for...'

My final pick from my fortnight of engaging with the cold callers was 'Sasha' from The Consumer Centre which, she fanfared, acted for leading UK businesses and charities (I will not name the firms she said she was representing but they are all highly regarded names who I imagine would run a mile from Sasha and her colleagues). I asked where Sasha was calling from. 'The Philippines,' came the reply and Sasha moved on to explain her survey would not take long. Intrigued I gave it a go for a few minutes. 'Please confirm your address?' I said I didn't want to confirm my address. 'What age are you?' I said I didn't want to reveal my age. 'What TV make do you have?' I said I did not want to reveal my TV make. And so it went on until I said that this was just a call to get marketing data on me that they would sell to other firms and I would get even more calls. I said that I wanted to complain and stop Sasha and her colleagues calling me. Then came the sinister bit as Sasha informed me that 'the only way we will stop calling is when you complete our marketing survey'. I restated that I wanted to complain and Sasha gave me a telephone number. I called the number and there was no answer – it was a dead line/or non-number. Subsequently I have learnt that some complaints lines for these cold callers are apparently premium rate numbers so they get you that way.

In summary, the first and most important learning point is to sign up for the TPS. Its powers in dealing with overseas callers are limited to information sharing with overseas authorities. However, armed with feedback from you they may be able to bring some pressure to bear on the way these overseas firms are intruding on our privacy and then preying on the elderly or naive. The TPS can definitely assist if UK-based callers are making nuisance marketing calls. The advice on overseas callers is just to state 'I am a member of the Telephone Preference Service and you should not be calling me. What is your name, where are you calling from and what is your telephone number'. Do not engage in any other conversation and then consider passing on the three facts to the TPS. In addition, new technology allows you to acquire telephones that display the inbound number and, even better, block certain numbers. This may be worth investing in if you or an elderly relative are plagued by such calls.

E-mail scammers

The ingenuity and creativity of the e-mail scammers is reaching new heights. In simple terms, someone somewhere has gathered thousands of e-mail addresses including yours and mass mails them with a piece of information designed with only one purpose in mind. That purpose is to gain your attention and engagement. All end up the same way which is you losing out. I see a few e-mails every week from my clients as they have apparently been offered a refund from HMRC or their bank is offering them a refund. The e-mail tells them that all they have to do is click on a link and then follow the instructions. These instructions usually end with you entering your bank account, credit card or paypal details to enable the refund to be processed. The quality of the websites you link to are usually convincing with lots of branding and official looking information. Unfortunately the reality is that they have been built by scammers and they want to steal your money. So never click on any refund links and always check with the organization directly. For instance HMRC advise that: 'HMRC will never ask you to provide confidential or personal information such as passwords, credit card or bank account details by e-mail. If you have received an HMRC related phishing/bogus e-mail, please forward it to the following e-mail address and then delete it: **phishing@hmrc.gsi.gov.uk**.'

Remember that many websites are not legitimate. Generally try to protect yourself by restricting yourself to known organizations and their websites. If it is a UK business they must clearly show the company or business operating the website (usually in the contact us or about us section) which you can then check out.

The other trigger that may help you spot a fraudster e-mail is that they usually want you to act immediately. At one point last year I began to think that I had a pretty unlucky bunch of clients as a few have been mugged while abroad. Apparently their mobile phone had been stolen but they had access to e-mail and needed me to urgently wire £500 until their credit cards had been cancelled and reissued. Recognizing the scam I usually telephone my clients. 'How are you?' and everything was, of course, fine. To cut to the end of the story e-mail accounts were hacked and the scammers had sent out £500 requests to every person on the client's e-mail address book. Coming from real e-mail addresses it had all seemed plausible but, as I say above, the ingenuity and creativity of the e-mail scammers is reaching new heights. On this point you should think about changing e-mail account passwords to a long weird password with a mix of characters and numbers. Passwords like 'Password123' or 'Letmein' or your name spelt backwards are ripe for picking off by the hackers.

Keeping your investments and savings safe

Always check that any proposed investment *and* the person giving the advice is regulated by the **Financial Conduct Authority** via **www.fca.org.uk** and their register of authorized firms or their consumer helpline on **0800 1116768**. If the investment fails and the firm is insolvent, the maximum that the UK safety net, the Financial Services Compensation Scheme, pays is £50,000 per person per firm.

The UK's depositor safety net, the Financial Services Compensation Scheme, safeguards savings and bank deposits of up to £85,000 per person per institution. Remember some UK banks run several different savings brands under a single licence and savers with money in these different accounts will only be protected up to the single limit.

More on the Financial Services Compensation Scheme including what is covered and how to make a claim can be found at **www.fscs.org.uk**.

Complaints and 'how to complain'

Things in life inevitably go wrong and sometimes you lose out when it was not your fault. It is always satisfying when you explain your complaint and an organization says: 'We are terribly sorry for the inconvenience we have caused you. Thank you for taking the time to set out your concerns. We have now fixed the issue and it will not happen again and we would like you to accept a bunch of flowers as our way of saying sorry.'

This sort of response is rare and I personally find it irritating the way more and more companies hide behind websites and it is almost impossible to find someone to talk to. Perhaps some businesses will see the benefit of reverting to decent two-way communications. I think that many consumers are willing to pay that little bit more for some decent service and the assurance that when something goes wrong there will be someone there to do something about it. Perhaps that is one of the reasons for the success of the John Lewis Partnership?

While the *Good Retirement Guide's* campaign for better customer service continues, my hints and tips on complaints might just help you get a better outcome:

- When something goes wrong contact the firm or organization responsible straight away and give them a chance to sort out the problem. It is only fair that they have a chance to look into your complaint as there are usually two sides to any story and perhaps you have simply misunderstood the situation. Clearly state your complaint. Spend time thinking about this beforehand so that you can be clear and concise about what has happened and what you expect. If you are vague and unclear when you complain you can expect a vague and unclear reply. If you want compensation, state how much and why.

    When you complain keep a note of who you spoke to, the date and time and what they said will happen next and by when. Ask whether it would help if you put your complaint in writing.

    If the issue is not resolved, take steps to make it a formal complaint. Ask the organization for the name, address, telephone number and e-mail of the person or department that deals with complaints. Write a letter and head it up 'FORMAL COMPLAINT' in capitals. Spend time getting it factually correct and attach supporting evidence. If it goes beyond two pages it sounds like you may be rambling so reread it and relegate some information to an attachment. Send it by recorded delivery and keep a copy together with the post office tracking receipt.

Take the case further if the organization rejects your complaint and you believe they have not addressed your concerns. Unfortunately some customer relations teams really don't care what you say or how unfairly you have been treated and will just go through a formula approach. At best they may say 'here are some discount vouchers to use against your next booking...' or words to that effect. If you remain dissatisfied say so and ask how you can escalate your complaint. If you do take your case further understand the costs you will have to pay. Some organizations have independent assessors and their service is completely free (for instance Companies House and other quasi government agencies). Some have a free Ombudsmen service (banks, financial advisers, mobile phones). Others have regulating bodies (solicitors, surveyors and chartered accountants) that may be able to intervene on your behalf. Help could also be at hand from Citizens Advice who also have very useful template letters and advice for complainants at **www.adviceguide.org.uk**.

If there is no external organization you could choose to use a complaints management service. These, however, charge a fee so make sure you understand the costs you will have to pay. You could also consider legal proceedings but again consider the costs you will pay including, perhaps, the other side's costs if the court decides you are wrong. Another useful route is to consider if mediation or arbitration is possible. The ABTA Arbitration scheme deals with alleged breaches of contract and/or negligence between consumers and members of ABTA the travel organization and has been in operation for over 40 years. The scheme is provided so that consumers can have disputes resolved without having to go to court and without having to go to the expense of instructing solicitors. It is important to understand that arbitration is a legal process; this means that if you do go through arbitration, but are not happy with the outcome, you cannot then go to court. You have to choose one or the other when pursuing your complaint.

The final and perhaps most important tip is to consider whether or not your complaint is really worth the effort of pursuing. Perhaps an organization has been wrong and you have been dealt with unfairly. You may take step 1 above if you feel it is worth it but then do you just vote with your feet and go elsewhere and tell your friends. Sadly I have to report that I have seen complainants who just went on and on (and on)

> making the same points that had been dealt with by the organization they are complaining against. The complainants then availed themselves of all appeal mechanisms including involving their MPs. Perhaps they just didn't fully understand the issues or maybe they had too much time on their hands but they just managed to dig themselves into a rut. There was also the occasional vexatious complainant – you know the sort of bitter person who just complains about everything and everyone and these people just sap your energy and in my view are best avoided.

I hope this chapter tunes up your ability to complain more effectively. There is some further help available for free at the government-funded 'The Money Advice Service'. I would recommend their booklet *Making a complaint*, which is available at **www.moneyadviceservice.org.uk** or on the Money Advice Line at 0300 500 5000.

Further reading

Our top four recommendations for further help, guidance and support on scams and complaints follow:

- The Police Service publication *The Little Book of Big Scams* published by the Metropolitan Police Service, PSNI and other forces. You can download the booklet at **www.met.police.uk/docs/little_book_scam.pdf**
- BBC's Rip Off Britain via **www.bbc.co.uk**, then Rip Off Britain and then their section on consumer advice.
- The Money Advice Service offering free, unbiased and independent help via **www.moneyadviceservice.org.uk**.
- Citizen Advice: **www.adviceguide.org.uk**.

Chapter Eight
Your home

" *Home is where you come to when you've nothing better to do.*

MARGARET THATCHER (MAY 1991)

You've worked all your life, saved hard and bought your family home, raised your children there and had many happy years in the property. For most of us in our 50s and 60s, our home becomes increasingly precious. There are around 10 million over-65s in Britain and the Office for National Statistics says that will increase to more than 16 million by 2033. Retired homeowners currently have a total property wealth owned outright of more than £752 billion recent figures have shown.

When we reach retirement we have the opportunity to consider whether our current home is still the place we really want to be. A report by Ipsos MORI (published in 2012) for the RIBA entitled 'The Way We Live Now – What People Need and Expect from their Homes' suggests the following: that as we grow older, locality is highly important. Retired people prefer to live somewhere within a safe community. Transport links which are good quality and suit our needs are important too, and expectations of our ideal home are powerfully shaped by the homes in which we have lived previously. Some of us may love period features and large rooms, for others mod cons are what matters. Many people put emotional considerations, such as the 'feel' of a home, as a priority. Whatever your preference, life stage is a major contributing factor in what makes the perfect home, with people of retirement age prioritizing different layouts, features and qualities to those with young families.

But is now the right time to consider moving home? According to a recent poll by Barclays Bank and *The Daily Telegraph*, among the over-50s many of us are looking to do exactly that. Some 31 per cent of those surveyed said they plan to move, with 53 per cent planning to downsize. A further 14 per cent are planning to do so to release equity from their property and 13 per cent are planning to move closer to their children. Before making a decision, however, it is wise to weigh up your options. If you are on benefits and you downsize, the capital you release could mean that you are no longer eligible for those benefits. Investing the capital you release to produce either income or capital growth could have tax implications for you – so this all needs consideration. A smaller property could mean that, if house prices should start rising again, the capital appreciation you see may also be lower than if you had stayed where you were. Most important of all you should consider whether downsizing will be liberating for you. Think about not just your current, but also your future needs. There is no point in moving house if you will have to do so again in a few years time should, say, your health deteriorate. Making your decisions carefully, not rushing into anything, doing your homework and being honest with yourself should help you to avoid making a costly mistake.

Staying put

Since moving house is said to be one of the most stressful things in life, and house prices unlikely to rise much over the next few years, many people may prefer to sit tight. Should this plan appeal to you, there may be ways of adapting your home to suit your needs once you've retired. Would it be sensible to turn a bedroom into an upstairs study, or convert a spare room into a separate workroom for hobbies? You could consider letting one or two rooms. As well as solving the problem of wasted space, it would also bring in some extra income.

Ways of increasing the size of your property

There are all kinds of ways to improve your property and maximize its potential. A loft conversion is popular as it can add an extra bedroom and possibly even a bathroom. Building an extra room as an extension is the next favourite, followed by adding a conservatory, a new kitchen, central heating, bathrooms and new windows. Any new work must comply with building regulations. Most important, under the Party Wall Act, where appropriate you must notify your neighbours. Adding an extension to the back of your property is the most practical option. Smaller extensions to the rear or side of a property can often be built without having to make a planning application, provided that the design complies with the rules for permitted development (see **www.planningportal.gov.uk**). It is wise always to check with your local authority first before committing to any work.

An ambitious scheme, of course, would be to become your own neighbour by purchasing the next-door property. Knocking through allows more space than an extension without incurring moving costs or leaving the neighbourhood. This option is neither cheap nor simple. Professional advice from an architect is essential, so that the finished conjoined house looks right. This also makes selling the property much easier in the future.

Alternatively, if you live in an apartment you might be able to buy the adjoining unit or the one above or below then knock through or install a staircase to achieve double living space. Any construction work being undertaken must, of course, adhere strictly to planning and building regulations and you must ensure the project is completed properly. With regard to any home extension or 'knock-through' option, provided you can remain living in the property while the building work is being carried out, the disruption is less dramatic. Owners living onsite often make for a smoother and swifter conclusion to the project.

Despite being pricier than a conventional extension, if there is no scope to go outwards or upwards, extending below ground level is proving increasingly popular. This is particularly so in higher-value areas such as central London. Planning permission is normally required but is not usually an obstacle, even within a conservation area, because the new space has no visual impact on the street-scape. Converting an existing cellar is less expensive and does not usually require planning permission (however, do check first with your local authority). For further information, see **www.basements.org.uk**.

Another popular way to increase space in your home is to build above a garage. A conversion of this kind is reasonably simple and increases the size of your home easily and quickly. Any scheme would be subject to appropriate planning permission being granted. This is needed because of the extra height and alteration to the roof line. Whether your garage is single size or double, attached or detached, this type of extension is one of the quickest 'wins' because you are working with what you've got and you are spared the necessity of digging new foundations. You could extend into the garage itself as well as building above, if it's not being used to house the car. Rooms above a detached garage make an ideal guest suite, office, study, granny or nanny flat (or somewhere to carry on a noisy hobby). Should this idea appeal, search the internet for specialist companies dealing solely with garage conversions.

Moving to a new home

Some people say that moving to a new home is one of the most stressful things in life. If you do decide to move, it makes sense that the sooner you start looking for your new home the better. If you are thinking of moving out of the neighbourhood, there are other factors to be taken into account such as access to shops and social activities, proximity to friends and relatives, availability of public transport and even health and social support services. If you are elderly or infirm, living in the country can create massive challenges, particularly if you have a long-term illness. Lack of public transport is one of the main causes of rural deprivation, with the loss of village shops and post offices being another. Anyone considering a major lifestyle change, such as moving to a rural location in retirement, should take time and review all options before coming to a decision.

Top tips if contemplating downsizing:

- Downsizing saves money. The costs of running a smaller property will be substantially lower. It makes sense to reduce outgoings just at the time your income reduces in retirement.

- You'll save because your family home may have more bedrooms than you need, require more maintenance and have higher council tax.

- The family home with a large garden could prove burdensome as you get older and are less agile.

- Releasing equity from your old property and the sale of your primary residence is free from CGT.

- Moving to a purpose-built property with the needs of older people in mind is popular. You could gain a ready-made community and it will be a safe environment.

The question of downsizing is something that affects many over-60s. If you are considering moving to a smaller property, you will have to face the painful challenge of deciding what to keep and what to discard. The best way to tackle this is rather than thinking 'What should I leave behind?' think 'What do I actually need?' Check with family members to see if there are any items they want, and let them take them now. Don't keep anything you don't use. Let it go to someone who could use it. For more information on how to downsize without pain, contact APDO UK (the Association of Professional Declutterers and Organisers, formed in 2004). Website: **www.apdo-uk.co.uk**.

If you decide a move is for you, even if you think you know an area well, check it out properly before coming to a final decision. If possible, take a self-catering let for a couple of months, preferably out of season when rents are low and the weather is bad. A good idea is to limit your daily spending to your likely retirement income rather than splurge as most of us do on holiday. Do your research and visit **www.upmystreet.com** or **www.neighbourhoodstatistics.co.uk**.

If you are thinking of moving abroad, you should take this decision only after careful consideration. The political climate of that country, being far away from friends, not having the same healthcare arrangements and having to learn a new language – to name a few. For more information on the financial implications of living overseas, see the section 'Retiring abroad', on page 68.

Counting the cost

Moving house can be an expensive exercise but, if you can afford to move, some good bargains can be had. It is estimated that the cost is between 5 and 10 per cent of the value of a new home, once you have totted up extras such as search fees, removal charges, insurance, stamp duty, VAT, legal fees and estate agents' commission. To find out the latest information about SDLT (stamp duty) see HM Revenue & Customs website: **www.hmrc.gov.uk**.

When buying a new home, especially an older property, it is essential to have a full building (structural) survey done before committing yourself. This will cost in the region of £500 for a small terraced house but is worth every penny. In particular, it will provide you with a comeback in law should things go wrong. A valuation report, while cheaper, is more superficial and may fail to detect flaws that could give you trouble and expense in the future.

If you are buying a newly built house, most mortgagees will lend on new homes only if they have a National House Building Council (NHBC) warranty or its equivalent. This is a 10-year 'Buildmark' residential warranty and insurance scheme under which the builder is responsible for putting right defects during the first two years. It is designed to protect owners of newly built or newly converted residential housing if a problem does occur in a new home registered with NHBC. See website: **www.nhbc.co.uk**. Also helpful to home buyers, the Land Registry allows members of the public to seek information directly about the 20 million or so properties held on its register via the **Land Registry** website: **www.landregistry.gov.uk**.

If you are selling your home, you no longer require a Home Information Pack (HIP), but the requirement for the Energy Performance Certificate (EPC) has been retained, whether you are selling or renting out.

Energy Performance Certificates (EPCs)

An EPC rates the property's energy use and suggests ways to make energy-saving improvements. The EPC rating is on an A–G scale (like the EU energy label used on fridges and other white goods); the higher the rating, the more energy efficient the home is. The average UK home has a 'D' rating, and the Energy Saving Trust suggests you think carefully before choosing any home with an 'F' or 'G' rating. Newer homes generally use less energy, so buyers or renters looking at a recently built home would expect to see an EPC rating of 'B' or above. EPCs are produced by accredited Domestic Energy Assessors and cost from £30 to £80, depending on the size of the property. Sellers are required to commission, but won't need to have received, an EPC before marketing their property.

Information

For details about local Domestic Energy Assessors see **EPC Register**; website: **www.epcregister.com**.

For a free and impartial home energy check visit **Energy Saving Trust**; website: **www.energysavingtrust.org.uk**.

For advice on leasehold legislation and policy, see the **Department for Communities and Local Government** section of website: **www.gov.uk**.

Bridging loans

Bridging loans are one way of solving the problem of moving house should the chain break between sale and purchase. But it can be an expensive option. Some of the major institutional estate agents operate chain-breaking schemes and may offer to buy your property at a discount (some 10 or 12 per cent less than the market price). For further information see website: **www.bridgingloans.co.uk**.

Estate agents

Finding your dream house is never easy. The National Association of Estate Agents (NAEA) runs a service called **Property Live,** a network of estate agents working with like-minded professionals committed to making the moving experience straightforward by providing access to a professional, friendly property service. See website: **www.propertylive.co.uk**.

There is a Property Ombudsman scheme to provide an independent review service for buyers or sellers of UK residential property in the event of a complaint. As with most Ombudsman schemes, action can be taken only against firms that are actually members of the scheme. See **The Property Ombudsman** website: **www.tpos.co.uk**.

Living in leasehold

An ever increasing number of people move into a flat as a retirement home. If acquiring a leasehold flat, there are one or two things to bear in mind before you buy. The freeholder of the building may be an investment company, a private investor, or ideally the leaseholders themselves in the form of a management company. With the advent of 'right to manage' leaseholders do not need to own the freehold but will be able to manage the building as if they were the freeholder. While it is important that leaseholders are aware of their rights, it is fundamental they are aware of their responsibilities. Principally this will be to keep the inside of their flat in good order, to pay their share of the cost of maintaining and running the building, to behave in a neighbourly manner and not to do certain things as set out in the lease, such as sublet their flat without the freeholder's prior consent.

As for rights, first and foremost, is the peaceful occupation of the flat, often referred to as 'quiet enjoyment'. In addition, the leaseholder has the right to expect the freeholder to maintain the building and common parts for which the leaseholder will be required to pay a 'service charge'. This is a payment made by a leaseholder to the freeholder or their managing agent to maintain, repair and insure the building as well as to provide other services, such as lifts, central heating or cleaners. These charges are liable to change from one year to the next, but must at all times be 'reasonable'. Leaseholders have a right to challenge the service charge if they feel it is 'unreasonable' via the Leasehold Valuation Tribunal (LVT). It is important to find out what the current charges are and the likely charges for future years and what, if any, reserves are held to cover the cost of major works such as external decoration of the building. For further information, see:

Leasehold Advisory Service (LVT): **www.lease-advice.org**.

Association of Retirement Housing Managers (ARHM): **www.arhm.org**.

Retiring abroad

Do you dream of retiring to the sun? A number of people contemplating an adventurous retirement raise funds on their family home in the UK and purchase a small property abroad, becoming what is known as 'residential tourists'. This means they travel to and from their other house without much luggage and spend several months at a time in their overseas home. Such a property abroad tends to fall into the category of 'lock up and leave' and it bridges the gap between selling up and moving completely from the country you've lived in for years. It allows a certain amount of thinking time before you make a decision on whether or not the foreign property will at some point become your 'forever' home.

Should you be considering retiring abroad, there are a number of additional costs, besides purchasing the property: legal expenses, notary fees, stamp duty, registration fees and local taxes, costs of a solicitor and surveyor and the cost of making a new will. Removal costs from the UK to the new country can be quite heavy too. So if you decide to retire overseas, be careful. Some ways of protecting yourself when buying property abroad include:

- Get all documents translated.
- If you are given something to sign, make sure you have a 14-day cooling-off period.
- Take the documents home to the UK and speak to a lawyer and financial adviser over here rather than in the country overseas.

- Make sure the lawyer you use is independent and not involved in the sale in any way.
- Do not use a lawyer recommended by the seller.
- If you are buying a repossessed property, find out what happened.
- If you are borrowing money, go to a reputable bank. The bank manager will want to be sure the deal is sound – this adds another layer of checks and protection.

There are many websites offering advice and information on retiring abroad. Look at:

www.gov.uk – Britons preparing to move or retire abroad.

www.propertyinretirement.co.uk – section on retiring abroad.

www.buyassociation.co.uk – section on advice on retiring abroad and homes abroad.

www.retirementexpert.co.uk – popular locations when retiring abroad.

www.shelteroffshore.com – information on living abroad.

www.expatfocus.com – provides essential information and advice for a successful move abroad.

Removals

Professional help is essential for anyone contemplating a house move. A reputable firm of removers and shippers will remove many of the headaches. A full packing service can save much anxiety and a lot of your time. Costs vary depending on the type and size of furniture, the distance over which it is being moved and other factors, including insurance and seasonal troughs and peaks. It pays to shop around and get at least three quotes from different removal firms. Remember, the cheapest may not necessarily be the best. Find out exactly what you are paying for and whether the price includes packing and insurance. The **British Association of Removers** (BAR) promotes excellence in the removals industry; for approved firms all of whom work to a rigorous code of practice, see website: **www.bar.co.uk**.

Retirement housing and sheltered accommodation

The demand for property that caters for older buyers is high, while the range of options available for purchasers has never been greater. You can choose from specially developed villages that provide independence, but also help and assistance where needed through to town centre developments aimed at 'empty nesters', and developments that have varying levels of care attached to them. The terms 'retirement housing' and 'sheltered accommodation' cover a wide variety of housing but are designed to bridge the gap between the family home and residential care. There are many well-designed, high-quality private developments of 'retirement homes' now on the market, for sale or rent, at prices to suit most pockets. As a general rule, you have to be over 55 when you buy property of this kind. While you may not wish to move into this type of accommodation just now, if the idea interests you in the long term it is worth planning ahead, as there are often very long waiting lists. For full details see Chapter 15, Caring for elderly parents.

Other options

Caravan or mobile home

Many retired people consider living in a caravan or mobile home. You may already own one as a holiday home that you are thinking of turning into more permanent accommodation. If you want to live in a caravan on land you own or other private land, you should contact your local authority for information about any planning permission or site licensing requirements that may apply. If you want to keep it on an established site, there is a varied choice. Check carefully, whichever you choose, that the site owner has all the necessary permissions. All disputes, since 30 April 2011, under the Mobile Homes Act 1983 are being dealt with by Residential Property Tribunals in place of the County Court.

Park mobile homes are modern, bungalow-style residential properties, usually sited on private estates. Impartial advice can be obtained from the NCC, the trade body that represents the UK park home (residential, caravan or mobile home) industry (**www.thencc.org.uk**). Before entering into a commitment to purchase a park home, it's well worth visiting an exhibition dedicated to park homes to gain useful information.

The main national exhibitions are: The National Park and Holiday Homes Show, The Park and Holiday Homes Show and The World of Park and Leisure Homes.

Park Home & *Holiday Caravan* magazine is the UK's biggest and best-selling park home magazine and is full of information for those interested in park homes. See website: **www.parkhomemagazine.co.uk**.

For companies that specialize in new homes for sale on residential parks, ready for immediate occupation, see **www.parkhome-living.co.uk**.

Self-build

More than 25,000 people a year now build their own homes. With typical cost savings estimated at between 25 and 40 per cent, it's very popular with the over-50s and many have successfully become self-builders. No prior building experience is necessary, although this of course helps. Obtaining planning permission from local councils is essential but can often be a protracted business. Individuals who wish to build on their own can make arrangements with an architect or company that sells standard plans and building kits. Be sure to do your research and seek professional advice first. Here are some useful websites for you to search:

www.homebuilding.co.uk: Information on all aspects of self-build including a self-build cost calculator.

www.buildstore.co.uk: Self-build, renovation, plots of land for sale, buying building materials.

www.builditthisway.co.uk: Self-build – the ultimate DIY project.

www.selfbuildland.co.uk: Self-build land for sale in the UK.

www.cat.org.uk: The Centre for Alternative Technology advice service on sustainable living and environmentally responsible building.

How green is your house?

Becoming eco-friendly is something everyone should consider: making your home as energy saving, economical and convenient as possible is going to save money. The sooner you start, the earlier you will reap the benefit.

Solar panels

Even though the cost of solar panels is falling, the returns from install-ing them are nowhere near as good as they were a few years ago. But as energy costs rise, a solar panel on your roof may still be worth the investment. Do you research on the Energy Saving Trust website: **www.energysavingtrust.org.uk**.

Insulation

One of the best ways of reducing those increasing utility bills is proper insulation. Heat escapes from a building in four main ways: through the roof, walls, floor and loose-fitting doors and windows. Insulation not only can cut the heat loss dramatically but will usually more than pay for itself within four or five years.

Loft insulation

As much as 25 per cent of heat in a house escapes through the loft. The answer is to put a layer of insulating material, ideally 220 to 270 millimetres thick according to the material used, between and across the roof joists. To employ a specialist contractor, you can find one through the **National Insulation Association** website: **www.nationalinsulationassociation.org.uk**.

Doors and windows

A further 25 per cent of heat escapes through single-glazed windows. If you wish to install double glazing there are two main types: sealed units and secondary sashes (which can be removed in the summer). It reduces noise as well as saving heat. Since April 2002, any replacement doors and windows installed have to comply with strict thermal performance standards and the installer must be registered under the FENSA scheme; see the **Glass and Glazing Federation** website: **www.ggf.co.uk**.

Effective draught proofing saves heat loss as well as keeping out cold blasts of air. For draught proofing older sliding-sash windows and doors, wiper seals, fixed with rustproof pins and screws, need to be used. If you do fit draught seals, make sure you leave a space for a small amount of air to get through, or you may get problems with condensation. For advice on durable products and contractors, see the **Draught Proofing Advisory Association** website: **www.dpaa-association.org.uk**.

Heat loss can also be considerably reduced through hanging heavy curtains (both lined and interlined) over windows and doors. If your curtains cover the windowsill or rest on the floor you will keep warmer. It is better to have curtains too long than too short.

Wall insulation

More heat is lost through the walls than perhaps anywhere else in the house: it can be as much as 50 per cent. If your house was built after 1930, cavity wall insulation should be installed. Grants are available, and you could expect a typical saving of around 25 per cent off your heating bill each year. Make sure that the firm you use is registered with a reputable organization; if a foam fill is used, the application should comply with British Standard BS 5617 and the material with BS 5618.

Solid wall insulation can be considerably more expensive, but will provide savings of around 25 per cent off your annual heating bill. It involves applying an insulating material to the outside of the wall, plus rendering or cladding. Alternatively, an insulated thermal lining can be applied to the inside. For further information see:

British Board of Agrément, website: **www.bbacerts.co.uk**.

British Standards Institution, website: **www.bsigroup.co.uk**.

Cavity Insulation Guarantee Agency (CIGA), website: **www.ciga.co.uk**.

Eurisol UK Ltd, website: **www.eurisol.com**.

Insulated Render & Cladding Association Ltd, website: **www.inca-ltd.org.uk**.

National Insulation Association, website: **www.nationalinsulationassociation.org.uk**.

Floor insulation

Up to 15 per cent of heat loss can be saved through filling the cracks or gaps in the floorboards and skirting and then ensuring a good felt or rubber underlay is laid under the carpet. Be careful, however, that you do not block up the underfloor ventilation, which is necessary to protect floor timbers from dampness and rot. Solid concrete floors can be covered with cork tiles or carpet and felt or rubber underlay. See Energy Saving Trust website: **www.energysavingtrust.org.uk**.

Hot water cylinder insulation

If your hot water cylinder has no insulation, it could be costing you several pounds a week in wasted heat. A British Standard insulating jacket fitted around your hot water cylinder will cut wastage by three-quarters. Most hot water tanks now come ready supplied with insulation. If not, the jacket should be at least 75 millimetres thick. See Energy Saving Trust website: **www.energysavingtrust.org.uk**.

Grants

There are many schemes for helping pensioners with heating bills and insulation costs. The big six electricity companies give a £120 annual rebate to certain customers, especially anyone on a small pension. Those receiving the guaranteed credit element of Pension Credit automatically get the money. At their discretion, energy companies can also give the refund to other vulnerable customers, including people with a disability or long-term illness. For information contact the Energy Saving Trust: website **www.energysavingtrust.org.uk**.

Here are some other websites that give advice and information on this subject:

www.insulationgrants.info: Home insulation grants – government grants for insulation.

www.freeinsulation.co.uk: government-backed grants available for cavity wall and loft insulation.

www.getinsulation.co.uk: New cavity wall and loft insulation. Apply for 100 per cent grants.

www.homeheatingguide.co.uk: grants for home insulation.

www.government-grants.co.uk: Grants for loft and cavity wall insulation available.

Heating

It may be possible to save money by using different fuels or by heating parts of your house by means of different systems. Your local gas and electricity offices can advise on heating systems, running costs and energy conservation, as well as heating and hot water appliances.

The **Solid Fuel Association** website gives advice and information on all aspects of solid fuel heating, including appliances and installation;

website: **www.solidfuel.co.uk**. The **Building Centre** website has a wide range of information on building products with consumer guidance; website: **www.buildingcentre.co.uk**.

Buying and installing heating equipment

When buying equipment, check that it has been approved by the appropriate standards approvals board.

For *electrical equipment*, the letters to look for are BEAB (British Electro-technical Approvals Board) or CCA (CENELEC Certification Agreement), which is the European Union equivalent.

For *gas appliances*, look for the CE mark, which denotes that appliances meet the requirements of the Gas Appliance (Safety) Regulations Act 1995. Domestic solid fuel appliances should be approved by the Solid Fuel Appliances Approval Scheme; check the sales literature.

Gas appliances should only be installed by a Gas Safe Register registered installer. Registration is compulsory by law. As a further safeguard, all registered gas installers carry a Gas Safe Register ID card. After a gas appliance has been installed, you should receive a safety certificate from the Gas Safe Register, which must be kept as you may need it should you want to sell your home in the future. See the **Gas Safe Register** website: **www.gassaferegister.co.uk**.

When looking for contractors, it is now a legal requirement for electricians as well as kitchen, bathroom and gas installers to comply with Part P of the Building Regulations. You would therefore be well advised to check that any contractor you propose using is enrolled with the relevant inspection council or is a member of the relevant trade association.

Electricians should be approved by the **NICEIC** and covered for technical work by the NICEIC Complaints Procedure and Guarantee of Standards Scheme and undertake to work to British Standard 7671. Any substandard work must be put right at no extra cost to the consumer. For local approved contractors see website: **www.niceic.org.uk**.

An alternative source for finding a reputable electrician is the **Electrical Contractors' Association**. See website: **www.eca.co.uk**.

Tips for reducing your energy bills

Energy can be saved in lots of small ways. Taken together, they could amount to quite a large cut in your bills. Here are some suggestions from **www.energychoices.co.uk**:

- *Switch suppliers.* This is one of the simplest ways of saving money. It is possible to cut bills by around £150 each, according to Ofgem.

- *Look after your boiler.* The current lifespan of a boiler is around 10 years. When replacing your boiler ensure you opt for an 'A' rated one displaying the Energy Saving Recommended logo.

- *Insulate your home.* Insulating your home is probably the most cost-effective way of reducing your home's fuel consumption. A significant amount of heat loss is through the roof; installing loft insulation is simple and you can do it yourself.

- *Turn down the temperature.* Turning down your thermostat by one degree centigrade can save up to 10 per cent on your heating bill.

- *Energy-saving light bulbs.* These typically last 12 times longer than ordinary bulbs and could save you approx £7 per year per bulb.

- *Change your habits.* Electrical appliances still use around 70 per cent of their usual energy when left on standby, so turning them off will trim your energy use. Closing curtains at dusk to stop heat escaping through the windows. If you are going away during the winter, leave your thermostat on a low setting to provide protection from freezing at minimum cost.

- *Watch your water usage.* Taking showers instead of baths uses 30 per cent less water. If you have more bedrooms than people in your home you could save over £200 by switching to a water meter, so you only pay for the water you actually use.

- *Change your appliances.* Domestic appliances account for 47 per cent of a household's total electricity consumption; fridges and freezers account for 18 per cent of the electricity bill in a typical house; washing machines, tumble-dryers and dishwashers for 14 per cent and cooking appliances for 15 per cent.

- *Insure your boiler.* For peace of mind take out boiler insurance, such as British Gas's Home Care (**www.britishgas.co.uk**).

- *Separate thermostats.* If you have separate thermostats for your heating system and hot water cylinder, you can set it at around 60 degrees Celsius to enable you to keep hot water for taps at a lower temperature than for the heating system.

If you have a disability, or are on a low income, you could qualify for the Social Tariff from your energy suppliers. You can ask also your gas or electricity supplier to put you on the Priority Service Register.

British Gas offers an **Essentials Programme** with a range of products, services and advice for vulnerable customers (such as those with low incomes and disabilities). See website: **www.britishgas.co.uk**.

The **Energy Saving Trust** has information on grants and money-saving ideas. See website: **www.energysavingtrust.org.uk**. Consumer Direct is the government-funded consumer advice service; **Citizens Advice** can give you advice about your consumer rights, see **www.adviceguide.org.uk/consumer**. Two other useful websites are: **www.moneysavingexpert.com** and **www. seniorsdiscounts.co.uk**.

Improvement and repair

If your house needs structural repairs, a wise first step would be to contact the **Royal Institution of Chartered Surveyors** to help you find a reputable chartered surveyor. See website: **www.rics.org**.

Disabled facilities grant (DFG)

This helps towards the costs of adapting your home to enable you to live there, should you become disabled, obtainable from your local council. It can cover a wide range of improvements, including the provision of suitable bathroom or kitchen facilities. Provided the applicant is eligible, a mandatory grant of up to £30,000 may be available in England, £25,000 in Northern Ireland and up to £36,000 in Wales.

As with most other grants, there is a means test. The local authority will want to check that the proposed work is reasonable and practicable according to the age and condition of the property, and the local social services department will need to be satisfied that the work is necessary and appropriate to meet the individual's needs. The grant can be applied for either by the disabled person or by a joint owner or joint tenant or landlord on his or her behalf. For further information, contact the environmental health or housing department of your local authority. See website: **www.gov.uk** – Disabled people.

Do not start work until approval has been given to your grant appli-cation, as you will not be eligible for a grant once work has started.

Community care grant

People on low incomes or the disabled may be eligible for help from the Social Fund: see website: **www.gov.uk** – Benefits.

Other help for disabled people

Your local authority may be able to help with the provision of certain special facilities such as a stair lift, telephone installations or a ramp to replace steps. Other useful contacts:

APHC Ltd (Association of Plumbing and Heating Contractors Ltd) holds a national register of licensed members. See website: **www.aphc.co.uk**.

Association of Building Engineers can supply names of qualified building engineers/surveyors. See website: **www.abe.org.uk**.

Association of Master Upholsterers & Soft Furnishers Ltd has a list of approved members; see website: **www.upholsterers.co.uk**.

The Building Centre can give guidance on building problems. See website: **www.buildingcentre.co.uk**.

Federation of Master Builders (FMB): lists of members are available from regional offices. See website: **www.fmb.org.uk**.

Guild of Master Craftsmen supplies names of all types of specialist craftspeople. See website: **www.guildmc.com**.

Institute of Plumbing and Heating Engineering lists professional plumbers. See website: **www.ciphe.org.uk**.

Royal Institute of British Architects (RIBA) has a free Clients Service that will recommend up to three suitable architects. See website: **www.architecture.com**.

The Scottish and Northern Ireland Plumbing Employers' Federation (SNIPEF) is the national trade association for plumbing and domestic heating contractors in Scotland and Northern Ireland. See website: **www.snipef.org**.

Home improvement agencies (HIAs)

Home improvement agencies (sometimes known as 'staying put' or 'care and repair' agencies) work with older or disabled people to help them remain in their own homes by providing advice and assistance on repairs, improvements and adaptations. They also advise on the availability of funding and welfare benefits, obtain prices, recommend reliable builders and inspect the completed job.

The British Legion and Age UK offer a handyman service to carry out small household repairs, and keep a list of Home Improvement Agencies:

Age UK website: **www.ageuk.org.uk**.

British Legion website: **www.britishlegion.org.uk**.

Foundations is the national body for Home Improvement Agencies in England. See website: **www.foundations.uk.com**.

Elderly Accommodation Counsel provides information on Home Improvement Agencies. See website: **www.housingcare.org**.

Anchor Trust offers comprehensive home care for the elderly. See website: **www.anchor.org.uk**.

Safety in the home

Accidents in the home account for 40 per cent of all fatal accidents, resulting in nearly 5,000 deaths a year. Seventy per cent of these victims are over retirement age, and nearly 80 per cent of deaths are caused by falls. A further 3 million people need medical treatment. Tragically, it is all too often the little things that we keep meaning to attend to but never quite get round to that prove fatal. Here are a few suggestions for you to make your home safer:

- *Steps and stairs* should be well lit, with light switches at both the top and the bottom. All stairs should have a handrail to provide extra support – on both sides if the stairs are very steep. You should keep proper steps, preferably with a handrail, to do high jobs in the house such as hanging curtains or reaching cupboards.

- *Floors*. Rugs and mats can slip on polished floors and should always be laid on some form of non-slip backing material. Stockinged feet are slippery on all but carpeted floors, and new shoes should always have the soles scratched before you wear them.

- The *bathroom* is particularly hazardous for falls. Sensible precautionary measures include using a suction-type bath mat and putting handrails on the bath or alongside the shower. For older people who have difficulty getting in and out of the bath, a bath seat can be helpful.

- In the *kitchen* spills should be wiped up immediately to avoid slips. Any items you use regularly should be kept easily within reach. If you are having trouble preparing meals or doing the cleaning, your local social services can assist you with advice on helpful equipment. The Disability Living Foundation can provide equipment such as handrails, automatic lights and kettle tippers.

- *Falls* are a great risk for older people. For every two people who fracture a hip in later life, one never regains the same level of mobility. So it pays to try to prevent such accidents. If you have a fall:

  - Stay calm. If you're unhurt, look for something firm to hold on to and get slowly to your feet again. Then sit down and rest.

  - If you are injured, try to get comfortable, stay warm, and shift position every half hour or so until help arrives.

  Should you have had several falls or fear falling, ask your GP to refer you to an NHS Falls Clinic. A falls prevention nurse can test your balance, recommend foot care and make sure you stay as fit as possible.

- *Fires*. If you have an open fire, you should always use a fireguard and sparkguard at night. The chimney should be regularly swept at least once a year, maybe more if you have a wood-burning stove. New upholstered furniture should carry a red triangle label, indicating that it is resistant to smouldering cigarettes. Furniture that also passes the match ignition test carries a green label.

- *Portable heaters* should be kept away from furniture and curtains and positioned where you cannot trip over them. Paraffin heaters should be handled particularly carefully and should never be filled while alight. Paraffin should be kept in a metal container outside the house. Never dry clothes near a portable heater or open fire.

- *Gas appliances* should be serviced regularly by British Gas or other Gas Safe Register registered installers. You should also ensure that there is adequate ventilation when using heaters. Never block up air vents: carbon monoxide fumes can kill.

  If you smell gas or notice anything you suspect could be dangerous, stop using the appliance immediately, open the doors and windows and call the National Grid 24-hour emergency line free: 0800 111 999.

- *Cookers* cause more than one in three fires in the home. Chip pans are a particular hazard. Pan handles should be turned away from the heat and positioned so you cannot knock them off the stove. If you are called to the door or telephone, always take the pan off the ring and turn off the heat before you leave the kitchen.

- *Cigarettes* left smouldering in an ashtray could be dangerous if the ashtray is full. Smoking in bed is a potential killer.

- *Faulty electric wiring* frequently causes fires, as does overloaded power points. The wiring in your home should be checked every five years and you should avoid using too many appliances off a single plug. It is a good idea to get into the habit of pulling the plug out of the wall socket when you have finished using an appliance. Where possible, have electric sockets moved to waist height to avoid unnecessary bending whenever you want to turn on the switch.

- *Electric blankets* should be routinely overhauled and checked in accordance with the manufacturer's instructions. It is dangerous to use both a hot water bottle and electric blanket – and never use an under blanket as an over blanket.

- *Gardening* with electrical appliances can be dangerous. They should never be used when it is raining. Always wear rubber-soled shoes or boots, and avoid floppy clothing that could get caught in the equipment.

- *Fire extinguishers* should be readily accessible. Make sure they are regularly maintained and in good working order. Portable extinguishers should conform to BS EN 3 or BS 6165. Any extinguishers made before 1996 should conform to BS 5423, which preceded BS EN 3. Many insurance companies now recommend that you install a smoke alarm, which should conform to BS 5446-1:2000 or BS EN 14604:2005, as an effective and cheap early-warning device.

Here are some useful websites:

www.dlf.org.uk;

www.saferhouses.co.uk

www.ageuk.org.uk

www.independentliving.co.uk.

Home security

According to the Home Office, the elderly are not more at risk from crime than any other section of society. Should you feel nervous or vulnerable, the crime prevention officer at your local police station will advise you on how to improve your security arrangements. He or she will also tell you whether there is a Neighbourhood Watch scheme and how you join it. This is a free service that the police are happy to provide.

If you are going away the **Royal Mail's Keepsafe** service will store your mail so as to avoid it piling up and alerting potential burglars to your absence. There is a charge for the service. See: **www.royalmail.com**.

If your home will be unoccupied for any length of time, it is sensible to ask the local police to put it on their unattended premises register. Finally, time switches (cost around £15) turn lights on and off when you are away and can be used to switch on the heating before your return.

If you want to know of a reputable locksmith, you should contact the **Master Locksmiths Association**; website: **www.locksmiths.co.uk**.

The BBC Crimewatch Roadshow (**www.bbc.co.uk/crimewatchroadshow**) offers the following tips to stay safe:

- Keep your possessions safe by securing your home. You may be entitled to help towards paying for security improvements from your local council. Check with the housing department about these payments.

- Don't keep large amounts of money in your home. Keep it in a bank or building society where it is much safer.

- Get to know your neighbours, as it will be helpful to both of you if you are aware of each other's routines.

- Make sure you have good exterior lighting on your home. Call the council and let them know if street lights have burned out on your road.

- It is especially important not to let strangers into your home. Fit a door chain and viewer.

- Never give out personal details, such as credit card information, to strangers who call to see you.

- Never let a maintenance or service man who has just turned up at your door into your home.

- Always check the ID of maintenance men that you are expecting. You can check these details with their employer before you let them in. If in doubt, ask them to come back when someone else is with you.

- If you're out after dark, leave a light and radio on in the sitting room.

- Get advice from the Crime Prevention Officer at your local police station. Some areas have schemes to help older people.

Further useful information is supplied by:

- **Victim Support,** a support and witness service for those affected by crime; see website: **www.victimsupport.com**.

- **Trustmark Scheme,** which finds reliable, trustworthy tradesmen; see website: **www.trustmark.org.uk**.

- **Trading Standards,** where you can search for trusted traders in your area; see website: **www.tradingstandards.gov.uk**.

- **Age UK Advice,** provide a booklet *Staying Safe*. See website: **www.ageuk.org.uk**.

- **Safe Partnership** runs local schemes providing free home security to vulnerable people: **www.safepartnership.org**.

Burglar alarms and safes

More elaborate precautions such as a burglar alarm are among the best ways of protecting your home. Although alarms are expensive they could be worth every penny. In the event of a break-in, you can summon help or ask the police to do what they can if you are away.

Many insurance companies will recommend suitable contractors to install burglar alarm equipment. The **National Security Inspectorate** website lists approved contractors: 700 recognized firms and some 1,000 branches. They also investigate technical complaints. See website: **www.nsi.org.uk**.

If you keep valuables or money in the house, you should think about buying a concealed wall or floor safe. If you are going away, it is a good idea to inform your neighbours. It is advisable to give them a key so that they can turn off and reset the alarm should the need arise.

Insurance discounts

According to recent research, seven out of 10 householders are under-insured, some of them unknowingly but some intentionally to keep premiums lower. Reassessing your policy makes sense for two reasons: first, because the number of burglaries has risen, so the risks are greater. Second, you may be able to obtain better value than you are getting at present. A number of insurance companies now give discounts on house contents premiums if proper security precautions have been installed.

Some insurance companies approach the problem differently and arrange discounts for their policyholders with manufacturers of security devices. If you would welcome independent advice on choosing a policy, you could contact British Insurance Brokers Associations and the Institute of Insurance Brokers. See website: **www.biba.org.uk**.

Personal safety

Older people who live on their own can be particularly at risk. A number of personal alarms are now available that are highly effective and can generally give you peace of mind. A sensible precaution is to carry a 'screamer alarm', sometimes known as a 'personal attack button'. A mobile telephone can also increase your sense of security. Older people feel particularly vulnerable to mugging so it is sensible to take precautions when out and about. Many councils run community alarm schemes for those who are housebound. For a small fee you get a panic button, usually on a pendant or wristband, so you can contact an emergency operator if you have a fall, are taken ill, or suspect a break-in. The operator phones a friend, relative or the emergency services. Age UK has been running its alarm scheme for 30 years but try your local council first.

Insurance

If your buildings and contents insurance was originally arranged through your building society, it may cease when your mortgage is paid off. If you buy a house with cash – for instance when moving to a smaller home – it is advisable to get a qualified assessor to work out the rebuilding costs and insurance value of your new home. The cost of replacing the fabric of your house, were it to burn down, could possibly be significantly greater than the amount for which it is currently insured. Remember, you must insure for the full rebuilding cost: the market value may be inappropriate. Your policy should also provide money to meet architects' or surveyors' fees, as well as alternative accommodation for you and your family if your home were completely destroyed by fire.

If you are planning to move into accommodation that has been converted from one large house into several flats or maisonettes, check with the landlord or managing agent that the insurance on the structure of the total building is adequate. When buying a new property you are under no obligation to insure your home with the particular company suggested by your building society. With all insurance, policies vary and it pays to shop around.

Owners of properties in flood-prone areas in the UK could soon have difficulty getting insurance. Even if they manage to find a policy that will cover them for flood damage, the premiums might well be unaffordable or impose huge excesses. It is advisable to check whether you live in a high-risk area and, if so, take steps to protect your property. Information on flood-risk areas and how to get help in obtaining insurance can be found on the Environment Agency website: **www.environment-agency.gov.uk**.

Another important extra feature of home insurance is 'public liability cover'. This is designed to meet claims against you as a home owner, tenant or landlord – for example if a visitor tripped and was injured in your home (contents insurance) or if a tile fell from your roof and damaged a neighbour's car (buildings insurance) – and you are found liable for the damage or injury.

Buildings insurance

If you rent your home, it's up to your landlord to arrange buildings insurance. If you own your own home, it's up to you. Even if you no longer have a mortgage, make sure your home is insured. BCIS, the **RICS's Building Cost Information Service,** provides cost information on all aspects of construction. It has an online calculator at **www.rics.co.uk** to estimate how much cover you need.

Contents insurance

It is important to have the right level of cover. Once you stop work, you may need to review the value of your home contents. With older possessions, you should assess the replacement cost and make sure you have a 'new for old' or 'replacement as new' policy. You should not forget to cancel items on your contents policy that you no longer possess. You must also add new valuables that have been bought or received as presents. In particular, do check that you are adequately covered for any home improvements you may have added.

Where antiques and jewellery are concerned, values can rise and fall disproportionately to inflation and depend on current market trends. For a professional valuation, contact the **British Antique Dealers' Association** (BADA), website: **www.bada.org** or LAPADA (Association of Art & Antiques Dealers), website: **www.lapada.org**. Photographs of particularly valuable items can help in the assessment of premiums and settlement of claims. Property marking, for example with an ultraviolet marker, is another useful ploy, as it will help the police trace your possessions should any be stolen.

The **Association of British Insurers** has information on various aspects of household insurance and loss prevention; see website: **www.abi.org.uk**.

The **British Insurance Brokers' Association** can provide information on registered insurance brokers in your area; see website: **www.biba.org.uk**.

Some insurance companies offer home and contents policies for older people at substantially reduced rates. See the following websites:

www.rias.co.uk;

www.castlecover.co.uk;

www.ageuk.org.uk;

www.staysure.co.uk;

www.50plusinsurance.co.uk;

www.saga.co.uk.

An increasing number of insurance companies offer generous no-claims discounts. Another type of discount-linked policy that is becoming more popular is one that carries an excess. Savings on premiums can be quite appreciable, if you check what terms they offer.

If you automatically renew your policy every year with the same company, you may find that your premiums have increased each year.

Financial institutions are keen on 'loyalty marketing' but loyalty should work both ways. Don't stay with a provider out of loyalty. Nowadays *disloyalty* pays because the winners are those customers who constantly switch from one provider to another.

Raising money on your home – equity release

Many home owners find that when they reach later life they have wealth tied up in their home but fewer savings or less income than they would like. If you don't want to move, or can't move, another option is equity release.

Taking money out of your home through an equity release scheme is a monumental – and one-way – decision. *Which?* magazine has a lot of advice on equity release, see their website: **www.which.co.uk**.

An equity release plan allows you to use some of the capital you have tied up in your home while keeping the right to carry on living there for as long as you need. It is an agreement between a home owner (aged 55 or over) and a provider, which enables the home owner to receive cash from the money tied up in their home. The money is free of tax and enables home owners to benefit from the value of their home. Releasing equity from your home could reduce your entitlement to some state benefits. It could also make a difference to your tax position, and it will reduce the value of your estate when you die. The important thing with equity release is to make sure your family knows all about your plans.

There are two main types of plan: a *lifetime mortgage* is where you raise money by taking out a mortgage against your property. The loan is repaid when the home is eventually sold. With a *home reversion plan* you sell part, or all, of your home now in return for a cash sum. You have the right to stay in your home as a tenant, paying little or no rent. Equity release plans are designed to run until you die or move out, for example if you move permanently into a care home. You can have a plan just for yourself, or for you and your partner. In the latter case, the plan runs until you both no longer need the home.

How a lifetime mortgage works

Like an ordinary mortgage, a lifetime mortgage is a loan secured against your home, but a lifetime mortgage is normally repaid only when you no longer need to live there. When taking out a lifetime mortgage you usually choose between borrowing a single lump sum or using a flexible or drawdown facility to provide a series of regular or ad hoc payments.

Most lifetime mortgages are 'roll-up loans'. This means you normally don't make any monthly repayments. Instead, interest is added to the loan and repaid only when your home is eventually sold. Usually interest is charged at a fixed rate. This means you can predict with certainty how the amount you owe will grow. Be wary of taking out a variable-rate plan where you do not have this certainty. With a roll-up loan, the amount you owe can increase quickly, so there may be little or nothing left from the proceeds after the loan is repaid. Most roll-up lifetime mortgages have a 'negative-equity guarantee' that promises the maximum you owe will not exceed the value of your home when it is sold.

How a home reversion plan works

With a home reversion plan you sell some, or all, of your home to a company (or in some cases, an individual investor) for less than the market value. In return you get a lump sum (which could be paid as a single sum or in instalments), a monthly income or both. You get the proceeds of the sale now. You no longer own your home, or the part you sold, but you have the right to stay there until you die or move out.

When your home is eventually sold, the reversion company gets all of the proceeds if you sold the whole of your home to them. If you sold part of your home, the reversion company gets its share. When you take out a home reversion plan, you don't get the full market value of your property on the part you sell. The difference between what you give up and what you get reflects the cost to the reversion company of waiting to gets its money back while letting you live in the property for little or no rent. The size of the difference depends on your:

- age – the older you are when you take out the plan, the shorter the period you are expected to live, so the larger the sum you can get;
- sex – women tend to live longer than men, but since 2013 insurers have not been allowed to take gender into account when fixing annuity rates. Rates for men will get worse – but might not improve much for women;
- health – if your life expectancy is reduced because of poor health, some providers may offer a higher amount.

Tips for choosing the right equity release scheme:

- Explore all other options first to make sure you find out how equity release would affect you and your entitlement to state benefits.

- Borrow the minimum amount you need to or choose a drawdown scheme that will give you the option to borrow money as and when you need it.

- Consider taking out a scheme that lets you make interest payments each month if you can afford to.

- Choose a scheme with no early-repayment charges, or ones that apply only for a limited period.

- 'Sale and Rent Back' schemes are not the same as, nor similar to, equity release. This is a sector to steer clear of. Companies typically offer to buy your home at a discounted price and there are serious pitfalls.

How much equity release might cost

- *Arrangement and administration fees*: the plan provider will normally charge an arrangement fee. With a drawdown mortgage or instalment reversion plan, there may be a separate administration fee for each withdrawal.

- *Valuation and legal fees*: you will have to pay for a surveyor to value your property and a solicitor to handle the paperwork and check the legal aspects of the agreement. You must pay the valuation fee in advance but the provider might reimburse this if the plan goes ahead. Some deals refund your legal costs too.

- *Insurance and maintenance*: in addition to the direct costs of the scheme, the provider will require you to have buildings insurance and to maintain the property to a reasonable standard.

Remember, equity release plans are complex. You are strongly recommended to get advice from an independent financial adviser specializing in equity release and a solicitor who is familiar with this type of plan. You should get legal advice – and use your own solicitor (not one appointed by the equity release firm). You should also ensure that the property is independently valued by a qualified surveyor. The adviser may charge a fee, be paid by commission, or a combination of both.

For further information, see the Money Advice Service website: **www.moneyadviceservice.org.uk**. You should also check with the **Equity Release Council**. This is the industry body for the equity release sector and represents the providers, qualified financial advisers, lawyers, intermediaries and surveyors who work in the equity release sector. For further information see website: **www.equityreleasecouncil.com**. Alternatively, the **Equity Release Information Centre** publishes a free 32-page guide to equity release. Visit **www.askeric.tv**.

The following websites offer further information:

www.homereversionschemes.co.uk;

www.sixtyplusonline.co.uk;

www.societyoflaterlifeadvisers.co.uk;

www.learnmoney.co.uk;

Using your home to earn money

Some people whose home has become too large are tempted by the idea of taking in tenants. There are three broad choices: taking in paying guests or lodgers, letting part of your home as self-contained accommodation, or renting the whole house for a specified period of time. In all cases for your own protection it is essential to have a written agreement and to take up bank references, unless the let is a strictly temporary one where the money is paid in advance. Otherwise, rent should be collected quarterly and you should arrange a hefty deposit to cover any damage. An important point to be aware of is that there is now a set of strict rules concerning the treatment of deposits, with the risk of large fines for landlords and agents who fail to abide by them.

Lodgers: In a move to encourage more people to let out rooms in their home, the government allows you to earn up to £4,250 (£2,150 if letting jointly) a year free of tax. Any excess rental income you receive over £4,250 will be assessed for tax in the normal way. For further information, see **HMRC** website: **www.hmrc.gov.uk** and **Gov.uk** website: **www.gov.uk**. If you have a mortgage or are a tenant yourself (even with a very long lease), check with your building society or landlord that you are entitled to sublet.

Paying guests or lodgers

This is the most informal arrangement, and will normally be either a casual holiday-type bed-and-breakfast let or a lodger who might be with you for a couple of years. In either case, the visitor will be sharing part of your home, the accommodation will be fully furnished, and you will be providing at least one full meal a day and possibly also basic cleaning services. You do not have to commit to having a lodger around the house full-time; some employees and lecturers need a room only between Monday and Friday. Foreign students are around all term time but not in the holidays. Foreign language students might need a room only for one six-week term. You can stipulate whether to take younger or older people.

There are few legal formalities involved in these types of lettings, and rent is entirely a matter for friendly agreement. As a resident owner you are also in a very strong position if you want your lodger to leave. Lodging arrangements can easily be ended, as your lodger has no legal rights to stay after the agreed period. A wise precaution is to check with your insurance company that your home contents policy will not be affected, since some insurers restrict cover to households with lodgers. Also, unless you make arrangements to the contrary, you should inform your lodger that his or her possessions are not covered by your policy.

If, as opposed to a lodger or the occasional summer paying guest, you offer regular B&B accommodation, you could be liable to pay business rates. Although this is not new, it appears that in recent years the Valuation Office Agency has been enforcing the regulation more strictly against people running B&B establishments.

Holiday lets

It is a good idea to register with your tourist information centre and to contact the environmental health office at your local council for any help and advice.

Letting rooms in your home

You could convert a basement or part of your house into a self-contained flat and let this either furnished or unfurnished. Alternatively, you could let a single room or rooms. As a general rule, provided you continue to live in the house your tenant(s) have little security of tenure and equally do not have the right to appeal against the rent. You would be advised to check your home contents policy with your insurance company. As a resident landlord, you have a guaranteed right to repossession of your property. If the letting is for a fixed term (eg six months or a year), the let will automatically cease at the end of that fixed period. If the arrangement is on a more ad hoc basis with no specified leaving date, it may be legally necessary to give at least four weeks' notice in writing. The position over notices to quit will vary according to circumstances. Should you encounter any difficulties, it is possible that you may need to apply to the courts for an eviction order.

Tax note

If you subsequently sell your home, you may not be able to claim exemption from capital gains tax on the increase in value of a flat if it is entirely self-contained. It is therefore a good idea to retain some means of access to the main house or flat, but take legal advice as to what will qualify.

Renting out your home on a temporary basis

If you are thinking of spending the winter in the sun or are considering buying a retirement home that you will not occupy for a year or two, you need to understand the assured short-hold tenancy rules. Unless notified in advance that you need the property back sooner (there are very few grounds on which you can make this notification) or unless earlier possession is sought because of the tenant's behaviour, your tenant has the right to stay for at least six months and must be given two months' notice before you want the tenancy to end. It is strongly advisable to ask a solicitor or letting agent to help you draw up the agreement.

The safest solution if possible is to let your property to a company rather than to private individuals, since company tenants do not have the same security of tenure. However, it is important that the contract should make clear that your let is for residential, not business, purposes. Before entering into any agreement, you should seek professional advice.

And some other ideas...

If you think a little extra cash might be useful, depending on where you live, you could turn your garden into a 'micro campsite' and earn up to £40 per night: **www.campinmygarden.com** gives information. Or you could hire out your garden for a number of uses – vegetable plots, storage, or even wedding receptions: **www.rentmygarden.co.uk**.

Should you have extra space in your house and don't mind renting out a room, by signing up to certain websites you can reach potential guests from all round the world. Try: **www.gumtree.com**; **www.airbnb.co.uk**; **www.wimdu.co.uk**; **www.spareroom.co.uk**; **www.crashpadder.com**; **www.hosts-international.com**.

If you'd rather not have people, you can make extra money out of the empty space in your house by renting out your cellar or loft as storage space to people who have too much stuff (**www.storemates.co.uk**). If parking is difficult or expensive in your area, drivers will pay to use your parking space or garage (**www.yourparkingspace.co.uk**; **www.parkonmydrive.com**).

You can offer your home for film and advertisement locations if you can cope with a lot of disruption. But it pays good money and film producers need other types of homes besides stately ones. Look at **www.film-locations.co.uk** or **www.amazingspace.co.uk**.

Holiday lets

Buying a future retirement home in the country and renting it out as a holiday home in the summer months is another option worth considering. This can prove a useful and profitable investment. As long as certain conditions are met, income from furnished holiday lettings enjoys most of the benefits that there would be if it were taxed as trading income rather than as investment income. This means you can claim 10 per cent writing down capital allowances on such items as carpets, curtains and furniture as well as fixtures and fittings. Alternatively, you can claim an annual 10 per cent wear-and-tear allowance. The running expenses of a holiday home, including maintenance, advertising, insurance cover and council tax (or business rates – see below), are all largely allowable for tax, excluding that element that relates to your own occupation of the property. Married couples should consider whether the property is to be held in the husband's or the wife's name, or owned jointly. A solicitor or accountant will be able to advise you.

To qualify as furnished holiday accommodation, the property must be situated in the UK, be let on a commercial basis, be available for holiday letting for at least 140 days during the tax year and be actually let for at least 70 days. Moreover, for at least seven months a year, not necessarily continuous, the property must not normally be occupied by the same tenant for more than 31 consecutive days. There is always the danger that you might create an assured tenancy, so do take professional advice on drawing up the letting agreement. Similarly, if you decide to use one of the holiday rental agents to market your property, get a solicitor to check any contract you enter into with the company. For more information see the **RICS** (Royal Institution of Chartered Surveyors) website: **www.rics.org**.

A further point to note is that tax inspectors are taking a tougher line as to what is 'commercial'. To safeguard yourself, it is important to draw up a broad business plan before you start and to make a real effort to satisfy the minimum letting requirements.

Tenants' deposits

The Tenancy Deposit Scheme which came into force in April 2007 was created to ensure tenants get back the amount owing to them, to make any disputes about the deposit easier to resolve and to encourage tenants to look after the property during the agreed term of their let. Landlords or agents must now protect it under an approved scheme. Failure to do so within 14 days of receiving the money could result in the landlord being forced to pay the tenant three times the deposit amount.

The two types of tenancy deposit protection schemes available for landlords and letting agents are insurance-based schemes and custodial schemes. All schemes provide a free dispute resolution service. The schemes allow tenants to get all or part of their deposit back when they are entitled to it and encourage tenants and landlords to make a clear agreement from the start on the condition of the property. The schemes make any disputes easier to resolve. For further information see the following:

www.gov.uk – Tenancy Deposit Protection;

www.rla.org.uk – Residential Landlords Association;

www.thedisputeservice.co.uk – Dispute Service.

Finally, property that is rented 'commercially' (ie for 140 days or more a year) is normally liable for business rates, instead of the council tax you would otherwise pay. This could be more expensive, even though partially allowable against tax.

Useful reading

The Complete Guide to Letting Property by Liz Hodgkinson, published by Kogan Page, £10.99 (website: **www.koganpage.com**).

Benefits and taxes

Housing Benefit

Provided you have no more than £16,000 in savings, you may be able to get help with your rent from your local council. You may qualify for Housing Benefit whether you are a council or private tenant or live in a hotel or hostel. For advice about your own particular circumstances, contact your local authority or your Citizens Advice Bureau.

The amount of benefit you get depends on five factors: the number of people in your household; your eligible rent (up to a prescribed maximum); your capital or savings; your income; and your 'applicable amount', which is the amount of money the government considers you need for basic living expenses. There have been cuts to housing benefit recently, sometimes dubbed 'the bedroom tax', so apply to your local authority to check if you are eligible for help.

If your income is less than your applicable amount you will receive maximum Housing Benefit towards your eligible rent (less any non-dependant deduction). You may be eligible for Income Support if your capital is less than £8,000, or less than £16,000 if you are aged 60 or over. If your income is equal to your applicable amount, you will also receive maximum Housing Benefit.

How to claim

If you think you are eligible for benefit you can apply online or ask your council for an application form. It should let you know within 14 days of receiving your completed application whether you are entitled to benefit, and will inform you of the amount. See website: **www.gov.uk** – Benefits.

Special accommodation

If you live in a mobile home or houseboat, you may be able to claim benefit for site fees or mooring charges. If you live in a private nursing or residential care home you will not normally be able to get Housing

Benefit to help with the cost. However, you may be able to get help towards both the accommodation part of your fees and your living expenses through Income Support or possibly under the Community Care arrangements. If you make a claim for Income Support you can claim Housing Benefit and Council Tax Benefit at the same time.

Council tax

Council tax is based on the value of the dwelling in which you live (the property element) and also consists of a personal element – with discounts and exemptions applying to certain groups of people.

The property element

Most domestic properties are liable for council tax, including rented property, mobile homes and houseboats. The value of the property is assessed according to a banding system, with eight different bands (A to H). The banding of each property is determined by the government's Valuation Office Agency. Small extensions or other improvements made after this date do not affect the valuation until the property changes hands. The planned council tax revaluation in England, due to take place in 2007, was postponed. Notification of the band is shown on the bill when it is sent out in April. If you think there has been a misunderstanding about the valuation (or your liability to pay the full amount) you may have the right of appeal.

Liability

Not everyone pays council tax. The bill is normally sent to the resident owner or joint owners of the property or, in the case of rented accommodation, to the tenant or joint tenants. Married couples and people with a shared legal interest in the property are jointly liable for the bill, unless they are students or severely mentally impaired. In some cases, for example in hostels or multi-occupied property, a non-resident landlord or owner will be liable but may pass on a share of the bill to the tenants or residents, which would probably be included as part of the rental charge.

The personal element

The valuation of each dwelling assumes that two adults will be resident. The charge does not increase if there are more adults. However if, as in many homes, there is a single adult, your council tax bill will be reduced by 25 per cent. Certain people are disregarded when determining the number of residents in a household: for full details see **www.gov.uk** – Council Tax.

Discounts and exemptions applying to property

Certain property is exempt from council tax, including:

- Property that has been unoccupied and unfurnished for less than six months.
- The home of a deceased person; the exemption lasts until six months after the grant of probate.
- A home that is empty because the occupier is absent in order to care for someone else.
- The home of a person who is or would be exempted from council tax because of moving to a residential home, hospital care or similar.
- Empty properties in need of major repairs or undergoing structural alteration can be exempt from council tax for an initial period of six months, but this can be extended for a further six months. After 12 months, the standard 50 (or possibly full 100) per cent charge for empty properties will apply.
- Granny flats that are part of another private domestic dwelling may be exempt, but this depends on access and other conditions. To check, contact your local Valuation Office.

Business-cum-domestic property

Business-cum-domestic property is rated according to usage, with the business section assessed for business rates and the domestic section for council tax.

Appeals

If you become the new person responsible for paying the council tax on a property that you feel has been wrongly banded, you have six months to appeal and can request that the valuation be reconsidered. Otherwise, there are only three other circumstances in which you can appeal:

- if there has been a material increase or reduction in the property's value;

- if you start, or stop, using part of the property for business or the balance between domestic and business use changes;
- if either of the latter two apply and the listing officer has altered the council tax list without giving you a chance to put your side.

If you have grounds for appeal, you should take up the matter with the Valuation Office. If the matter is not resolved, you can then appeal to an independent valuation tribunal. For advice and further information, contact your local Citizens Advice Bureau.

Council Tax Benefit

If you cannot afford your council tax because you have a low income, you may be able to obtain Council Tax Benefit. People on Pension Credit (Guarantee Credit) are entitled to rebates of up to 100 per cent. Even if you are not receiving any other social security benefit, you may still qualify for some Council Tax Benefit. The amount you get depends on your income, savings, personal circumstances, who else lives in your home (in particular whether they would be counted as 'non-dependants') and your net council tax bill (ie after any deductions that apply to your home). If you are not sure whether your income is low enough to entitle you to Council Tax Benefit, it is worth enquiring. If you disagree with your council's decision, you can appeal. For further information see:

Citizens Advice Bureau, website: **www.citizensadvice.org.uk.**

Federation of Private Residents' Associations Ltd (FPRA) website: **www.fpra.org.uk.**

Chapter Nine
Leisure activities

There is no pleasure in having nothing to do; the fun is in having lots to do and not doing it.

MARY WILSON LITTLE

Do you have plans for the second half of your life? If you are intending to age well, and enjoy your leisure, it's important that you should get organised. A charity called 'The Second Half Centre' was set up in London in January 2013 to promote better ageing for all. The Centre (founded by Jill Shaw Ruddock and located in the NHS St Charles' Centre for Wellbeing) is based on the premise that as we're all living longer, soon reaching the age of 100 will be the norm. But how well we age is up to each individual. The purpose of the centre is to help people who want to stay well and stave off age-related diseases. Keeping active mentally and physically is the best way forward. Whether you enjoy art history, needlepoint, gardening or jujitsu, you will find an activity at The Second Half Centre to suit you, and at an affordable price. Oldies in the area should be kicking down the doors to cross this threshold, as it combines an unfogeyish club, community centre and further education college.

(Source: Modern Life – The Oldie, April 2013)

With regard to our new-found leisure in retirement, anti-ageing strategies vary considerably. Some of us might read about them while sitting in our armchair and spend the next few months thinking or researching carefully before committing ourselves. Others might feel impelled immediately to get up and involved with enthusiasm. Despite the wide range of our age, state of health and depth of pockets, it is really important for us, the over-55s, to find leisure activities that will help us enjoy a long and happy retirement.

Top tips for ageing well. Some people use a five-a-day plan:

- daily engagement with community and/or family and friends;

- regular exercise;

- wholesome diet;

- mental stimulation;

- cultivating a passion or purpose – a leisure pursuit or volunteering.

Whatever you feel about it, ageing well and making the most of our leisure is up to each of us and a vital part of enjoying our retirement. Here are plenty of suggestions for you if your 'Second Half of Life' planning needs a nudge. This chapter is best read in conjunction with Chapter 14, Holidays, as many of the organizations listed there would be equally relevant here. However, those that appear in Chapter 14 would probably involve most people spending a few days away from home. The latest information is always available on the relevant website, so do check there for further details.

Adult education

Whether you cherish the hope of taking a degree, learn about computing, studying philosophy or archaeology, opportunities for education abound, and there are scores of subjects easily available to everyone, regardless of age or previous qualifications. Not all educational courses are free, however there are a number of different funding options available for those over 50. Those who have never taken any form of educational course through a university or college may also be able to obtain financial assistance. Where to find help? Agencies such as Saga, AgeUK and LaterLife will supply information on free and subsidized educational courses. Local libraries are another place to find information on educational matters.

Learning new skills is always beneficial and can lead to new opportunities. Many retired people have actually found new careers in later life. Here are some websites for available courses throughout the UK:

Adult Education Finder: **www.adulteducationfinder.co.uk**.

BBC Learning: **www.bbc.co.uk/learning/adults**.

Home Learning College: **www.homelearningcollege.com**.

National Extension College (NEC): **www.nec.ac.uk**.

National Institute of Adult Continuing Education (NIACE):
www.niace.org.uk.

Open and Distance Learning Quality Council (ODLQC):
www.odlqc.org.uk.

Open University (OU): **www.open.ac.uk**.

Pearson's Love to Learn: **www.lovetolearn.co.uk**.

University extra-mural departments – non-degree and short courses

Many universities have a department of extra-mural studies that arranges courses for adults, sometimes in the evening or during vacation periods. If you live near a university, ask there, but here are a few websites to check:

Birkbeck, University of London: **www.bbk.ac.uk**.

U3A (The University of the Third Age): **www.u3a.org.uk**.

Workers' Educational Association (WEA): **www.wea.org.uk**.

Animals

If you are an animal lover, it is likely that you already have connections with charities and organizations that relate to your favourite animals, but here are some suggestions, which include online publications:

Birdlife International Community: **www.birdlife.org**.

British Beekeepers Association: **www.bbka.org.uk**.

Your Cat magazine: **www.yourcat.co.uk**.

Dogs Monthly magazine: **www.dogsmonthly.co.uk**.

Horse and Hound magazine: **www.horseandhound.co.uk**.

RSPCA: **www.rspca.org.uk**

Wildfowl & Wetlands Trust (WWT): **www.wwt.org.uk**.

Arts

Wherever you live you can enjoy the arts. Whether you are interested in active participation or just appreciating the performance of others, there is an exhilarating choice of events. Many entertainments offer concessionary prices to retired people.

The Arts Council England works to get great art to everyone by championing, developing and investing in artistic experiences that enrich everyone's lives. For information and details of each regional office, see website: **www.artscouncil.org.uk**.

If you're passionate about the creative arts, you can study with the specialists. For courses ranging from art history, creative writing, fine art, illustration, graphic design, music, painting, photography, textiles and visual communications, see the **Open College of Arts** website: **www.oca-uk.com**.

For those who wish to join in with amateur arts activities, most public libraries keep lists of choirs, drama clubs, painting clubs and similar in their locality.

Films

Cinema is a hugely popular art form and should you enjoy film, you could join your community cinema, local film society or visit the National Film Theatre. Here are some other websites to look at:

British Federation of Film Societies (BFFS): **www.bffs.org.uk**.

British Film Institute (BFI): **www.bfi.org.uk**.

Music and ballet

You might consider becoming a Friend and supporting one of the famous 'Houses' such as Covent Garden, or prefer music making in your own right; whatever your taste, here are some suggestions:

Covent Garden: **www.roh.org.uk**.

English National Opera (ENO): **www.eno.org**.

Sadler's Wells: **www.sadlerswells.com**.

Scottish National Opera: **www.scottishopera.org.uk**.

Southbank Centre: **www.southbankcentre.co.uk**.

Welsh National Opera: **www.wno.org.uk**.

Music making

Whatever style of music you enjoy, there are associations to suit your taste.

Handbell Ringers of Great Britain: **www.hrgb.org.uk**.

Making Music: **www.makingmusic.org.uk**.

National Association of Choirs:
www.nationalassociationofchoirs.org.uk.

Society of Recorder Players: **www.srp.org.uk**.

Poetry

There is an increasing enthusiasm for poetry and poetry readings in clubs, pubs and other places of entertainment. Special local events may be advertised in your neighbourhood. **The Poetry Society** is a charitable organization providing support and information and aims to create a central position for poetry in the arts. See **www.poetrysociety.org.uk**.

Television and radio audiences

People of all ages, backgrounds and abilities enjoy participating as members of studio audiences and contributors to programmes. For those wishing to take part there are a couple of websites that can help:

Applause Store: **www.applausestore.com**.

BBC Shows: **www.bbc.co.uk/showsandtours/tickets**.

Theatre

For all keen theatregoers, details of current and forthcoming productions for national and regional theatres, as well as theatre reviews, are well advertised in the press and on the internet. Preview performances are usually cheaper, and there are often concessionary tickets for matinees. Here are some useful websites:

ATG Tickets: **www.atgtickets.com**.

Barbican: **www.barbican.org.uk**.

Donmar Warehouse: **www.donmarwarehouse.com**.

National Theatre: **www.nationaltheatre.org.uk**.

National Theatre of Wales: **www.nationaltheatrewales.org**.

Official London Theatre: **www.officiallondontheatre.co.uk**.

Scottish Community Drama Association (SCDA): **www.scda.org.uk**.

Theatre Network: **www.uktheatre.net**.

The Old Vic: **www.oldvictheatre.com**.

TKTS: **www.tkts.co.uk**.

Visual arts

Attending exhibitions and lectures, if you enjoy art, is something you should have more time for in retirement. Some of the following art societies offer a good choice of such activities:

Art Fund: **www.artfund.org**.

Contemporary Art Society: **www.contemporaryartsociety.org**.

National Association of Decorative & Fine Arts Societies (NADFAS): **www.nadfas.org.uk**.

Royal Academy of Arts: **www.royalacademy.org.uk**.

Tate: **www.tate.org.uk**.

Painting as a hobby

If you are interested in improving your own painting technique, art courses are available at your local adult education institute. Your library may have details of local art groups and societies in your area. The **Society for All Artists** (SAA), which exists to inform, encourage and inspire all who want to paint, whatever their ability, provides all that you need to enjoy this hobby: **www.saa.co.uk**.

Computing and IT

With the constant advance of new technology, computing is one of the most popular classes for retired people. In most cases, learning these skills is completely free. Local libraries have set times throughout the week for retired people to either learn computing skills or update skills they already have. The plus point of learning skills such as the internet is that it can lead on to other free learning applications. There is a huge range of free learning resources available on the internet, if you know where to look. Here are a few possibilities:

Digital Unite: **www.aboutacademy.digitalunite.com**.

Pearson's Love to Learn: **www.lovetolearn.co.uk**.

Which? Guides have four *Made Easy* titles to help you understand computers and the internet; step-by-step guides you can trust: *Internet Made Easy for the Over-50s*; *Using your PC Made Easy*; *Laptops and Mobile Devices Made Easy*; *PC Problem Solving Made Easy*. See website: **www.which.co.uk/books**.

Crafts

The majority of suggestions are contained in Chapter 14, Holidays, variously under 'Arts and crafts' and 'Special interest holidays', since many organizations offer residential courses and painting holidays. If you are interested in a particular form of craft work many of the societies and others listed in Chapter 14 should be able to help you. Here are a couple more:

Crafts Council: **www.craftscouncil.org.uk**.

Open College of the Arts (OCA): **www.oca-uk.com**.

Creative writing

It is said that there is a book in everyone, and many retired people have a yen to write. As this is a solitary occupation you may find that joining a writing group is a worthwhile and pleasurable thing to do. The **National Association of Writing Groups – www.nawg.co.uk –** is one place to find a local one; though not all creative writing groups are linked to that site. Whatever the style, creative writing groups provide company, support and a degree of critique too. Some specialize, but many take fiction, non-fiction and poetry in their stride, so you can write anything from an essay to an article, from a rant to a novel – and, who knows, you might even get published and earn some money.

If any of this interests you, something else to check is *Writing Magazine*. This is a monthly journal designed to help aspiring and actual writers. Patrick Forsyth (a many-times-published Kogan Page author) writes regularly for that magazine, and is a great fan of writing groups. 'They are,' he says, 'if not essential, a very great help to those who love to write, but lack confidence, want a bit of advice, support or motivation. I certainly recommend you give attendance a go. Getting published in not easy, and it is said that the single word that best describes a writer with no persistence is *unpublished*. But it *is* possible and seeing a book or article with your name on, and having it followed by a cheque, is very satisfying.' Patrick knows; one of his recently published books, a hilarious critique of inappropriate public writing, is called *Empty when Half Full*.

Dance/keep fit

Clubs, classes and groups exist in all parts of the country offering ballroom, old-time, Scottish, folk, ballet, disco dancing and others. Additionally, there are music and relaxation classes, aerobics and more gentle keep-fit sessions. To find out what is available in your area, ask at your library, or see the list below (there are further suggestions in Chapter 13, Health, 'Keep fit'):

British Dance Council: **www.british-dance-council.org**.

English Folk Dance and Song Society: **www.efdss.org**.

Imperial Society of Teachers of Dancing: **www.istd.org**.

Keep Fit Association (KFA): **www.keepfit.org.uk**.

Royal Scottish Country Dance Society: **www.rscds.org**.

Sport and Recreation Alliance: **www.sportandrecreation.org.uk**.

Games

Many local areas have their own backgammon, bridge, chess, whist, dominos, Scrabble and other groups that meet together regularly in a club, hall, pub or other social venue to enjoy friendly board games. Information on any local clubs should be available from your library. Here are some national organizations which will put you in touch with local groups:

Boardgame Players Association: **www.boardgamers.org**.

English Bridge Union: **www.ebu.co.uk**.

English Chess Federation: **www.englishchess.org.uk**.

Scrabble Clubs UK: **www.absp.org.uk**.

Gardens and gardening

Courses, gardens to visit, special help for people with disabilities, and how to run a gardening association; these and other interests are all catered for by the following organizations:

English Gardening School: **www.englishgardeningschool.co.uk**.

Garden Organic: **www.gardenorganic.org.uk**.

Gardening for Disabled Trust: **www.gardeningfordisabledtrust.org.uk**.

National Gardens Scheme: **www.ngs.org.uk**.

National Society of Allotment & Leisure Gardeners Ltd:
   www.nsalg.org.uk.

Royal Horticultural Society: **www.rhs.org.uk**.

Scotland's Gardens Scheme: **www.scotlandsgardens.org**.

Thrive: **www.thrive.org.uk**.

Welsh Historic Gardens Trust (WHGT): **www.whgt.org.uk**.

History

People with an interest in the past have so many activities to choose from – visit historic monuments, including ancient castles and stately homes, in all parts of the country; explore the City of London; study genealogy or research the history of your local area. There are many organizations to consider, but here are a few websites to give you some ideas:

Age Exchange: **www.age-exchange.org.uk**.

Architectural Heritage Society of Scotland: **www.ahss.org.uk**.

British Association for Local History: **www.balh.co.uk**.

City of London Information Centre: **www.cityoflondon.gov.uk**.

English Heritage: **www.english-heritage.org.uk**.

Federation of Family History Societies: **www.ffhs.org.uk**.

Garden History Society: **www.gardenhistorysociety.org**.

Georgian Group: **www.georgiangroup.org.uk**.

Historic Houses Association (HHA): **www.hha.org.uk**.

Historical Association: **www.history.org.uk**.

Monumental Brass Society: **www.mbs-brasses.co.uk**.

National Trust: **www.nationaltrust.org.uk**.

National Trust for Scotland: **www.nts.org.uk**.

Northern Ireland Tourist Board: **www.discovernorthernireland.com**.

Oral History Society: **www.ohs.org.uk**.

Society of Genealogists: **www.sog.org.uk**.

Victorian Society: **www.victorian-society.org.uk**.

Magazines

There are a growing number of magazines dedicated to the over-50s with articles and features on topics that include health, travel, finances and lifestyle. Here are some of the most popular, a number of these publications are available online:

50 Plus Magazine: **www.50plusmagazine.co.uk**.

55 Life Scotland: **www.55life.co.uk**.

Giddy Limits: **www.giddylimits.co.uk**.

Healthylife: **www.healthylife-mag.co.uk**.

Laterlife: **www.laterlife.com**.

Mature Times: **www.maturetimes.co.uk**.

Over 65 Magazine: **www.over65magazine.co.uk**.

Retirement Today: **www.retirement-today.co.uk**.

Savista Magazine: **www.savistamagazine.com**.

The Oldie: **www.the.oldie.magazine.co.uk**

Third Age: **www.thirdage.co.uk**.

YOURS Magazine: **www.yours.co.uk**

Museums

Most museums organize free lectures and guided tours on aspects of their collections or special exhibitions. If you join as a Friend, you can enjoy certain advantages, such as access to private views, visits to places of interest, receptions and other social activities. Apart from the famous national museums, there are many fascinating smaller ones to be found around the country, depending on your area of interest. Enjoy your research, but here are a few useful websites to start you off:

British Association of Friends of Museums (BAFM):
www.bafm.org.uk.

Ashmolean Museum of Art and Archaeology:
www.ashmolean.org.

British Museum: **www.britishmuseum.org**.

Fitzwilliam Museum: **www.fitzmuseum.cam.ac.uk**.

National Museums of Scotland: **www.nms.ac.uk**.

Natural History Museum: **www.nhm.ac.uk**.

Royal Museums Greenwich: **www1.rmg.co.uk**.

Science Museum: **www.sciencemuseum.org.uk**.

V&A (Victoria and Albert Museum): **www.vam.ac.uk**.

Nature and conservation

Many conservation organizations are very keen to recruit volunteers; the majority are therefore listed in Chapter 12, Voluntary work. Also many of those concerned with field studies arrange courses and other special activity interests where there is usually a residential content, so more are listed in Chapter 14, Holidays. Here are a few that don't appear elsewhere in this book:

Field Studies Council: **www.field-studies-council.org**.

Forestry: **www.forestry.gov.uk**.

Inland Waterways Association: **www.waterways.org.uk**.

Wildlife Trusts: **www.wildlifetrusts.org**.

Public library service

The public library in the UK is an endangered species and needs your support. Library services that are run by local authorities provide free services that empower people to access resources. Libraries still fulfil their traditional role of lending books, but also improve people's lives through a whole range of activities and services. The UK library service is a huge resource, which not only lends millions of books free each year, but also CDs and DVDs. Most are now equipped with the internet, so visitors can browse websites and do research. One of its traditional main attractions is as a source of masses of information about both local and national activities. Additionally, there are reference sections containing newspapers and periodicals as well as a wide selection of reference books covering any subject.

The UK's public library service is excellent – please help to keep it going by using your local facilities.

Sciences and other related subjects

If astronomy, meteorology or geology fascinate you, there are several societies and associations that may be of interest:

British Astronomical Association: **www.britastro.org**.

Geologists' Association: **www.geologistsassociation.org.uk**.

Royal Meteorological Society: **www.rmets.org**.

Special interests

Whether your special enthusiasm is stamp collecting or model flying, most of the associations listed organize events, answer queries and can put you in contact with kindred spirits:

British Association of Numismatic Societies (BANS):
www.coinclubs.freeserve.co.uk.

British Model Flying Association (BMFA): **www.bmfa.org**.

Central Council of Church Bell Ringers (CCCBR): **www.cccbr.org.uk**.

Miniature Armoured Fighting Vehicle Association (MAFVA):
   www.mafva.net.

National Association of Flower Arrangement Societies (NAFAS):
   www.nafas.org.uk.

National Philatelic Society: **www.ukphilately.org.uk**.

Railway Correspondence and Travel Society: **www.rcts.org.uk**.

Sport

Retirement is an ideal time to get fit and take up a sporting hobby. To find out about opportunities in your area, contact your local authority recreational department or your local sports or leisure centre. In addition, here are some relevant websites:

Angling

Whether you are an experienced angler, or are thinking of taking up fishing as a hobby, this sport offers a wide variety of opportunities. Particularly good news for women whose pheromones apparently attract fish onto their rods....

Angling Trust: **www.anglingtrust.net**.

UK Fishing: **www.ukfishing.com**.

Badminton

Badminton is a popular sport for all ages. Most people play it for leisure but it can be competitive as well as keeping you fit. For more information see:

Badminton England: **www.badmintonengland.co.uk**.

Play Badminton: **www.playbadminton.co.uk**.

Bowling

Bowls is enjoyed by millions of people throughout the world and the vast majority of them are over 50. The game of bowls comes in a variety of forms: Crown Green Bowls, Lawn Bowls, Short Mat Bowls and Carpet Bowls. For further information:

British Crown Green Bowling Association: **www.crowngreenbowls.org**.

English Bowling Association: **www.bowlsengland.com**.

English Indoor Bowling Association: **www.eiba.co.uk**.

English Short Mat Bowling Association: **www.esmba.co.uk**.

Clay pigeon shooting

Clay pigeon shooting is enjoyed by people from 9 years to 90, of either sex.

It is a hobby that can provide great personal fulfilment on an informal basis, or in a more organized and competitive fashion.

Clay Pigeon Shooting Association (CPSA): **www.cpsa.co.uk**.

Clay Shooting: **www.englishsportingclays.co.uk**.

The Big Shoot: **www.thebigshoot.co.uk**.

Cricket

There are lots of different playing opportunities for all ages and abilities, such as club cricket, indoor cricket and new shorter formats of the game. If playing is not for you, there are many places to watch matches:

England and Wales Cricket Board (ECB): **www.ecb.co.uk**.

Kia Oval – Surrey County Cricket Club: **www.kiaoval.com**.

Lord's Cricket Ground: **www.lords.org**.

Croquet

Croquet has been popular in England since it was first introduced in 1851 at The Great Exhibition. It can be played as a recreational pastime or competitive sport. See:

Croquet Association: **www.croquet.org.uk**.

Cycling

If you want to get into cycling, either for leisure or as a competitor, there are plenty of ways into the sport.

British Cycling: **www.britishcycling.org.uk**.

CTC (Cyclists' Touring Club): **www.ctc.org.uk**.

Road Cycling UK (RCUK): **www.roadcyclinguk.com**.

UK Cycling Events: **www.ukcyclingevents.co.uk**.

Darts

As well as being a professional competitive sport, darts is also a traditional pub game. Today it is played by over 6 million people regularly, and watched by millions on television.

British Darts Organisation (BDO): **www.bdodarts.com**.

Golf

National Golf Unions can provide information about municipal courses and private clubs, of which there are some 1,700 in England alone. Additionally, many adult education institutes and sports centres run classes for beginners.

England Golf: **www.englandgolf.org**.

Golfing Union of Ireland: **www.gui.ie**.

Scottish Golf: **www.scottishgolf.org**.

Welsh Golfing Union: **www.golfunionwales.org**.

Running

Regardless of age, fitness level, aspiration, background or location, running is good for you. There are many benefits so why not become one of the UK's running community. To help get you started, here are a few websites:

ARC (Association of Running Clubs): **www.runningclubs.org.uk**.

Good Run Guide: **www.goodrunguide.co.uk**.

Run England: **www.runengland.org**.

Runners Forum: **www.runnersforum.co.uk**.

Swimming

Did you know that over 450 people in the UK die from drowning each year. Swimming is the only sport that can save your life. Whether you are a beginner, seasoned-swimmer, or planning to make a return to the pool after years (or decades) away, the following website will give you lots of information.

British Swimming: **www.swimming.org**.

Table tennis

Table tennis is a cheap and accessible sport, played by 2.4 million people in the UK. For people of all ages and abilities, table tennis clubs provide the best place to learn and play the sport.

English Table Tennis: **www.englishtabletennis.org.uk**.

Veterans English Table Tennis Society: **www.vetts.org.uk**.

Tennis

Tennis is enjoyed by millions of recreational players, including seniors, and is also a hugely popular worldwide spectator sport.

International Tennis Federation: **www.ifttennis.com**.

Lawn Tennis Association: **www.lta.org.uk**.

Veterans' Lawn Tennis Club of Great Britain:
www.vltcofgb.org.uk.

Veteran rowing

Rowing has enthusiasts aged from 31 to well past 80. Since 2010 'veteran' rowers have been known as 'Masters'. There has also been a change in the lower age so that rowers from 27 to over 80 can now compete in Masters events. See:

British Rowing: **www.britishrowing.org**.

Walking

Walking is an excellent form of exercise which can keep you fit, active and improve your mental health. Walking can also help you recover from illness as well as prevent it.

Ramblers' Association: **www.ramblers.org.uk**.

Windsurfing

Windsurfing as an activity in middle age can lead to a more active, healthier and happier old age. If you need a bit of encouragement to enjoy the challenge of windsurfing, see:

Seavets (Senior and Veteran Windsurfers Association): **www.seavets.co.uk**.

Yachting

If you want to try sailing to see if you like it, there are ways to go without any major financial commitment. Your nearest sailing club may be able to arrange a trial sail, or you could try a water sports holiday.

New To Sailing: **www.newtosailing.com**.
Royal Yachting: **www.rya.org.uk**.

For people with disabilities

Facilities for the disabled have improved dramatically recently. Here are some sporting organizations which cater specifically for the disabled.

British Blind Sport: **www.britishblindsport.org.uk**.
British Disabled Fencing Association (BDFA): **www.bdfa.org.uk**.
British Wheelchair Sport: **www.wheelpower.org.uk**.
Disabled Skiing UK: **www.disabilitysnowpsort.org.uk**.
English Federation of Disability Sport: **www.efds.co.uk**.
UK Deaf Sport: **www.ukdeafsport.org.uk**.

Women's organizations

Here are some women's clubs and organizations that are enormously popular:

Association of Inner Wheel Clubs UK:
   www.associationofinnerwheelclubs.

Federation of Women's Institutes of Northern Ireland:
   www.wini.org.uk.

Mothers' Union (MU): **www.themothersunion.org.**

National Association of Women's Clubs: **www.nawc.org.uk.**

National Women's Register (NWR): **www.nwr.org.uk.**

Scottish Women's Rural Institutes (SWRI): **www.swri.org.uk.**

Townswomen: **www.townswomen.org.uk.**

Women's Institute (WI): **www.thewi.org.uk.**

Chapter Ten
Starting your own business

ALLAN ESLER SMITH

Allan is a fellow of the Institute of Chartered Accountants and specializes in helping people start up in business. He has helped thousands of mature people do this, and shares his hints and tips in this chapter.

You can find Allan at **www.allaneslersmith.com**.

> *Perfect freedom is reserved for the man who lives by his own work and in that work does what he wants to do.*
>
> **R G COLLINGWOOD (1889–1943)** *SPECULUM MENTIS*

More and more people are setting up their own business and becoming their own boss. So whether it is earning £5,000 to supplement a pension or building a business that can keep you earning and occupied for years to come, this is the chapter for you. While financially rewarding, this is not the only reason people want to start a business as social and emotional benefits also feature. This chapter will show you how easy it is to start a small business and it is packed with hints and tips to grow an existing small business. Indeed you could start tomorrow and it could cost you only £15. Importantly, in starting a small business you will not be alone and this chapter will signpost you to plenty of help and support and most of it is free (it is just a matter of knowing where to look!). You are also in good company as 91 per cent of businesses in the UK have fewer than four staff and the enterprise culture in the UK is gathering momentum again.

This chapter will give you the confidence to get started and has plenty of straightforward simple advice. The key issues covered are:

- Understanding the differences between starting a small business and employment, especially if both options are still open to you.

- Failing to plan usually means you're planning to fail. So what's the plan?

- Getting off to a good start – practical and emotional tips and buying your first equipment.

- Administration, finance and tax – keep on top of the paperwork or it will keep on top of you!

- Filling the diary with work and some clever tips for marketing that will make a difference.

- The trading format – should you set up your own limited liability company or work as a sole trader or maybe go into partnership?

- Other ways of getting started and operational issues.

- Where you can go for further help – remember you are not alone and these are enterprising times in the UK.

Additionally, in the three real-life case studies featured at the end, you will see how Phil, Debbie and Paul are coping after starting up in business. What did or did not work for them? Finally a useful summary checklist has been included to help you tick off the key issues once you decide to get started in business.

Yes, you can!

Broadcaster Liz Barclay and Maree Atkinson of the Federation of Small Business share their insights into starting a business and share some tips and reveal that 'Yes, you can!'

Liz Barclay is one of the most recognized voices on British radio today with her common-sense approach to money and finance on *You and Yours*. Liz also writes for several monthly personal finance and small business magazines and shares her experience and tips below.

First, forget about the salary spiral where you will only consider taking a job that offers you as much as or more than you have earned in the past. Do your calculations carefully and work out how much you need to make to pay your bills and enjoy life. That shift in thinking alone opens up all sorts of possibilities. You can do work that pays less but that you enjoy more, choose your own working hours and when to take breaks and mix work with rest, play, retraining, learning and even unpaid voluntary work. The world is your oyster.

Many of the people I talk to, who are moving out of full-time employment, are thinking of retraining or brushing up long-disused skills at a further education college, or about how they can turn a hobby into an income-generating venture. Self-employment or starting a small business after a lifetime of being an employee can be daunting but it can be done and Allan's chapter will help you on the way. The people I know who are most successful are those who are doing something they love. Judith is writing verses for greetings cards and taking photos for postcards – using her creative side after retiring from social work. Dawn is going back to her artistic roots and Diane is teaching older people Pilates and complementary therapies. They're passionate about their businesses and willing to give them the time and TLC they need to make them flourish. Hard work doesn't seem like a chore so they're less likely to give up when the going gets tough, as it will.

The section within this chapter on 'Marketing tips to fill your diary' will assist you with your marketing and research. The case studies at the end of this chapter show how new start-up businesses have secured their very first few clients. On generating business ideas and marketing, Liz adds:

> There are ideas everywhere. You don't have to come up with something new. You might do what you did before as an employee but on a consultancy basis with new customers. The more important thing is research. Be sure there are enough people who will pay you for what you do and that they have easy access to your products or services. Just because two tanning salons on the high street are buzzing doesn't mean there are enough customers to support a third. Many businesses that I saw fail had not done enough market research before spending money. Ask your customers what they like about your business and what they don't. Listen, act and add value – like the butcher in Glasgow who has long queues because he gives his customers recipes for the meat they buy. Talk to your employees who often know the business and customers better than you do. Keep building those relationships so that you spot the trends and stay ahead of the competition.

Liz's concluding advice is that 'success comes with having a positive and optimistic attitude to your business. This is a must – yes, you can. The glass is always half full! Be passionate about your business. Do not just turn up to work, but enjoy what you do. Put your life and soul into achieving a good day's work.'

Maree Atkinson runs her own business and sees hundreds of small businesses start up in her role as an award-winning membership adviser for the Federation of Small Business (FSB). The FSB has around 200,000 members and promotes and protects the interests of the self-employed and owners of small firms. For Maree the watchwords are 'Yes, you can,' but take special care over your marketing.

Certainly starting a business later in life may be daunting – I can personally vouch for that. But one big advantage for mature entrepreneurs is the wealth of experience and contacts gathered in work and general life over many years. The more successful start-ups that I see have a real passion to succeed and normally a willingness to adapt. I would agree with Liz Barclay about the importance of market research and really getting to know your customers and the competition you face. This is also a key part of the business plan process that Allan details within this chapter. I definitely agree with Allan that the first draft of your business plan does not need to run on for pages and pages. Indeed some business plan 'templates' that I have seen put people off the whole planning process.

I would encourage you to start the planning process by getting something down in writing to show you have researched and understood your target customers. Where are they? What is their profile and what might they need? What price are they prepared to pay? How will you get your product or service to them? These are all good starting questions and you can then build things from there by investigating the competition. With further help from your advice network your plan will start to take shape. Remember that there is a lot of help out there and you are definitely not alone. I see lots of idea sharing, hints and tips and introductions at the various members' networking and social events we run at the FSB.

Maree goes on to advise:

There are also many courses, seminars and training events to help businesses start up and your accountant, FSB contact and Enterprise Agency (contact details are at the reference section of this chapter) should be able to point you in the right direction. As a bonus you may find that many are subsidized or free. I have some words of caution on this subject and then another tip. In my day-to-day work I find that new mature business owners might be shy or perhaps feel uncomfortable as it has been many years since they attended a course. Also, for various reasons some people think they have no need to take advice or go on training courses or perhaps they just feel out of their comfort zone. In my experience these folk tend to struggle in the first year or two. I would strongly recommend that you take advantage of external support in the early years especially if it is free and of good quality. You'd be daft not to!

One other challenge that I see is new business owners becoming overwhelmed by the many hats they have to wear. People also underestimate the time it takes to do even the simplest of tasks. Perhaps this is because they came from larger organizations with in-house functions for marketing, legal, accounts and health and safety. Unless you bring in specialists to deal with these areas you are left with a choice: deal with the issues or they will simply get left behind. My top tip is therefore about managing your time and it is no shame to work with lists to make sure the must dos are tackled first and the other tasks scheduled in. If you find your precious family time is being spent on disliked jobs, think about hiring in help if you can afford it. I would also recommend checking out trade and professional associations (including the Federation of Small Business, which I represent) as these can provide a high level of support and contacts who can assist.

Maree's concluding advice is:

I must have seen over 4,000 people start up in business over the past nine years. Those that have taken time to research their product or service, sought input from others, understood the financial requirements and developed the plans needed to launch and continue have a much better prospect of success.

Some further marketing tips from Maree feature in the 'Marketing tips to fill your diary' section of this chapter.

Some of the differences between starting a small business and employment

In some cases where there is an opportunity to start a small business there could be a similar opportunity to take a full- or part-time employed position that might be quite similar in the actual work undertaken. Which route is right for you? Here are some of the many reasons for starting a small business:

- focus on what you are best at or enjoy;
- be your own boss;
- provide a legacy for your children;
- flexibility (around other interests/responsibilities);
- freedom to organize things your way;
- no commuting;
- less direct involvement in internal politics and no more useless meetings;
- enjoy working on your own;
- try something new/an experiment;
- getting paid for overtime.

On the other hand here are some of the reasons for seeking a part- or full-time employed position:

- a local employer;
- security of income;
- benefits of holiday pay, pension, paid sick leave, and perhaps private health and life cover;
- bonuses and perhaps a car;
- team aspect and friendship of colleagues;
- known travel requirements;
- no personal liability if things go badly wrong;
- staff discounts or other perks.

Why bother with a plan?

Before getting into plans and 'Why bother?' it is probably useful to gain an overview of some common reasons why businesses fail and set this in context with the specifics of running a small business to help you succeed.

There are thousands of success stories about those who took the plunge nearing or post-retirement to build a business that provided involvement, fun and income, plus a legacy for their children. However, for every two success stories there is a business that does not work out and your money could disappear fast if you set up in the wrong way or overstretch yourself. Worst of all you could lose your home if things go really badly wrong so the reasons below and tips throughout this chapter should help you understand and then deal with the risks.

Why businesses fail – learning the lessons

Businesses can fail for many reasons. Learn from the mistakes of others and you will be doing yourself a favour. The number-one reason why businesses fail is that *the market moves on and you are left behind*. Take time out to think and keep abreast of what your customers really want (have you tried asking them recently?); where are your competitors and what are they doing to keep on top of or ahead of the market and, overall, how is the market moving? Once you get left behind, you'll find the demand for your services declining and your income reducing – a rather toxic mix.

A second reason (and one that may increase in 2014) is the *failure to deal with tax affairs properly*. The implications of penalties and interest levied by HMRC (Her Majesty's Revenue & Customs) are often ignored and only hit home when it is too late. Keep your books properly and retain all records for six years after the year end – in brief, if you can't prove it, you may lose the tax benefit and pay additional tax, penalties and interest. If there is a problem, HMRC can go back and inspect previous years' accounts (for up to five years or even longer). If you fail to pay your tax fully when it is due, HMRC will pursue you vigorously and you are giving HMRC a reason to have a closer look at you and your business. On the other hand, if you have genuine cash flow difficulties and cannot pay your tax on the due date, talk to HMRC and you may find their attitude refreshing if it is the first time you have stumbled.

A third reason (and again one that may increase in 2014) is a *failure to manage your cash flow and this includes a lack of access to funding*. Vee Bharakda is a director of Business Recovery specialists Wilkins Kennedy and advises that 'access to funding is becoming a real issue! If you go to a bank they will want to know exactly why the business requires funding and will be vigilant in their lending criteria. They will require, in most cases, security over the business assets or the owners' residential homes.' Vee adds that 'in certain cases businesses have found alternative funding through invoice discounting and factoring which can be an effective way to fund an expanding business'. So for someone setting up in business in later life the scale of the anticipated business will be a key issue. On the one hand you may not need external finance if you fund the business from your own resources or if you start small and grow organically. On the other hand if external finance is needed you may have to 'get real' and recognize that banks and others are not in the habit of lending money to unviable propositions. It is often the case that the bank will be the largest stakeholder in a business. For this reason security is normally required, which may well include a charge on your home.

A failure to plan and poor management are a fourth reason for businesses failing. Vee Bharakda comments that the failure to plan and basic management deficiencies are often interlinked: 'Over the years we have seen various examples of inadequate management skills. The day-to-day running of the business sadly seems to take priority rather than planning for the future. Unfortunately the owners are so busy in immediate and minor issues that they fail to recognize the need to spend time on longer-term planning and strategic decisions and the business spirals downwards to failure.'

One common mistake by business owners is that they fall victim to the old excuse that 'my plan is in my head'. This is short-sighted as they usually take a triple hit because of:

- lack of clarity on objectives;
- lower-quality input from those that can help them;
- poor monitoring of how well they are actually doing.

Break the writer's block and set down your plan in writing for the year ahead. The starting point can be as simple as three handwritten pages defining a few well considered objectives, and a cash flow and profit-and-loss forecast for the year ahead linked to those objectives, plus a robust marketing plan. More hints and tips on this basic, but effective, approach to a business plan are set out in the next section of this chapter. Don't expect perfection for the first draft, but do keep it under review; with focus and some decent effort it will start to pay off. Why not set yourself some stretching objectives? You never know, you may be surprised at what you are capable of achieving!

A fifth reason for business failure is *bad debts* (where the customer goes bust and cannot pay your invoices), as this will come off your bottom-line profit and can really hurt. There are a few simple steps that you can take to reduce the potential of taking such a hit. What are your credit terms and have you encouraged all customers to pay electronically? Do you contact them as soon as your invoices become overdue? Do you require cash on delivery or prepayment? (PayPal and mobile credit card machines are transforming the payment services.) In some cases it is worth remembering that a bad customer is sometimes worse than no customer at all.

Vee Bharakda comments that 'Businesses tend to fail for the reasons Allan has mentioned and one additional reason that we have seen recently – trying to expand too quickly.' Vee goes on to explain: 'Some businesses start on the right track, but tend to expand far too quickly either by overtrading, selling more than their cash flow will allow, over-production of stock or not researching the marketplace or competitors adequately.

'The most common mistake that we see in this area is businesses employing the wrong staff and additional staff rather than first looking to motivate and incentivize the existing workforce. Extra staff increases overheads and decreases profit. Beware!'

So 'Why bother' when it comes to planning? The answer should now be evident from the above – you are improving your chances of succeeding and may even do rather better than you first thought. On that positive note Vee remembers many positive turnaround stories from her career in business recovery and believes that 'success comes from having a positive and optimistic attitude to your business. Business owners need to be open-minded and realize that they do not need to know everything and must always be willing to learn and adapt with the business in mind. And with that in mind if a business owner is experiencing financial difficulties and is worried about the risk they could be facing it is always best to talk to a business recovery specialist sooner rather than later.'

What goes into a plan?

The starting point is to make a promise that you will put your plan down in writing. Too many people run a mile when the subject of a plan comes up, especially the notion of a grand-sounding business plan. Perhaps armed with some confidence gained from a book on setting up a business, business banking literature, or even after attending a setting-up-in-business course, some new businesses start a plan but never get it finished.

The reason for this is twofold: first, fear of the planning process and, second, intimidation by some daunting plan templates and spreadsheets seen in books or banking literature. The prescription is a three-stage plan that will get you started and then, with experience, you can tweak it and make it that bit slicker.

Stage 1 of the plan: objectives

What, financially, do you need to set as objectives to bring you in that £5,000 or £20,000 or £60,000 that you want in your pocket? This takes a bit of thinking through and ties into the stage 3 section detailed below. Typically you should be able to come up with two or three simple objectives based on income, gross profit (if you sell stock) and overheads.

For a high-powered full-time management consultant who does not sell stock there could be just two objectives. *Objective 1*: I aim to invoice £40,000 in my first year of trading based on working at least 100 days at an average billing rate of £400 per day. I will review my billing rates quarterly and my performance monthly. *Objective 2*: I will aim to keep my overheads (after expenses recharged to clients) in my first year to £5,000.

For businesses that sell stock, *Objective 3* will be something like: I will aim to achieve the following gross profit percentages:

Product line A: 30 per cent;

Product line B: 40 per cent;

Product line C: 50 per cent.

Gross profit percentages are calculated using:

(Sales price less cost of materials/product sold ÷ sales price) × 100

The key point with objectives is that less gives more: you don't want a long list of objectives. Just isolate what is important, set them down and double-check that they are SMART (specific, measurable, achievable, realistic and timed).

Stage 2 of the plan: your market research

The next page of your plan should be all about your marketing effort, a topic often misunderstood and mistaken for advertising. Think about approaching this section under the following three headings.

Products

Start with your main product or service and think about the features and benefits of what you are selling. Understanding these and discussing them with your trusted advisers will allow you to start thinking about other related services or goods which you could offer.

Customers

For each main product area ask lots of questions to tease out your research. Who are my customers? Where are they based? When do they tend to buy? How and where do they tend to buy and at what price? How should I contact them? Keep asking those important questions of who, what, why, where, when and how and they will help you tease out all sorts of gems. This part of the plan is vital, as you will have read from the tips provided by Liz Barclay and Maree Atkinson in the 'Yes, you can!' section of this chapter.

Competitors

Again, ask yourself who, what, why, where, when and how?

This should lead to a series of activities that you can do to help secure new quality work and customers (note that the marketing section later on in this chapter has further tips). If you end up with a jumble of un-focused ideas try ranking each idea on the basis of priority, impact and cost (free is good!).

Stage 3 of the plan: your income and expenditure forecast

This is your income and expenditure forecast for the year and this third page is the tricky one. It is your map for the year ahead financially and will allow you to monitor your actual performance against the plan. You can then do something about it when you are off target. You should be able to do this yourself but if it becomes a struggle, ask your accountant to help.

Is there more?

Once you have completed your first plan the secret is to keep it alive and keep reviewing how you are doing against it. Your plan can then be improved and extra sections or pages added to make it an even better tool, or you may find that the simple three-stage approach is all you need.

The *top tips* on your plan are:

- Don't worry about calling it a business plan or such other high-powered term. Think of it only as a tool to help you get from where you are to where you want to be.

- Commit your plan to writing – three or four pages initially are fine. If you don't write it down you will not be able to use it to tease out other opportunities, review it with your trusted advisers (a family member or friend who runs their own business, your accountant and perhaps a business adviser or mentor) and build on it.

- Don't expect perfection as no one gets it right on the first, second or even third draft but do keep coming back to it and try to make it that little bit better each time.

Practical and emotional tips

If you are married or in a civil partnership your partner's attitude is crucial. Even if not directly involved, he or she will have to accept (at least) the loss of a room in the house being used as your office. There will be the added distractions of out-of-hours phone calls and, perhaps, suddenly cancelled social engagements. The points below will help you identify other issues that are either of a practical or emotional nature:

- First and foremost will you be doing something you really enjoy? If so the work itself is the motivator: you do it because you want to do it.

- Are you willing to turn your hand to support jobs (eg bookkeeping/secretarial tasks such as invoicing)?

- Have you space available to work from home initially or would you need/prefer to rent accommodation?

- Can your family/partner cope with having you and your business in the house?

- Can you cope without the resources/back-up provided by an employer (IT/HR/training)? When you run your own business you have to do it yourself or buy it in.

- Have you the funds to manage any initial outlay (eg stock, equipment, new car or van, computer) or are the essential resources already to hand?

- Can you afford a period without income while you get yourself established?

This list is by no means exhaustive but the questions give an idea of the things that anyone contemplating starting their own business will face.

Keep on top of the paperwork

Generally, this one topic causes the most groans! But simple bookkeeping, if done properly, is just a by-product of your business and flows naturally from raising sales invoices and paying for purchases. After all, you want to ensure that you are invoicing or charging the right amount to clients, that they pay the correct amount on the invoice (not all manage to do this) and identify any that do not pay at all. For a small business with only a few clients each month, the last issue will be picked up quickly. But if you have multiple clients you may miss an invoice that was never paid. You will never miss an unpaid invoice if you are on top of your bookkeeping.

An even more compelling reason for doing your own bookkeeping is that HMRC has a 'prove it or lose it' view if enquiring into an aspect of your tax return. Under the system of self-assessment, HMRC relies on you completing your tax returns. In the case of an enquiry, HMRC tells you precisely what part of your tax return is under investigation; you are then expected to be able to validate every payment (excluding coin-operated vending machines that do not give a receipt) that you have made, with a supporting invoice or receipt (ie not a credit card payment slip with no substance detailing what was actually bought). HMRC will also track the invoice through to the payment on the bank or credit card statement to verify that it was valid expenditure. HMRC can also go to third parties directly for any further confirmation it needs. Understanding the approach that HMRC takes helps you to appreciate the need to retain all invoices and to record how and when they were paid. If you are unable to prove the expenditure, you lose it as far as HMRC is concerned, resulting in fewer purchases being accepted as a deduction from your profits and more tax to pay. There will also be penalties and interest to pay and the scope of its enquiries into your tax affairs will be widened.

Basic bookkeeping

All incoming and outgoing payments therefore need to be recorded throughout the year. When recording income, you will need to differentiate between your fees and your expenses (or other 'recharged' items). You will also need to keep a record of income from other sources, such as bank/building society interest. Records of outgoings need to be categorized according to type and examples of some categories you might need to consider are: stock, subscriptions/meeting fees, office equipment, office supplies, post and courier costs; travel fares, parking and subsistence; telephone and internet; sundry; accountancy and professional fees; and insurance.

Many small business owners opt to do their own bookkeeping, with or without the help of a computer software package. If you opt for a software package choose one that your accountant understands and fees should be less. For many small businesses your accountant should be able to provide some Excel spreadsheets that will do the job together with a bookkeeping guide to help get you started.

If you are really averse to bookkeeping yourself, consider hiring a bookkeeper. Bookkeepers currently charge between about £15 and £23 per hour, depending on geographical location and experience and can be found by recommendation from your accountant or business network contacts.

Accountants

Depending on qualifications and experience, accountants assisting new small start-up businesses could charge from £35 to about £120 per hour to assist you in setting up in business and prepare your accounts and tax. A good accountant who knows your industry area will be able to help with general guidance and input to your plan on marketing and pricing, drawing on experience beyond accounting and tax.

Some accountancy firms offer a combination of bookkeeping, accountancy and tax services and, if so, you can expect to pay a premium on the bookkeeping hourly rates quoted above. Always ask your trusted family members or friends if they can recommend an accountant. Remember to ask for confirmation of the accountant's qualifications (the type of qualification and whether their practising certificate has been issued by a recognized professional body) and check that they hold professional indemnity insurance. It is advisable to meet at least two accountants and see how you feel about rapport and the availability of proactive hints and tips. Will the person you meet be the person who does your accounts and tax and provides proactive advice? Always request written confirmation of hourly rates plus an estimate of fees for the year and obtain a proposed retainer specifying what you and the accountant will do and by when.

Finally, there is sometimes some confusion over the term 'audit of accounts'. Many years ago, smallish companies in the UK had to have an audit of their accounts. The turnover threshold (one of three thresholds) for being required to have an audit has been increased and currently stands at £6.5 million, so the vast majority of start-ups need not concern themselves with audited accounts.

Paying tax and national insurance

Sole traders

Self-employed individuals running their own businesses are usually called 'sole traders'. All new businesses that trade as sole traders need to register as self-employed with HMRC. While tax can be daunting, some sole traders with relatively straightforward billing and overheads have been able to undertake their own tax returns after researching the position. In the UK, sole traders pay income tax on their profits. With income tax, you first have a personal allowance, which gives you a tax-free amount and then any excess income (including your profits) is taxed at 20 per cent, then 40 per cent and then 45 per cent. The precise yearly limits are available from the HMRC website or your accountant. In very broad terms, if you are under 65, you currently (summer 2013) have a tax-free allowance of £9,440. You are then taxed on the next £32,010 at 20 per cent and then 40 per cent tax applies to further taxable income up to £150,000. Anything above £150,000 gets taxed at 45 per cent. Many sole traders choose to run their bookkeeping for the year to 5 April to coincide with the tax year end (or 31 March, which HMRC effectively accepts as equivalent to 5 April).

If you are past the state retirement age there will be no National Insurance Contributions (NICs) to pay. Subject to this, sole traders are liable for Class 2 NICs (currently a nominal amount of £2.70 per week), which are collected by direct debit either monthly or quarterly. The mandate is set up automatically when you register as self-employed. After starting, you have three months to register and if you forget there is an automatic £100 fine. You are also liable for the much more significant Class 4 NICs that are assessed and collected by HMRC at the same time as assessing your income tax on profits. Currently these are at 9 per cent on profits between £7,755 and £41,450 and this reduces to just 2 per cent on profits over £41,450.

The payment of sole-trader income tax is reasonably straightforward but there is a twist in your first year of trading. Assuming that you have a year end of 5 April 2015, the first payment will be due by 31 January 2016 so you have a long period of (effectively) interest-free credit, as some of the profits on which the tax is due may have been earned as long ago as May 2014. With the first payment, however, you get a 'double whammy' as you also have to pay on 31 January 2016 a payment on account of your second year's trading. Then on 31 July 2016 you have to make a second on-account payment of the second year's trading. Both on-account payments are set by default on the basis of your Year 1 profits. You can 'claim' a reduction if year 2 is proving to have lower profits than year 1; your accountant will help you with this if it is appropriate.

After this initial tax famine, followed by double payment of tax, you will thereafter receive a tax demand twice a year. Payments need to be made by 31 January (during the tax year) and then by 31 July after the end of that tax year, with any over-/underpayment sorted out by the following 31 January. Many sole-trader businesses set up a reserve bank account in addition to their current account, and place a percentage of their income aside, which is earning interest each month (albeit not amounting to much in the current climate). This tactic should help you resist the temptation to raid money that is not for spending – and ensure you can pay your tax on time.

Additionally, as a self-employed person you are allowed certain other reliefs. Ask your accountant, but the following expenses and allowances are usually tax deductible:

- *Business expenses*. These must be incurred 'wholly and exclusively' for the purposes of the trade. Office supplies that you buy will probably qualify; however, any business entertaining will not.

- *Partially allowable expenses.* These mainly apply if you are working from home. They include such items as the part of your rent, heating, lighting and telephone usage that you devote to business purposes, and also possibly some of the running expenses on your car, if you use your car for your business.

- *Spouse's wages.* If you employ your partner in the business, his or her pay (provided this is reasonable) qualifies as a legitimate expense, in the same way as any other employee's, but must be accounted for through a PAYE system.

- *Pension contributions.* Tax relief is generally available for pension contributions at the higher of £3,600 (gross) or 100 per cent of relevant earnings up to a maximum of £50,000 for 2013/14 which reduces to £40,000 for 2014/15.

- *Capital allowances.* There is an annual investment allowance (AIA) which provides tax relief on many types of expenditure on equipment up to £250,000 per annum of expenditure (except on certain items such as cars). This is then supplemented by writing-down allowances of between 8 and 18 per cent. This can be a complex area and if significant expenditure on plant and equipment is envisaged, you should discuss this with an accountant.

- *Research and development.* There are generous reliefs available if you can meet the stringent qualifying conditions. Best advice is to check with an accountant.

- *Interest on loans.* Tax relief is given on money borrowed to invest in business expenses and equipment in most normal circumstances.

Partnerships

Partnership tax is broadly similar to the process described for a sole trader as above with the exception of some more paperwork. In addition to submitting each partner's individual personal self-assessment tax return a composite partnership tax return must also be submitted.

Limited company

Companies pay corporation tax on their profits (currently 20 per cent). There is a higher rate of corporation tax of 23 per cent on profits above £300,000 which reduces to 21 per cent from 1 April 2014 and then again to 20 per cent from 1 April 2015. Your company accounts need to be finalized and any corporation tax paid nine months after your year end.

The key point with a company is that the money coming in is not your money – it is the company's money – so how do you extract your money? The first option is salary and this means running a 'Pay As You Earn' (PAYE) system: another form of tax with a rigorous calculation regime and payments that have to be made to HMRC. PAYE carries the income tax rates as featured for the sole trader but NICs (National Insurance Contributions) can be much higher as these are a composite of employee *and* employer NICs (as the company is an employer). Currently these are 12 per cent employee NICs on £7,748 to £41,444 reducing to 2 per cent for amounts above £41,444 and then an additional 13.8 per cent employer NICs on everything above £7,696. Salary and employer's NICs are deductible when calculation corporation tax.

There is a daunting year-end routine involving a whole series of forms beginning with the letter P. Overall, the system is capable of being run by a business person with some oversight from an accountant and a decent piece of payroll software (and the free HMRC online service is good). An alternative is to ask a bookkeeper, payroll bureau or your accountant to do it for you.

The second option for extracting funds is dividends (taking for granted that you have repaid expenses and any loan to get the company started). Dividends are not deductible when calculating your corporation tax. The big selling point for dividends is that, at face value, they are not subject to NIC. This leads us neatly into a possible 'tax trap' for the unwary. As a director, you can decide whether or not to pay yourself a salary, dividends or both. The appeal of dividends is the lack of NICs. However, this is before we have outlined HMRC regulation number 35 (IR35) that came into force in April 2000.

HMRC is particularly interested in ex-employees setting up service companies that work exclusively for their former employer and also 'personal service companies', to use an HMRC term. This is an extremely wide-ranging and difficult subject but, in very simplified terms, 'personal service companies' are one-person companies that provide services to one or a few clients. In fact the individual concerned could be seen to 'look like, act like and smell like an employee'. This situation is one of the subject matters of IR35 and is to be avoided if at all possible! Remember, IR35 only applies to companies (not sole traders).

There are many hints and tips and some urban myths about IR35 and you may encounter advice such as having substitution clauses in your contracts; having clauses in your contracts that mean you are not obliged to work certain days and the client is not obliged to give you work; having all the trappings of a 'genuine' business (business cards, headed paper, advertising, seeking to agree a 'price for the job', rather than an hourly rate, holding your own professional indemnity insurance and having your own website, etc).

The bottom line as we go into 2014 is that HMRC is strengthening its specialist compliance teams that investigate IR35. HMRC is also seeking to provide more information to assist businesses in understanding whether IR35 affects them. For instance, in 2012 HMRC specified tests and depending on your answers you obtain a risk rating – the higher the score the lower your risk to IR35. You can quickly build up your score with some big hitting points, for instance operating from your own premises and actually substituting another person in the delivery of your services. There are also some modest point earners (such as maintaining professional indemnity insurance and having a written business plan). On the other hand you can almost wipe out your points by going back to work for an employer that you were on PAYE with 'within the 12 months which ended on the last 31 March'. HMRC provides some examples of freelancers and provides its view on the likely IR35 status. For some these tests will provide a quick fix to IR35 (own premises and a substitution 'arrangement') but for most freelancers it is now even more complex and seems to be a step backwards.

Tips and hints on IR35 are outside the scope of a guide like this. It is a big issue and one that you have first got to recognize and then do something about. One of the key players in helping freelancers guide themselves through the minefield of IR35 is the Professional Contractors Group (PCG) at **www.pcg.org.uk**. This organization, working in conjunction with a chartered accountant who understands IR35, is probably your next step if you are a freelancer and you trade as a company. Briefly, if ·you fall foul of IR35, the tax inspector will seek to set aside the dividends you have paid and treat the dividend payment as if it were subject to PAYE and NICs (including employer NICs). If you do find yourself subject to IR35 there is a complex eight-step calculation called a 'deemed payment' and there is a deemed payment calculator on HMRC's website: **www.hmrc.gov.uk/leaflets/calc_deempyt.htm**.

Registering for VAT

Value Added Tax (VAT) was introduced back in 1973 and it seems that many people have lost sight of the name of this tax and especially the word 'added'. You are, in effect, adding a tax and are an unpaid tax collector.

If your taxable turnover is likely to be more than £79,000 in the first 12 months or less you must register for VAT unless your supplies/ services are outside the scope of VAT. Remember that any expenses that you recharge to clients need to be included in the calculation of taxable turnover. Form VAT1 must be completed and sent to HMRC within 30 days of the end of the month in which the value of your taxable turnover exceeded £79,000 over a rolling 12 months.

UK business clients are invariably registered for VAT so are not concerned about having it added to your invoice. To avoid adding VAT to invoices for business clients in other EU countries it is essential to quote the client's VAT number on the invoice.

In addition, note that you can claim back VAT on pre-start/pre-registration expenditure involved in setting up the business. If you elect for 'Cash Accounting' status, this means that VAT only becomes payable or reclaimable when invoices are actually paid. It avoids having to pay the VAT on your own invoices before slow-paying clients pay you, which can add significantly to cash flow problems. On the other hand, if you have a client who pays you promptly, remember not to spend the cash before the quarter end when you have to submit your VAT return and payment. The VAT regime carries with it onerous fines and penalties for late payment and evasion, and is not to be taken lightly.

If your taxable turnover is below the limit, you may apply for voluntary VAT registration. Before applying, consider carefully whether registration will really be of benefit to you, that is, whether reclaiming the VAT paid on items needed for your business (such as office equipment) is worth the trouble of sending in mandatory, quarterly VAT returns and keeping separate VAT records for possible inspection by visiting VAT officers. One final positive if you do register for VAT is that it seems to give you added credibility with clients.

VAT flat rate scheme

HMRC introduced the flat rate scheme in 2004, with the aim of simplifying record keeping for small businesses. This allows you to charge VAT to your clients at the standard rate of 20 per cent and to pay VAT as a percentage of your VAT-inclusive turnover (instead of having to work out the VAT payable on your sales less purchases). You can apply to join the scheme if your taxable turnover (excluding VAT) will not be more than £150,000 in the next 12 months.

HMRC publishes a list of business categories from which you need to decide which best describes your business. A further bonus is that you can deduct 1 per cent from the flat rate that you use for your first year of VAT registration. As a tip, do not do anything without checking it out with your accountant as there are a few twists and turns that could make the VAT flat rate scheme unsuitable. But, at face value, it seems to have been beneficial to many small businesses. Further information can be gained from HMRC's website and inserting 'VAT flat rate scheme' into the internal search engine on that site.

Marketing tips to fill your diary

When you start a small business there are three marketing 'must haves'. The first is that you have something that people will want to buy. The second is you and your ability to present and be the face of a viable business. The third 'must have' does not come naturally to many people but it can be learnt and it can be improved. It is all about the ability to market the business.

It is a sad fact that many new owners/managers genuinely believe that marketing simply means placing an advert in some well-known directory. Unfortunately this view of marketing means achieving only a fraction of the sales of any comparable business with a decent grasp of marketing.

The objective is to plan ahead, generate sales for your new business, anticipate when your sales will end or dip and start looking for ways you can promote your business before that happens. The following eight tips should help you. Why not use these to assess your marketing to date and what more you can do?

Your own website and/or social media

Now that businesses rely so heavily on the internet have you thought about a website and/or harnessing social media to promote your business?

Is there a vital domain name (website unique address) that you need to secure and register? If you search 'domain names and how to register them' you will find lots of offers of advice. Instead, try asking friends who operate their business using a website and don't ignore help that is right in front of your nose: young friends or relatives may know more than you do about this subject.

It is also worth checking out other websites including those run by trade or professional associations which may allow you to register and set up a profile. If you do not want to have your own website, you can set up profiles on various social media 'networking websites' such as LinkedIn. Depending on your business, Facebook and Twitter can provide the benefits of building your online contacts (giving potential accessibility) and allowing you to showcase your expertise in a certain area.

Personal contacts and networking

Once you decide to set up your own business your personal contacts, such as ex-colleagues or other small business owners, will be a potential source of work. Too many small businesses forget that behind every contact there is another layer of potential contacts, who are just one introduction away; so ignore this multiplier effect at your peril. In your first year you should be re-educating your contacts to think of you not as 'Jane who used to work at IBM' but Jane who now runs her own business advising small businesses on their IT needs. Do not be afraid to pick up the phone or send business cards explaining your new business and what you can offer. Joining the best trade or professional association you can find will be a great way of networking with the added bonus of research facilities, information and other fringe benefits. Currently the Federation of Small Business and Professional Contractors Group receive very positive feedback and represent reasonable value for money. See also 'Further help, advice and training' on page 218.

Discounts and offers

These can be used to great effect during seasonal dips, introducing a new service or clearing old stock. Whether it is 20 per cent off, a buy-one-get-one-free offer or the numerous variations of this basic approach there are three golden rules:

- Always state the original or usual price (to show the value in the offer).
- Always specify an expiry date.
- Always explain that the offer is subject to availability.

Flyers and business cards

Generally speaking a response rate of 1 per cent to a flyer is considered fairly good. With some clever thinking you can increase the response rate. Have you targeted the flyer? A good example would be the wedding gown designer who neatly persuades the reception of a sought-after wedding location hotel to keep a flyer dispenser in their foyer.

Are you able to include your professional or trade association logo on your flyer and business cards? Have you asked if this is possible?

There are two sides to a flyer and business card – have you thought about putting information on the blank reverse side? Could this contain some useful tips or, perhaps, a special offer or discount? Anything that ensures the card or flyer is kept rather than dumped will help your business to edge ahead.

Testimonials

People generally buy on trust and never like to be made to look a fool. The intangible benefit of testimonials is simply that it shows prospective customers that you have done a good job and can be relied upon. Looked at in this way, the benefit flowing from positive testimonials can be powerful and should never be underestimated.

Agencies

Agencies will be especially important for prospective consultants or contractors, as most recruitment agencies also deal with full- and part-time contract positions. When marketing yourself to an agency the same rules apply as when marketing yourself to a potential employer. Good personal and written presentation will help the agency to sell you on to its clients, so take the time to get it right. Remember that it is in the agency's interest to find you work as it receives a fee for placing you.

Advertising

There are many options for advertising yourself and your business such as website banners, sponsored links on search engines such as Google, free and paid-for directory listings and sponsorships.

Another approach could be 'free' advertising through creating a press release that you forward to local or trade press with an interesting story. Could you also publish it on your website, or send it to your customers and ask them to refer to it with anyone that could be interested? You can also advertise yourself and your skills by writing articles in professional or trade journals – what do you have that is news or novel or leading edge?

Another subset of advertising is sponsorship. The driving instructor who sponsored the playing shirts on the local under-17 football team is a great example of cost-effective sponsorship.

Learn when to say 'no'

This contradicts all the positive tips above, but is generally the hardest lesson to learn and will probably only come with experience. The fear of losing a sale to a competitor, or the uncertainty of where the next piece or work or sale will come from if you reject this one, may induce you to overstretch or undercut yourself. If you continually face this dilemma it will only place unrelenting stress on you and you may not survive in business for long. So learning how to say 'no' in a way that does not burn bridges is important.

Maree Atkinson of the Federation of Small Business (see the 'Yes, you can!' section of this chapter) has some additional tips to help you learn to say 'no'.

Maree advises:

Be wary of the promises of business. You will want to help customers and will want to secure those early sales. You may even find yourself bending over backwards to help. But have you given away your ideas and spent hours of your time with no prospect of the work? A very talented garden designer was asked to redesign a large garden. Excited by the project he prepared some initial plans and the client made a number of changes which he incorporated. The client did go ahead with the work but used the plans with another contractor. I guess it is a balance between 'marketing time' and showing your wares but not going too far – all of which you will learn in time!

Marketing to the wrong people. In the early days of starting a small business you will receive invitations for a meeting from possible business partners or joint ventures, who want to 'see if there's a way we could do some work together'. Networking is vital to many businesses, but don't network with random people just because you think you're supposed to network. Do some research about the offer and listen to your 'gut feeling' before you say 'yes'. In time work out what sort of networking is best for you and what offers to explore further.

Maree's words remind me of Lord Alan Sugar's words on what makes an entrepreneur in his latest book *The Way I See It*. Lord Sugar's straight-forward advice was that 'If you have partners, they have to bring something to the party.'

Trading formats

Sole trader

A self-employed person is someone who works for him/herself, instead of an employer, and draws an income from their personally run business. If the profits from the work are accounted for on one person's tax return, that person is known as a sole trader. If the profits are shared between two or more people, it is a partnership (see below).

There is no clear definition of self-employment. Defining an employee, on the other hand, is slightly easier as it can generally be assumed that if income tax and NICs are deducted from an individual's salary before they are paid, then that individual is an employee.

Importantly, the business has no separate existence from the owner and, therefore, all debts of the business are debts of the owner who is personally liable for all amounts owed by the business. This strikes fear into the hearts of many business owners. You only need to think of the number of business owners who go bust every time a recession comes around and lose their house. Should this be a worry?

First and foremost, you must consider the risk to you in any work that you do. Could it go wrong and could you be sued? Is that a realistic prospect or so remote that it does not even warrant thinking about? Or is it somewhere in the middle? Can insurance help (see the section below)? Remember that such insurance is only as good as the disclosures you make and the levels of cover provided. At the end of the day you know your business, your customers and the work that you do, so the risk assessment can only be done by you.

How to start up as a sole trader

You can start trading immediately.

You can trade under virtually any name, subject to some restrictions that are mostly common sense, such as not suggesting something you are not (connection to government, royalty or international pre-eminence). A B Jones trading as Super Lawns is fine.

The full name and address of the owner and any trading name must be disclosed on letters, orders and invoices.

A phone call to HMRC's helpline for the newly self-employed (0845 915 4515) must be made within three months of starting up.

Partnership

Two or more self-employed people who work together on a business and share the profits are trading in partnership. The profits from the work are accounted for on a partnership tax return and extracts from that partnership tax return are then copied into the partner's individual tax returns.

The business has no separate existence from the partners and, therefore, all debts of the business are debts of the partners, so they are personally liable for all amounts owed by the business. In addition, partners are jointly and severally liable for the debts of the business or, put more simply, the last person standing pays the lot. There is a saying that you need to trust your business partner better than your husband/wife/civil partner.

As with sole traders, the first consideration is the potential for business risk, since your personal wealth is backing the debts of the business. First and foremost you must consider the risk to you in any work that you do and, given the 'joint and several liability' point explained above, the trust and faith you have in your business partner. As mentioned above, could it go wrong and could you be sued? Is that a realistic prospect or so remote that it does not even warrant thinking about? Or is it somewhere in the middle? Can insurance help? Again, remember that such insurance is only as good as the disclosures you make and the levels of cover provided. At the end of the day you know your business, your business partner, your customers and the work that you do, so the risk assessment can only be done by you.

How to start up as a partnership

You can start trading immediately.

You can trade under virtually any name, subject to some restrictions that are mostly common sense, such as not suggesting something you are not (connection to government, royalty or international pre-eminence). A B Jones and A B Smith trading as J & S Super Lawns is fine.

You will need to consult a solicitor to assist with the preparation and signing of a partnership deed. The partnership deed is for your protection and is essential because it sets out the rules of the partnership including, for example, the profit or loss split between partners, what happens if one partner wishes to leave or you wish to admit a new partner.

The full name and address of the partners and any trading name must be disclosed on letters, orders and invoices.

A phone call to HMRC's helpline for the newly self-employed (0845 915 4515) explaining that you are starting a partnership must be made within three months of starting up.

Limited company

A limited liability company (often the shorthand of 'limited company' is used to describe this trading format) is a company whose liability is limited by shares and is the most common form of trading format. The company is owned by its shareholders. The company is run by directors who are appointed by the shareholders.

The shareholders are liable to contribute the amount remaining unpaid on the shares – usually zero as most shares are issued fully paid up. The shareholders therefore achieve limited liability.

How to start up a limited company

A company needs to be registered with Companies House and cannot trade until it is granted a Certificate of Incorporation. The registration process is a quick and inexpensive process using Companies House's web incorporation service (it currently costs £15 and is completed within 24 hours). Some people use a company formation agent (Google this term to find such an agent – there are plenty of them) and the process should cost less than £100.

The company name needs to be approved by Companies House and no two companies can have the same name. Names that suggest, for instance, an international aspect will require evidence to support the claim and certain names are prohibited unless there is a dispensation. An example of this latter category would be the word 'Royal'.

You must appoint a director and this 'officer' of the company carries responsibilities that can incur penalties and/or a fine. The appointment of directors should therefore not be done lightly. The full range of responsibilities is set out in The Companies Act; further guidance is available from the Companies House website (**www.companieshouse.co.uk**). Some examples of the responsibilities include the duty to maintain the financial records of the company, to prepare accounts, to retain the paperwork and to avoid conflicts of interest. Small businesses no longer have to have a separate company secretary but it can be useful to have another office-holder signatory and the risks associated with this position are relatively light. In addition you will need to appoint a registered office, which is a designated address at which official notices and communications can be received. The company's main place of business is usually used as the registered office but you could also use the address of your accountant or solicitor (there may be a charge for this).

The advantages and disadvantages of the three formats are shown in Table 10.1.

This guide can only give an overview of how to set up and run a limited company and you are strongly advised to obtain a book on directors' duties and running a company. There are many on the market and a web search will identify several.

TABLE 10.1

Advantages	Disadvantages
SOLE TRADER	
Simple to set up.	Personal liability.
Simple to run and you are in complete control of the business and make all the business decisions. You also enjoy the greatest freedom from regulation and paperwork.	Additional cost of the payment for insurance if considered appropriate.
Strictly speaking, you don't even need to maintain a separate bank account but it is advisable to do so.	

TABLE 10.1 *continued*

Advantages	Disadvantages
Much lower National Insurance Contributions (NICs) than a limited liability company.	Perceived lack of credibility.
Taxation is covered by a few extra pages on your income tax self-assessment and paid twice a year (January and July).	
Accountancy fees will be lower than if you run your own limited liability company.	
Only you, your accountant and HMRC need know your turnover, profits and income.	Employment agencies in certain sectors will not deal with sole traders. Instead they may ask you to take up a consulting or contracting position through a limited company which you set up, or through an umbrella company that they may introduce you to.
Tax breaks can be potentially more attractive than a company for a business with losses in the early years. Generally there are more attractive tax breaks for use of home office and use of a car for work.	
Simple to shut down. It is possible to start off as a sole trader and then convert to a company later on as the business grows or risks increase.	

PARTNERSHIP

Can be useful in husband-and-wife businesses and is simple to set up.	Personal liability and joint and several liability.
Simple to run but there are now at least two people making the decisions so not quite the same control as for a sole trader.	Cost of partnership deed.

TABLE 10.1 *continued*

Advantages	Disadvantages
Much lower NICs than a limited liability company.	Additional cost of insurance if considered appropriate.
Taxation is covered by a partnership tax return and extracts from this are copied on your income tax self-assessment and paid twice a year (January and July).	
Only you, your partners, your accountant and HMRC need know your turnover, profits and income.	
Tax breaks can be potentially more attractive than a company for a business with losses in the early years. Generally there are more attractive tax breaks for use of home office and use of a car for work.	

LIMITED COMPANY

Advantages	Disadvantages
Limited liability of shareholders.	In certain circumstances, directors may incur unlimited liability if they are found liable for fraudulent or wrongful trading.
Perceived credibility.	Formal accounts have to be prepared and filed at Companies House within nine months of the accounting year end. An annual return detailing the ownership of the company also has to be filed each year. Failure to deliver documents on time will result in a fine.
	An accountant will generally be required to prepare annual accounts but no audit is required for companies with a turnover of less than £6.5 million.

TABLE 10.1 *continued*

Advantages	Disadvantages
	Transparency of company name, accounts and directors at Companies House (if operating an especially sensitive business, consider obtaining a confidentiality order that helps mask personal information).
Employment agencies and recruitment consultants may require you to work through a limited company (or umbrella company).	More taxes to deal with.
	Every trading company must submit a corporation tax return.
	Directors who are also shareholders will usually receive their income via salary and/or dividends. Salaries are paid through PAYE and, therefore, a PAYE scheme will need to be set up and administered.
	HMRC requires all directors to submit self-assessment tax returns.
	NICs paid by a limited company may come as a surprise to new owner-directors. NICs are dependent on the salary drawn and are paid by both the company and the employee. This double NIC 'hit' means that a director taking profits as salary will pay more than double the NICs of a sole trader taking the same level of income. Income paid as dividends is not liable for NICs. Due to the significant savings derived, this has caused HMRC to review contracts and the level of dividends closely, under a regime known as IR35 which has been in place since 6 April 2000.
	IR35 and other tax 'pitfalls' (one of which is 'income shifting') will need to be understood and, if applicable, addressed.

Alternative ways of getting started

Rather than start a new business, you could buy into one that is already established, or consider franchising.

Buying a business

Buying an established business can be an attractive route to becoming your own boss, as it eliminates many of the problems of start-up. The enterprise is likely to come equipped with stock, suppliers, an order book, premises and possibly employees. It is also likely to have debtors and creditors. Take professional advice before buying any business, even one from friends. In particular, you should consider why the business is being sold. It may be for perfectly respectable reasons – for instance, a change of circumstances such as retirement. But equally, it may be that the market is saturated, that the rent is about to go sky-high or that major competition has opened up nearby.

Before parting with your money, make sure that the assets are actually owned by the business and get the stock professionally valued. You should also ensure that the debts are collectable and that the same credit terms will apply from existing suppliers. Get an accountant to look at the figures for the last three years and have a chartered surveyor check the premises. It is also advisable to ask a solicitor to vet any legal documents, including staff contracts: you may automatically inherit existing employees.

The value of the company's assets will be reflected in its purchase price, as will the 'goodwill' (or reputation) that it has established. For more information, contact the agents specializing in small businesses, **Christie & Co**, see website: **www.christie.com**.

Franchising

Franchising has become an increasingly popular form of business, with attractions for both franchisor and franchisee. The franchisor gains as their 'brand' is able to expand quickly. The advantage to the franchisee is that there are normally fewer risks than starting a business from scratch.

A franchisee buys into an established business and builds up his or her own enterprise under its wing. In return for the investment plus regular royalty payments, he or she acquires the right to sell the franchisor's products or services within a specified geographic area and enjoys the benefits of its reputation, buying power and marketing expertise. As a franchisee you are effectively your own boss. You finance the business, employ the staff and retain the profits after the franchisor has had its cut. You are usually expected to maintain certain standards and conform to the broad corporate approach of the organization. In return, the franchisor should train you in the business, provide management support and give you access to a wide range of backup services.

The amount of capital needed to buy a franchise varies enormously according to the type of business, and can be anywhere between a few hundred pounds and £500,000 or more. The franchisee is normally liable to pay an initial fee, covering both the entry cost and the initial support services provided by the franchisor, such as advice about location and market research.

The length of the agreement will depend both on the type of business involved and on the front-end fee. Agreements can run from three to 20 years and many franchisors include an option to renew the agreement, which should be treated as a valuable asset.

Many franchises have built up a good track record and raising money to invest in good franchises may not be too difficult. Most of the leading high street banks operate specialist franchise loan sections. Franchisors may also be able to help in raising the money and can sometimes arrange more advantageous terms through their connections with financial institutions.

The **British Franchise Association** (BFA) represents 'the responsible face' of franchising, and its members have to conform to a code of practice. The BFA publishes a *Franchisee Guide*, which provides comprehensive advice on buying a franchise, together with a list of BFA member franchisors and affiliated advisers. It is well worth attending a franchise seminar to find out more and compare the various franchise options on offer.

A good franchisor will provide a great deal of invaluable help. However, some franchisors are very casual in their approach, lacking in competence, or even downright unethical. Make careful enquiries before committing any money: as basic information, you should ask for a bank reference together with a copy of the previous year's accounts. Also check with the BFA whether the franchisor in question is a member and visit some of the other franchisees to find out what their experience has been. Before signing, seek advice from an accountant or solicitor.

For more information, see the British Franchise Association website: **www.thebfa.org**.

Operational and other issues

Inventions and intellectual property

If you have a clever idea that you would like to market, you should ensure that your intellectual property is protected. For information about patenting an invention and much more, look at the **UK Intellectual Property Office** website: **www.ipo.gov.uk**.

Licences

Certain types of business require a licence or permit to trade; these include pubs, off-licences, nursing agencies, pet shops, kennels, mini-cabs or buses, driving instructors, betting shops, auction sale rooms, cinemas, street traders and, in some cases, travel agents and tour operators. You will also require a licence to import certain goods. Your local authority planning office will advise you whether you require a licence, and in many cases your council will be the licensing authority.

Permissions

Depending on the nature of your business, other permissions may need to be obtained, including those of the police, the environmental health department, licensing authorities and the fire prevention officer. In particular, there are special requirements concerning the sale of food, and safety measures for hotels and guest houses. Your local authority will advise you on what is necessary.

Employing staff

Should you consider employing staff, you will immediately increase the complexity of your business. Sole traders who need to take on staff would be sensible to take advice before doing so on what roles and responsibilities this will involve. Many people starting a business wisely limit recruitment to the minimum in the early days, until they are sure that they can afford the cost of having permanent staff.

Once you become an employer, you take on responsibilities. As well as paying salaries, you will have to account for PAYE, keep National Insurance records and conform to the multiple requirements of employment legislation. While this may sound rather daunting, the government provides a service, staffed by new business advisers, to help small businesses employing staff for the first time get to grips with the tax and National Insurance systems. For further information see website: **www.hmrc.gov.uk**.

If you are still worried or don't want the bother of doing the paperwork yourself, your accountant is likely to be able to introduce you to a payroll service which will cost you money but will take the burden off your shoulders.

Personnel records

Many businesses find it useful to keep personnel records covering such information as National Insurance numbers, tax codes, appraisal reports and so on. For information on data protection see the **Information Commissioner** website: **www.ico.gov.uk**.

Employment legislation

As an employer, you have certain legal obligations in respect of your staff. The most important cover such issues as health and safety at work, terms and conditions of employment and the provision of employee rights including, for example, parental leave, trade union activity and protection against unfair dismissal. Very small firms are exempt from some of the more onerous requirements and the government is taking steps to reduce more of the red tape. However, it is important that you understand in general terms what legislation could affect you.

Minimum wage

There are now three main levels of minimum wage. For all workers aged 16–17 who are no longer of compulsory school age, the minimum hourly rate is £3.72; for those aged 18–20, the minimum is £5.03; and for those aged 21 and above, the minimum is £6.31 an hour. The apprentice rate for apprentices under 19 or 19 or over in the first year of their apprenticeship is £2.68.

Health and safety at work

The Health and Safety at Work Act applies to everyone in a business, whether employer, employee or self-employed. It also protects the general public who may be affected by your business activity. **The Health and Safety Executive** has a useful website: **www.hse.gov.uk**.

Discrimination

An employer, however small the business, may not discriminate against someone on the grounds of sex, race, disability, religion, marital status, sexual orientation or, since October 2006, age. This applies to all aspects of employment, including training, promotion, recruitment, company benefits and facilities. For further information see the **Equality and Human Rights Commission** website: **www.equalityhumanrights.com**.

Contract of employment

A contract of employment is an agreement entered into between an employer and an employee under which they have certain mutual obligations. It comes into being as soon as an employee starts work, when it is taken that he or she accepts the job on the terms offered. Within two months of the job starting, the employer must normally give the employee a written statement highlighting the key terms and conditions of the job, together with a general description of the duties.

Entitlement to a written statement applies to all staff, including part-timers and employees working on fixed-term contracts. By law, they are required to be treated no less favourably than comparable full-timers or permanent employees in respect of their terms and conditions of employment, including access to training, holiday entitlement and benefits. For further information and advice consult your Professional Association's advice line, local Citizens Advice Bureau or your solicitor.

Disputes

If you find yourself with a potential dispute on your hands, it is sensible to approach **ACAS**, which operates an effective information and advisory service for employers and employees on a variety of workplace problems, including employment legislation and employment relations. It also has a wide range of useful publications, giving practical guidance on employment matters. See website: **www.acas.org.uk**.

Insurance

Insurance is more than just a wise precaution. It is essential if you employ staff, have business premises or use your car regularly for commercial purposes. Many insurance companies now offer 'package insurance' for small businesses, which covers most of the main contingencies in a single policy. This usually works out cheaper than buying a collection of individual policies. An insurance broker should be able to guide you through the risks and insurance products available:

- *Employers' liability.* This is compulsory if you employ staff. It provides indemnity against liability for death or bodily injury to employees and subcontractors arising in connection with the business.

- *Product and public liability.* This insures the business and its products against claims by customers or the public.

- *Professional indemnity.* This is essential if a client could suffer a mishap, loss or other damage in consequence of advice or services received.

- *House insurance.* If you operate your business from home, check that you have notified your house insurer of this fact.

- *Motor risks.* Check that you have notified your insurer if you use your motor vehicle for your business.

- *Life assurance.* This ensures that funds are available to pay off any debts or to enable the business to continue in the event of your death.

- *Permanent health insurance.* Otherwise known as 'income protection', it provides insurance against long-term loss of income as a result of severe illness or disability.

- *Key person insurance.* This applies to the loss of a key person through prolonged illness as well as death. In small companies where the success or failure of the business is dependent upon the skills of one or two key executives, key person insurance may be demanded by lenders.

You should discuss these points with your insurance company or a broker. To find an insurance broker, see the **British Insurance Brokers' Association** website: **www.biba.org.uk,** or the **Association of British Insurers** website: **www.abi.org.uk**.

Property investment

A frequent avenue that some people explore when nearing retirement is property investment either in the UK or abroad. Since they may be armed with spare funds and perhaps have the advantage of more time available and perhaps even some maintenance skills, you can understand why this happens. Up until 2007 people thought they had it made in property investment with the magic mix of good capital growth and decent returns on their investment through rental income. The capital growth bubble burst in the summer of 2007 and some people have been nervous about this sector ever since. It is beyond the scope of this text to comment on whether or not the tide is turning but it can alert you to some of the key issues and potential sources of further help. Some of the issues are around minimizing your property tax bill, deciding whether to use a letting agent or not, complying with all the red tape and avoiding 'tenants from hell'.

Remember there are many players in this market including mortgage lenders, mortgage brokers, developers, property syndicates, letting agents, and most will know more than you and all will want some of your money. Some even pay for your flights and travel to visit property abroad and then play on this in a subsequent high-pressure sales environment. I strongly advise you never to give in and sign up. There will always, of course, be another day, another deal. The best advice I can give to anyone thinking about property investment is to invest £10 in David Lawrenson's best-selling property book *Successful Property Letting* and review his website, **www.lettingfocus.com**. This will open your eyes to some of the issues I have touched upon and will give you straight-forward and clear advice and information on this market. For instance, one of David's candid tips is 'You must like property. So, if houses bore you stiff, you're probably better off doing something else.'

Armed with this and advice from friends and relatives who have invested in property, you might then be ready to put your toe in the water and start to explore this area.

Further help, advice and training

The very first paragraph of this chapter promised: '*Importantly, in starting a small business you will not be alone and this chapter will also signpost you to plenty of help and support and most of it is free (it is just a matter of knowing where to look!).*' This chapter alone will help you get started but you will need further help and information. Fortunately, small businesses are well served when it comes to general help and training. A number of organizations offer subsidized or free advice and training schemes. The best ones feature below.

Organizations providing free or subsidized help

Government resources

www.gov.uk contains the government's online resource for businesses. Regional or country-specific support is also available at:

Regional help – **www.nationalenterprisenetwork.org.**

Northern Ireland – **www.nibusinessinfo.co.uk.**

Scotland – **www.business.scotland.gov.uk.**

Wales – **www.business.wales.gov.uk.**

Start up Britain

Start up Britain has been set up by the government to help you find information about starting a business and contains offers and discounts available to new business start-ups. Further information is available from **www.startupbritain.org.**

HMRC

Your local HMRC Business Education & Support Team provides free training events aimed at start-up businesses and on how to run a payroll. Further information is available at **www.hmrc.gov.uk/bst/index.htm.**

Adult education centres

Short courses in specific business skills are run by business schools and colleges of higher and further education. Various trade and professional associations also run courses. Further information is available from **www.learndirect.co.uk** and the Workers Education Association on **www.wea.org.uk.**

PRIME

PRIME (The Prince's Initiative for Mature Enterprise) helps people over the age of 50 set up in business for themselves. PRIME offers free information, workshops and business networking events. It can refer people to accredited advisers for free business advice, and in some parts of the country can also offer free mentoring and other services. Should you be interested in self-employment, PRIME is full of practical ideas and helpful business information. See website: **www.prime.org.uk**.

Tax Volunteers

Tax Volunteers is an independent free tax advice service for older people on low incomes who cannot afford to pay for professional advice. Website: **www.taxvol.org.uk**.

Other useful organizations

Lawyers for Your Business is a network of 1,000 solicitor firms in England and Wales offering specialist advice to small- and medium-sized businesses. To help firms access business-related legal advice, Lawyers for Business offers a free half-hour initial consultation with a lawyer in your area who is a member of the scheme. Advice can be sought on a range of issues. To obtain a list of members, see website: **www.lawsociety.org**.

Federation of Small Businesses (**www.fsb.org.uk**). The FSB represents great value for money. The networking opportunities and fringe benefits it provides makes it a 'must have' for most new small businesses.

Professional Contractors Group (PCG) The PCG's 'Guide to Freelancing' is free and can be downloaded from its website (**www.pcg.org.uk**). PCG's knowledge of and guidance on IR35 for consultants and contractors is second to none.

Business start-up websites. These are packed with free hints and tips and a useful one is **www.bstartup.com** and their exhibitions are free, well attended and have some excellent free workshops and guest speakers.

Useful reading

An extensive list of books for small and start-up businesses is published by Kogan Page, website: **www.koganpage.com**, including *Start Up and Run Your Own Business* and *Working for Yourself. An Entrepreneur's Guide*, both by Jonathan Reuvid, *Soul Trader*, by Rasheed Ogunlaru, *The Rebel Entrepreneur: Rewriting the Business Rulebook* by Jonathan Moules and *Successful Property Letting: How to Make Money in Buy-to-Let*, by David Lawrenson.

Case studies

Debbie Coupland – Owner/Director of Great War Tours Ltd

*Debbie served in the army as an officer for five years, worked in business administration, gained a degree as a mature student and then worked for the Ministry of Defence recruiting officers for the army. In late 2011 following a restructure Debbie took the opportunity to leave and create her own business: Great War Tours Ltd, dedicated to providing private, bespoke, luxurious trips to the memorial sites and battlefields of the Great War in northern France and Belgium (*www.greatwartours.co.uk*).*

What encouraged you to create your own company?

I have been a keen student of the First World War since childhood and over the years have visited a variety of battlefield sites through a variety of tour styles. I felt that there was a gap in the battlefield tour market which I could use to advantage; my unique selling point would be to offer very small tours (to no more than four clients), using a vehicle not usually associated with such tours (a classic, six-door Cadillac de Ville Limousine) and accommodating my clients in top class hotels and restaurants not usually on the battlefield routes. I have spent the last 14 months proving through rigorous testing that my idea was valid and have now completed the first tour with paying clients.

What was the best tip you were given when you set up?

Within the first few days of talking about my proposed business, I was sent a list of six tips for business start-up, the first of which was *'No more excuses – got a business or business idea, then do it or ditch it!'* I failed to embrace fully only one, *'Be prepared to sell, sell, sell – too many businesses spend too much time developing the product or service and not enough time planning how to take it to market and sell it. Until you have customers you don't have a business.'* In my own defence I was still working on my marketing strategy in an effort to garner more! I have also been very lucky to find some very professional people to help me – business mentor, accountant, solicitor, web-designer and marketing co-ordinator, to mention a sample – who have offered me sterling advice delivered through the friendliest of working environments.

How did you find your first few clients?

I have engaged with networking and social media as well as events through which I could distribute leaflets and business cards. In the end I actually found my first clients through personal contact! And I suspect that, in the end, while I am also beginning to embrace radio advertising in a bid to raise awareness of my product, my client base will grow primarily through personal recommendation. My website benefits me by being able to engage directly with potential clients through a video clip and enabling new clients to read previous clients' reports via the testimonial page. This provides potential clients with essential re-assurance that Great War Tours Ltd is a trustworthy brand.

If you were starting again, what would you do differently?

Several different clichés come to mind as being appropriate here from 'Ignorance is bliss' to 'If I wanted to get there I wouldn't have started from here' and finally, the suitably military one, 'Ignorance is no excuse'! But none of these quite ring true enough so that I must admit that, even with the gift of hindsight, I probably wouldn't do anything differently. How could I possibly say such a thing, I hear you ask? Hasn't she learned anything? Well, recently I was privileged to watch a demonstrator working on behalf of the National Association of Flower Arrangement Societies. She advised that the best way to start an arrangement was to visualize the end product and then work backwards! Which observation, I think, describes most aptly, the way I have worked over the last 15 months. I have held my vision of the final product – a private, bespoke, luxurious tour through northern France and Belgium, for no more than four clients – clearly in my head. And everything that I have done since has been geared towards achieving that goal.

Phil Champ, FIMMM, MSLL, MFSB – product, industrial, mechanical designer; sole trader trading as Champ Industrial Design

Phil set up his own business in 2011 having worked as an employee in and around the design industry for over 30 years. In early 2011 Phil's then employer decided to restructure and ceased to offer product design as an activity. This left Phil wondering 'What now?' During the time spent creating a new CV and updating his portfolio and wondering if any of his interview suits would still fit, his phone started to ring. Past clients wondered whether he could carry out design projects for them as his former employer no longer offered this service. After some initial meetings and a consultation with his wife who is an AAT qualified book-keeper, Phil decided to bite a big bullet and set up on his own business and Champ Industrial Design was born.

Why did you decide to set up as a sole trader rather than a limited company?

After consulting with my accountant (by the way, finding a good accountant was pretty much the first thing on my list of things to do before I even decided that I would try to set up on my own), I came to the conclusion that it would be the quickest and simplest way to get up and running. There is, I believe, less paperwork involved in being a sole trader and I didn't want to overload my wife with too much paperwork.

How have you found your first years of trading?

A vertical line of learning – there has been no 'curve'! Business has been great but the new skills that you need to develop quickly can be very distracting and time consuming. These include: writing non-disclosure agreements, terms and conditions, checking that you have the right insurance policies in place. Also, making sure that your terms and conditions are legal and binding brings you into contact with the legal profession.

How did you obtain your first few clients?

I was actually very lucky in that several of the clients from my previous job liked my work and approached me directly to see if I would like to work on certain projects for them. Articles in trade journals helped my services – who says you have to pay for advertising? I see this done by more and more businesses now that I know what to look for. Articles seem to be a good win–win for all concerned.

What were the best tips you were given when you set up?

Get a good accountant who understands your industry, which I did. His first bit of advice was to join the Federation of Small Businesses, which again I did. This proved to be very useful in the first few months as the advice available was invaluable. They also help you realize that you are not alone and that there are other people out there in exactly the same boat as you are. Another good tip came from an unusual source. I had taken up the offer to meet with a 'business mentor' and had spent a whole morning with him. It was useful but I came away asking myself more questions than I had gone to see him with. On my way home, I popped into my local off-licence for a couple of bottles of wine for the weekend and there was an assistant there who I hadn't seen for a couple of years. He explained that he had now come back as manager. I asked him how it felt to be responsible, to which he replied, 'I have always been responsible; the difference is that I am now accountable.' I found this one small statement more useful than the whole three or so hours with the business mentor, as it had totally highlighted my inner feeling of disquiet that I had felt since setting up. Once I realized that this was what the disquiet was about, I could set about dealing with it. I started to sleep a little better after this.

If you were starting again, what would you do differently?

I do constantly make an effort to be more organized but as a designer, your natural thought process is quite chaotic, lateral, and tangential. Thinking in logical straight lines sometimes takes a lot of a very different kind of concentration. If it weren't for having a wife who does do the straight-line thinking, is very thorough, methodical and logical, I would probably have given up and tried to find another 'normal' PAYE job. This makes me conclude that you do need a good bookkeeper to keep you on the straight and narrow if your business exists in any 'creative' industry.

I think self-discipline is important together with strict allocation of time, as there is a tendency to knee jerk every time a client asks something of you. This approach does not best serve their needs, or allow you to fully concentrate on whatever the task at hand is. I have also become something of a workaholic, so taking time out for other things is important. I guess that this is partly due to having my office at home. I need to learn how to shut the door and stay out sometimes! Have a look at my website at **www.champ-id.co.uk** and if I can be of help please just get in touch via the site.

Paul Riley – fire safety business; company

Paul served in the battle of the Falklands with the Royal Navy, where he mastered a number of trades including serving as a fireman. Paul subsequently became the chief fire safety trainer for Kidde Thorn fire protection and later set up his own business in 1997 which subsequently went bust. But Paul is starting up again.

Why did you set up as a company?

I set up as a limited company because I simply asked my potential customers what would they prefer and the majority said they would much rather deal with a company than a sole trader. It seems that companies can carry more credibility.

What services did you provide?

The core business was fire safety training and the style and method of delivery were well received. Bolt-on services including fire extinguisher servicing, fireproofing and fire risk assessments were subsequently supplied. Basically if a client asked, 'Paul can you...?' and it was about fire safety the answer was always 'yes'!

In 2004 a major bank asked me to provide my 'off the wall' training style electronically with something called e-Learning. To cut a long story very short, it was successful and then another bank said they would like it. We ended up in three of the largest banks in the world as clients, without advertising. At this point I thought, 'Hang on – there's a real market out there,' so I took a large second mortgage on the house and I had eight people working for me and things were looking very rosy.

Where did it all go wrong?

In the autumn 2008 the banking crisis hit: soon banks cancelled orders and development of our software stalled. I tried lots of different ways to maintain cash flow and looked at credit control and invoice factoring. The company became insolvent and in September 2009 I placed my company into administration.

What did you lose?

I lost my house and cars (oh, and a wife), but now I've finished licking my wounds and decided it's time to start afresh. However, this time I, and not my bank, will be in control! I have a £1,000 loan from my sister and in the summer of 2012 I started My Fire Safety Ltd with the tag line 'Because fire safety is all about you'. I am the sole employee, pulling in expertise as required and already have a few very nice clients.

What have you learnt?

Being on Working Tax Credits has humbled me, and now I count every single penny. In purchasing I look for and find quality at a good price and use technology to talk with customers (Skype, etc), instead of visiting all customers. The recession has taught businesses to be selective and careful in their spending. I can see now that clever businesses are embracing new communications technologies.

Perhaps the most important message is that when the going gets tough the bank manager is *not* your friend, as he is there to get as much money out of you as possible! I had a great relationship with my bank manager – even on the day I placed my company into administration he said, 'Don't worry, Paul, there is no way they will take your house.' They did – the local manager has no influence at head office. I don't blame my manager, I just wish he had warned me 12 months earlier.

As we now move into 2014, I continue to keep costs to a minimum. I also invest time in talking to accounts departments, which has worked wonders as I get paid well within 30 days. Asking old customers to refer me has paid massive dividends. Over 70 per cent of my work is now from new clients. Offering great customer service has been key and helping the Prince's Trust resulted in me being invited to meet Prince Charles at the grand opening of their head office. 'My Fire Safety' is permanently exhibited in their reception area! Business is good but this time it's on my terms and in my control!

My biggest message is put the past behind you. Constantly looking back with anger is damaging and it eats you up. Things *do* get better. I have my youngest daughter back living with me and I am happy, and I'm looking forward to building my second business!

Starting and running a business – checklist

When starting or running a business, you will encounter a vast range of information and this can sometimes lead to you feeling swamped. This checklist has been developed to help you along the path of starting and running a small business. You should annotate each item as:

N: Not applicable; W: Work on now; A: Review with Accountant; C: Complete

1 If you want to travel somewhere you use a map. In business it's just the same except you get yourself a **plan**.

It is crucial to commit it to writing and don't expect to get it right first time (no one does!). A few pages are fine to start with based on:

- a few 'SMART' objectives (ie if each objective is not specific, measurable, achievable, realistic and timed then have another go). Also try to make your objectives a bit challenging – you might just surprise yourself; and:

- a profit-and-loss forecast for at least the year ahead (and the basic assumptions you have used as supporting notes); and:

- your marketing research (what the products are that you offer and who the customers are and the competitors for each); and finally:

- your marketing plan setting out, based on your market research, what you plan to do and when you plan to do it.

The plan can then develop with review, time and further research and grow as your business evolves. Review it with your accountant, a trusted friend who runs their own business and perhaps a business adviser or mentor – don't keep it to yourself. The plan will then start to develop and grow. There are some useful free templates available on the web but, right at the very start, don't feel you have to follow them slavishly if you find yourself bogged down and uninspired.

2 Choose your **trading format**, ie company (usually signified by 'limited') or sole trader or partnership or limited liability partnership. This is an important step and one to talk through with your accountant, or a business adviser if you have one, as they may have ideas on this that you have not considered.

You can set up a company for £15 with Companies House. See **www.companieshouse.gov.uk** 'web incorporation service'.

Understand your obligations and risks as a director (if trading as a company); see **www.companieshouse.co.uk** and their 'Life of a Company' guidance parts 1 and 2.

Understand the personal liability risks of sole trader/partnership and, indeed, joint and several liability if trading in partnership ('last person standing pays the lot'!). If things go badly wrong your personal wealth could be at risk – but perhaps insurance could help?

3 Choose your **accountant** – there are many accountancy organizations and the word accountant is not protected in the same way as, say, 'solicitor'. Chartered accountants can be found at **www.icaew.co.uk** (England and Wales); **www.icas.org.uk** (Scotland) and **www.charteredaccountants.ie** (Ireland). Accountants are usually prepared to see you for an initial 'no obligation' meeting. Be clear about who your regular contact will be and their qualifications, what they will do and you will do, an estimate of costs and ask for their hourly charging rates. All of this should be confirmed in writing to help avoid 'confusion'. Consider your rapport with your accountant and their knowledge of your industry.

4 Make sure you have a source of **legal help**. Could your local solicitor help? Alternatively your trade association may offer a free legal helpline which may get you by initially. Whether you need a solicitor or not depends very much on two things. First, the nature of your trade and the risks you are exposed to. Second, what crops up once you are in business (buying another business, litigation, claims etc; having a solicitor on standby can be useful and many solicitors will provide an initial free one-hour no-obligation consultation at the outset). An early legal question that will usually arise is about your terms and conditions of trade.

5 There is some **free government help** which you will find at **www.gov.uk** which contains the government's online resource for businesses.

You should also check out the government-backed initiative **www.startupbritain.org** for inspiration and ideas.

Regional or country-specific support is also available at:

Regional help – **www.nationalenterprisenetwork.org**;

Northern Ireland – at **www.nibusinessinfo.co.uk**;

Scotland – at **www.business.scotland.gov.uk**;

Wales – at **www.business.wales.gov.uk**.

For the over-50s try **www.prime.org.uk**.

6 Consider taking help and advice from trusted friends or family that are in business already. Often this can yield great hints and tips. Can they help with your business plan? Remember you are not alone – there are about 4.7 million businesses in the UK and 91 per cent have fewer than four people.

7 Join the best **trade or professional association** that you can identify and consider the extra benefits each provides in the areas of research information, networking events, helplines, tax investigation help and insurance offerings. Consider joining the Federation of Small Business, **www.fsb.org.uk**. For consultants/ interim managers also consider the Professional Contractors Group, **www.pcg.org.uk**.

8 Choose and if appropriate protect your **business name**. There is some useful free help available on **intellectual property** (patents, brands, etc) at the Intellectual Property Office at **www.ipo.gov.uk**.

9 Determine your ability to stay afloat during the first year by taking your profit-and-loss forecast from step 1 and then plan your **cash flow**. In addition, work out how much money you'll also need for equipment and other capital items when starting up.

   If you need financial help review your options for obtaining finance (personal loan, bank finance, bank overdraft, invoice discounting and grants).

10 Choose a business **bank** account. Shop around for the best deal that suits your business (often a trade-off between the convenience of a local 'bricks and mortar' branch accompanied by internet banking versus free or reduced charges for internet-only accounts). Once the bank account is set up always reconciling your bank account to your business accounts is a crucial control.

11 Assess your **pension** needs. See **www.unbiased.co.uk** for finding an Independent Financial Adviser or IFA.

12 Sort out your **tax and record keeping** (documents need to be kept for six years and you need to become a receipt/invoice hoarder with a logical 'system for filing), as the taxman might say 'prove it or lose it'.

13 Check with your accountant that your proposed bookkeeping and record-keeping systems are acceptable before you buy them or start to build a system (whether manually written up or Excel

or accounting software). Most accountants should be able to provide you with a free do-it-yourself Excel solution and book-keeping guide or point you to an online or software accounting solution.

14 Understand the implications of failing to deal with your **tax** affairs properly. This can be penalties ranging from 30 per cent to 100 per cent and interest. Indeed, failing to deal with tax affairs properly is one of the common reasons for a business failing. Some trade associations (for instance FSB and PCG mentioned above) include 'free' tax investigation cover – a very useful benefit but the best way to cover yourself is to maintain decent books and records and become a receipt hoarder.

15 Understand your **income tax obligations** and deadlines as a sole trader. Register with the newly self-employed helpline 0845 9154515 within three months of obtaining an income. This does not need to be done if you set up as a company.

16 For companies you need to understand your payment obligations (and timescales) on **PAYE and National Insurance** (this can also apply to sole traders who have employees) and corporation tax. HMRC run some useful free online courses to help with payroll which you can find under 'Business Support Team' at **www.hmrc.gov.uk**. Alternatively you may want to outsource PAYE/payroll to a payroll agent where the costs are usually about £16 to £23 per hour.

For companies you are obliged to file your annual accounts at Companies House and pay your corporation tax to HMRC nine months after your year end. When you start a business this may seem a long time away and your accountant would usually be expected to undertake these tasks. It is usually better to complete these tasks sooner rather than later after your year end so you can pick up learning points.

17 Understand your obligations regarding your company **Annual Return** (if trading as a company). This is a really straightforward routine and completed on the anniversary of setting up a company each year. There is good-quality free help at Companies House, **www.companieshouse.gov.uk**.

18 Understand your obligations on **VAT**. The current registration
    threshold for compulsory registration is £79,000. If you do
    register for VAT consider VAT schemes especially the VAT flat
    rate scheme for small businesses. Once registered, diary your
    quarterly online VAT returns and payments and upon registering
    with HMRC they can also provide you with an alert/reminder
    service. The penalties for late filing of VAT returns increase with
    each late return.

19 Set up your **premises** so that you can work effectively. If you
    work from home manage your family's and neighbours'
    expectations – suddenly the phrase 'Time is money' takes on
    a new meaning.

20 Set up your **suppliers** (set up contracts and bills in the company
    or business name) and, if appropriate, set up stock control and
    delivery systems.

21 Consider **insurance** policies for identified business risks
    (professional indemnity, public liability, product liability, etc).
    An insurance broker can advise on this and you should also
    consider policies available via trade associations as these can
    provide increased cover at less cost.

22 Consider protecting the income you take from your business
    (especially if you have dependants) in the event of long-term
    illness or of **death** (**www.unbiased.co.uk** for finding an
    Independent Financial Adviser or IFA).

23 If running your **business at home** you must tell your insurer that
    you run a business from home.

24 **Marketing and selling** will be massively important to your
    success. If you are not from a selling/marketing background talk
    to trusted friends who run their own business and your
    accountant/adviser or mentor about your market research and
    marketing plan. Understand your customers and what they need.
    Do not underestimate the importance of networking.

25 Plan the **pricing** strategies for your product or service. A different
    package means a different price. How have you benchmarked
    your price and how have you differentiated your offering
    (features and benefits) to allow you to charge that little bit

more? Conversely what features and benefits have you stripped out to allow you to offer a headline price that comes in beneath the competition?

26 Plan your **marketing promotion strategy**. Remember that 'folk are different' and that it is a bit like fishing – you use different hooks depending on what you are trying to catch.

27 Get paid promptly for your sale. What are your **payment terms** (terms and conditions)? Follow up on outstanding debts. If you sell stock have you included a reservation of title clause to help you retrieve unpaid stock if your client goes bust?

28 Set up your **IT system** and support and have a system to back up your data securely. A stolen laptop or hard drive failure can be catastrophic on your business continuity if you have not backed up your data and systems.

29 Check whether you need to notify the Information Commissioner under the **data protection** laws (**www.ico.gov.uk**).

30 Consider other **red tape**, especially if your area is a specialized sector (food, health and safety, etc). Investigate and apply for the licences and permits that your business may need. To help understand any special needs of your business sector check with your trade association, which usually has a wealth of information and guidance available.

31 Review and update your business plan in the light of experience and keep it a living document.

Chapter Eleven
Looking for paid work

> *If you really want something in this life, you have to work for it. Now quiet, they're about to announce the lottery numbers.*
>
> **HOMER SIMPSON QUOTED IN *THE OBSERVER***

According to recent research by Primetime Retirement (**www.primetimeretirement.co.uk**), the number of people working past the age of 65 could hit 2 million within the next decade. Increasing longevity and the need to boost retirement income means an increasing number of older people in Britain are working past the current pension age. Between 2008 and 2010 the number of over-65s in the workforce increased by nearly 20 per cent, and this growth can only continue as changes in employment law and state pensions mean more will have the opportunity to stay in work. One of the reasons for the increased number of post-retirement age workers is the tough economic climate, but it is good news that many older people who wish to continue working are not being locked out of the job market because of their age. However, for some older workers the picture is not so rosy – 45 per cent of unemployed people aged 50–64 have been out of work for more than a year. This is significantly higher than any other age group, so it is vitally important that employers do not overlook the skills and experience older workers have to offer. So how difficult is it to find paid work in your 60s? Would you be willing to work into your 70s and beyond?

Top tips: Motivators for continuing to work in your 60s and beyond

- keeping mentally and physically active;
- ensuring sufficient funds to meet rising living costs;
- retaining good levels of self-esteem – job status;
- continuing social contact with others;
- preference for being/doing something useful.

Should you be considering remaining in employment beyond retirement age, there are a number of options available. You could continue to work full time, should your employer wish to keep you on. With years of experience and useful skills, this is something of value to employers. You might prefer to work part-time or flexible hours. Some people wish to have a complete change and set up in business for themselves (see Chapter 10). If you are looking for employment you could contact previous employers, if you have enjoyed working for them. They might consider you for any vacancies they have. Many employers do welcome older workers, as they are viewed to be reliable and have good workplace experience. Over the course of your working life you will have picked up many skills – some of which are transferable and could be utilized in a whole host of jobs. Be ready to show potential employers how keen you are to learn. Be able to demonstrate that taking on new training and learning new skills and working methods are not a problem to you.

You may have to be prepared to work for less money than you previously earned, and show your potential employer that you are more than willing to pass on some of your skills to other less experienced colleagues. However, one of the older workers' trump cards is reliability, and this can be reinforced by references from previous employers. Provided you come across well at interview, potential employers are likely to value your stability. Whatever your reason, enjoy your job hunting.

Financial considerations

Since the abolition of the earnings rule, no matter what age you are or how much you earn there is no longer any forfeit to your state pension, although of course you may have to pay tax on your additional income. If you are working close to a full-time week and/or have enough money to live on, there could be an advantage in asking the DWP to defer your pension, as this will entitle you to a bigger one in the future. Each year of deferral earns an increment of about 10.4 per cent of the pension.

Another advantage is that, if you choose to defer your pension by at least a year, you will have the option of taking the money as a taxable lump sum instead of in higher weekly pension payments. For other information concerning your pension, tax, and working for yourself refer to Chapters 3, 4 and 10.

Age discrimination and equality

Age discrimination legislation came into force in October 2006, and The Equality Act was enshrined in 2010. These laws make it illegal for employers to discriminate against older candidates on account of age as regards recruitment, training and promotion. In particular, provided individuals are still physically and mentally capable of doing their job, an employer can no longer oblige them to retire at a 'default' retirement age. Employers also now have a duty to consider requests by employees who want to postpone their retirement and will need to give those they want to retire at least six months' written notice of their decision. The government scrapped 65 as the UK's default retirement age, with effect from April 2011.

Assessing your abilities

Knowing what you have to offer a potential employer is an essential first step. Make a list of everything you have done, in both your formal career and ordinary life, including your outside interests. In particular, consider adding any practical or other skills, knowledge or contacts that you have acquired over the years. These could now prove especially useful. If, for example, you have done a lot of public speaking, fundraising, committee work or conference organization, these would be excellent transferable skills that would make you attractive to a prospective employer. As a result of writing everything down, most people find that they have far more to offer than they originally realized. In addition to work skills, you should include your personal attributes and any special assets that would attract an employer. The list might include health, organizing ability, a good telephone manner, communication skills, the ability to work well with other people, use of a car and willingness to do flexible hours. Maturity can also be a positive asset.

If you spend some time working on your personal branding, how to market yourself and to whom, you will become much more focused. It will help you form a clearer idea of the sorts of jobs that would suit you. As a general rule when job hunting, the more accurate and targeted you can be in the application process, the more likely you are to succeed. If you intend to do something completely different do your research carefully. Talking to other people helps. Friends, family, work colleagues or business acquaintances may have useful information. It could also be sensible to consult outside experts who specialize in adult career counselling. Whatever you decide to do, remember that with age and experience comes wisdom. You have the power to negotiate and you have the power to decide what you want to do next. Make sure you take a job that is right for you.

Job counselling

This is usually a mixture of helping you to identify your talents in a vocational sense combined with practical advice on successful job-hunting techniques. Counsellors can assist with such essentials as writing a CV, preparing for an interview and locating job vacancies. They can also advise you of suitable training courses. There are numerous companies offering this service; a search on the internet will reveal them. Best advice is to ask for recommendations from other people before signing up with a company. If you want to make really certain they can help, you could ask to speak to one or two of their former clients to find out whether they found the service useful.

Training opportunities

Knowing what you want to do is one thing, but before starting a new job you may want to brush up existing skills or possibly acquire new ones. Most professional bodies have a full programme of training events, ranging from one-day seminars to courses lasting a week or longer. Additionally, adult education institutes run a vast range of courses or, if you are still in your present job, a more practical solution might be to investigate open and flexible learning, which you can do from home.

Open and flexible learning

Open and flexible learning is successfully helping to provide a greater range and flexibility of vocational education and training opportunities for individuals of all ages. In particular, it is designed to increase the scope for participants to learn at a time, place and pace best suited to their own particular circumstances.

The following organizations offer advice and an excellent range of courses:

Adult Education Finder: **www.adulteducationfinder.co.uk**.

Home Learning College: **www.homelearningcollege.com**.

Home Learning Courses: **www.homelearningcourses.com**.

Learn Direct: **www.learndirect.co.uk**.

National Extension College: **www.nec.ac.uk**.

National Institute of Adult Continuing Education (NIACE): **www.niace.org.uk**.

Open and Distance Learning Quality Council (ODLQC): **www.odlqc.org.uk**.

Open University (OU): **www.open.ac.uk**.

IT skills

If you are considering a change in direction, some new qualifications may be advantageous. IT skills are essential, so if you are not confident about your computer literacy and don't have much IT experience or specialist knowledge, here are some websites to look at:

Affordable Training: **www.affordabletraining.co.uk**.

Computeach: **www.computeach.co.uk**.

Home and Learn: **www.homeandlearn.co.uk**.

National Skills Academy: **www.itskillsacademy.ac.uk**.

Help with finding a job

If you plan to work in retirement, the best way is to start looking while you still have a job. Prospective employers may prefer applicants who are busy and actively working rather than those who have had a period of non-employment for whatever reason. However, whether you are hoping to go straight from one job to another, or have had an enforced period of not working, this should not affect the way you approach your job search. If you have been retired for some time and want to return to work, you might consider doing some voluntary work in the meantime (see Chapter 12, Voluntary work). This would provide a ready answer to the inevitable interview question 'What have you been doing?'

When starting to look for work, make sure you tell your friends and acquaintances that you are in the market for work, and include your present or recent employer. Some firms encourage consultancy links with former executives, or at least are prepared to respond to a good idea. A greater number are more than happy to take on previous employees over a rush period or during the holiday season. If you are a member of a professional institute, talk to them and tell them of your availability. Many institutes keep a register of members wanting work and, encouragingly, receive a fair number of enquiries from firms seeking qualified people for projects, part-time or temporary work, interim management or sometimes even permanent employment. Any clubs to which you belong could provide useful leads, as well as any committees you sit on, or any other group with which you are involved. Often someone you know will be the perfect link between you and your next employer.

With so many vacancies being advertised online, it pays to have a CV and covering letter ready for submission straight away. Sign on to a select number of sites that will keep you posted about work opportunities. Check out where there are skills shortages and see if any of your transferable skills would help plug that gap. When applying for jobs, remember that enthusiasm counts. Keep in regular contact, by telephone, e-mail or personal visit. Sometimes being on the spot and available at the right time are the keys to success. A direct approach to likely employers is another possible option. Ask your colleagues, contacts and friends for their advice on which organizations might be interested in employing someone with your abilities. If someone you know can prepare the ground in advance by way of introduction, and act as referrer, this is far more likely to get you noticed.

The following websites may be useful:

Laterlife: **www.laterlife.com**.

Really Caring 60+ Recruitment Co: **www.applegate.co.uk**.

Redundancy Expert: **www.redundancyexpert.co.uk**.

TAEN (Experts in Age & Employment): **www.taen.org.uk**.

Wise Owls: **www.wiseowls.co.uk**.

CV writing

Regardless of whether you use contacts, advertisements or agencies – or preferably all three – a prime requirement will be to have a well-presented Curriculum Vitae. This is your personal sales document and it will be helpful if it can be e-mailed to prospective employers. It should contain:

- your name and address;
- contact numbers – land line and mobile;
- e-mail and website addresses;
- key achievements to date;
- qualifications and work experience, past employers, positions held and responsibilities;
- referees.

Your CV should be no longer than two pages of A4. It should be targeted to the job on offer, emphasizing those elements of your experience and skills that are relevant. There are plenty of websites where CV templates can be downloaded for free, with tutorials explaining the entire process. A well set out CV can make all the difference when it comes to catching an employer's interest. Older workers should concentrate on their main employment skills and employers when updating a CV. See:

CV Library: **www.cv-library.co.uk**.

Interview technique

If you have worked for the same employer for a number of years, your interview skills may be a little rusty. It is a good idea to list all the questions you expect to be asked (including those you hope won't be brought up) and then get a friend to rehearse you in your answers. In addition to questions about your previous job, have answers prepared for the following: what you have done since leaving employment; whether your health is good; why you are interested in working for this particular employer; and, given the job requirements, what you think you have of special value to offer. You may also be asked what you know about the organization, so do your research. Obvious mistakes to avoid are claiming skills or knowledge that you do not possess; giving the impression that you have a series of stock answers to problems; and criticizing your former employer. Be prepared to have an answer to the question: how much money would you expect? With the economy still struggling, you may have to strike a balance between what you would like and what is realistic in the current market. Here are some websites that have some useful advice about how to prepare for interviews.

CV Tips: **www.cvtips.com**.

Fish4Jobs: **www.fish4.co.uk**.

Job Search News: **www.job-hunt.org**.

Useful reading

Preparing the Perfect CV (5th edition), *Preparing the Perfect Job Application* (5th edition) and *Successful Interview Skills* (5th edition), all by Rebecca Corfield and published by Kogan Page; website: **www.koganpage.com**.

Part-time openings

With the job market so competitive, many part-time or temporary assignments offer the perfect way into employment that may develop into full-time work in future. With the average job now lasting between 1.8 and three years, temporary or project-based professional and executive assignments that last a specific time are becoming increasingly common. People with specialist expertise are actively sought, so it is important to be aware of the growth areas in employment. Over a fifth of all new jobs are now on a contract basis, the average being for six months or a year. Mature candidates have everything to gain here because of the greater turnover of jobs. Serial part-time or freelance work can easily develop into a full-time occupation. Many retired businesspeople take on two or three part-time jobs and then find themselves working as hard as they have ever done in their life. See:

High 50 UK: **www.high50.com**.

Over Fifties Friends: **www.overfiftiesfriends.co.uk**.

Skilled People: **www.skilledpeople.com**.

Employment ideas

Consultancy

A number of retired executives hire themselves back to their former employer in a consultancy capacity. They undertake specific projects for which they are paid a fee. This may be structured as a lump sum or, as many consultants do, they may negotiate a day rate. Consultancy, by definition, is not limited to a single client. By using your contacts judiciously plus a bit of marketing initiative, it is quite possible to build up a steady list of assignments on the basis of your particular expertise. Marketing and organizational skills are always in demand, as are knowledge of IT, website design, accountancy, HR issues and public relations experience and fundraising. Small firms are often a good bet for consultants, as they normally buy in expertise as and when it is required. Many established consultancies retain a list of reliable associates – a sort of freelance register – whom they call on, on an 'as needed' basis, to handle suitable assignments. Have a look at the following websites for suggestions:

Consulting UK: **www.consulting.co.uk**.

Institute of Consulting: **www.iconsulting.org.uk**.

Mindbench Management Consultancy: **www.mindbench.com**.

Interim management

Interim managers represent a huge growth area in recruitment over the past few years. An interim manager gives a company instant access to a 'heavyweight yet hands-on executive' with proven track record to meet its needs. Typically hired for three to nine months, interim managers help organizations undergoing major change, implement critical strategies or plug a crucial management gap. Many of the best jobs go to those who have recently taken early retirement or been made redundant. Assignments could be full time or involve just one or two days' work a week. For more information:

Aim Recruitment Ltd: **www.aiminterims.co.uk**.

Executives Online: **www.executivesonline.co.uk**.

Interim Management Association (IMA): **www.interimmanagement.uk.com**.

Interim Partners: **www.interimpartners.com**.

Openings via a company or other reference

Secondment from your current employer to another organization is something worth considering. This can be part time for a few hours a week or full time for anything from a few weeks to two years. It can also often lead to a new career. Normally only larger employers are willing to consider the idea since, as a rule, the company will continue to pay your salary and other benefits during the period of secondment. If you work for a smaller firm it could still be worth discussing the suggestion, as employers benefit from the favourable publicity the company attracts by being seen to support the local community. See:

Business in the Community: **www.bitc.org.uk**.

Whitehall & Industry Group: **www.wig.co.uk**.

Public appointments

Opportunities regularly arise for individuals to be appointed to a wide range of public bodies, such as tribunals, commissions and consumer consultative councils. Many appointments are to local and regional bodies throughout the country. Some are paid but many offer an opportunity to contribute to the community and gain valuable experience of working in the public sector on a part-time, expenses-only basis. Public appointments vacancies at local and regional levels across UK are found on **www.gov.uk/public-appointments**.

Non-executive directorships

Many retiring executives see this as the ideal solution; however, these appointments carry heavy responsibilities made more onerous by recent legislation. If you are able and committed and have the necessary experience, see these websites:

First Flight Placements: **www.ffplacements.co.uk**.

NED Exchange: **www.nedexchange.co.uk**.

Non-Executive Directors' Club: **www.non-execs.com**.

Market research

In addition to the normal consultancy openings in marketing, there is scope for those with knowledge of market research techniques. The work covers a very broad spectrum, from street or telephone interviewing to data processing, designing questionnaires, statistical analysis and sample group selection.

Market Research Society: **www.mrs.org.uk.**

National Centre for Social: **www.natcen.ac.uk.**

Paid work for charities

Although charities rely to a very large extent on voluntary workers (see Chapter 12), most charitable organizations of any size have a number of paid appointments. Other than particular specialists that some charities may require for their work, the majority of openings are for general managers or administrators, fundraisers and those with financial skills. Salaries in general are considerably below the commercial market rate. Anyone thinking of applying for a job in a charity must be in sympathy with its aims and style. Agencies specializing in charity recruitment advise that it is a good idea to work as a volunteer before seeking a paid appointment, as this will provide useful experience. The following organizations may help:

CF Appointments: **www.cfappointments.com.**

Charity JOB: **www.charityjob.co.uk.**

Charity People: **www.charitypeople.co.uk.**

Harris Hill: **www.harrishill.co.uk.**

ProspectUs: **www.prospect-us.co.uk.**

TPP Not for Profit: **www.tpp.co.uk.**

Working for a Charity: **www.wfac.org.uk.**

Sales

Almost every commercial firm in the country needs good sales staff. Many people who have never thought of sales could be excellent in the job because of their specialist knowledge in a particular field combined with their enthusiasm for the subject. There is always a demand for people to sell advertising space. Also, many firms employ demonstrators in shops or at exhibitions for special promotions. The work is usually temporary or freelance by definition, and while pay is normally good, the big drawback is that you could be standing on your feet for long periods of the day. If the idea of selling fires you with enthusiasm, there are many opportunities to tempt you.

Career Builder: **www.careerbuilder.co.uk.**

Employers Jobs: **www.employersjobs.com.**

Tourist guide/holiday reps

Tourist guide work is something that will appeal to extroverts, with stamina and a liking for people. It requires an academic mind as well, since you will need to put in some fairly concentrated study. While there are numerous possible qualifications, some are easier than others. Training for the coveted Blue Badge takes 15 months. The Blue Badge itself is no guarantee of steady work, and most tourist guides are self-employed. Opportunities are greatest in London, especially for those with fluency in one or more foreign languages. See:

Guild of Registered Tourist Guides: **www.britainsbestguides.org.**

You could sign on as a lecturer with one of the growing number of travel companies offering special interest holidays. To be eligible you need real expertise in a subject, the ability to make it interesting and have an easy manner with people. Pay is fairly minimal, although you may receive tips – plus of course the bonus of a free holiday.

Travel Job Search: **www.traveljobsearch.com.**

Travel Weekly: **www.jobs.travelweekly.co.uk.**

Other tourist work

If you live in a popular tourist or heritage area, there is a whole variety of seasonal work, including jobs in hotels, restaurants, shops and local places of interest. Depending on the locality, the list might also include jobs as deckchair attendants, play leaders for children, caravan site staff, extra coach drivers and many others.

Teaching and training skills

If you have been a teacher at any stage of your career, there are a number of part-time possibilities.

Coaching

With examinations becoming more competitive, demand has been increasing for ex-teachers with knowledge of the public examination system to coach youngsters in preparation for A and AS levels, GCSE and common entrance. Research local schools, search the internet or contact a specialist educational consultancy:

Gabbitas Education Consultants: **www.gabbitas.co.uk**.

Specialist subjects

Teachers are in demand for mathematics, physics, chemistry, technology and modern languages. People with relevant work experience and qualifications may be able to teach or give tuition in these subjects. A formal teaching qualification is required to teach in state-maintained schools. Before engaging with children, you will need a DBS check (see page 246). Retired teachers, linguists and others with specialist knowledge can earn good money from tutoring.

Further Education Jobs: **www.fejobs.com**.

Home Tutors: **www.hometutors.org.uk**.

English as a foreign language

There is an ongoing demand for people to teach English to foreign students. Opportunities are concentrated in London, but most cities that have universities offer language courses during the summer. Good English-language schools require teachers to have an initial qualification in teaching English to those who have a different first language.

British Council: **www.britishcouncil.org**.

Intensive Tefl Courses: **www.tefl.co.uk**.

Tefl Courses: **www.teflengland.co.uk**.

Working in developing countries

There are various opportunities for suitably qualified people to work in the developing countries of Africa, Asia, the Caribbean and the Pacific on a semi-voluntary basis. Skills most in demand include civil engineering, mechanical engineering, water engineering, architecture, urban, rural and regional planning, agriculture, forestry, medicine, teaching English as a foreign language, maths and physics training, and economics. All air fares, accommodation costs and insurance are usually covered by the organizing agency, and pay is limited to a 'living allowance' based on local levels. As a general rule, there is an upper age limit of 65 (VSO accepts volunteers up to 75), and you must be willing to work for a minimum of two years.

The following are the major agencies involved in this kind of work (more details are contained in Chapter 12, Voluntary work):

International Service: **www.internationalservice.org.uk**.

Progressio: **www.progressio.org.uk**.

Skillshare International: **www.skillshare.org**.

Voluntary Service Overseas (VSO): **www.vso.org.uk**.

Publishing

Publishers regularly use freelance staff with appropriate experience for proofreading, copyediting, design, typography, indexing and similar work as well as for writing specialist copy. See:

The Bookseller: **www.thebookseller.com**.

The Society for Editors and Proofreaders: **www.sfep.org.uk**.

Caring for other people

There are a number of opportunities for paid work in this field. If you are considering working with vulnerable people (young or old), you will be required to have a full Disclosure and Barring Service (DBS) check. This was formerly the Criminal Records Bureau (CRB) check. This is designed to protect those who need to rely on other people and to ensure that no one unsuitable is appointed to a position of trust who is likely to abuse it. These checks are extremely thorough and can take several weeks or even months to process. Please be patient and as accurate as possible when asked to provide information by prospective employers, charities or not-for-profit organizations. For further information about

DBS checks and why they are required, see website: **www.gov.uk** – Employing people (select the 'Recruiting and hiring' link).

Domestic work

A number of private domestic agencies specialize in finding temporary or permanent companions, housekeepers and extra-care help for elderly and disabled people or for those who are convalescent. Pay rates vary depending on which part of the country you live in and the number of hours involved.

Anchor Care: **www.anchor.org.uk**.

Consultus Care & Nursing Agency Ltd: **www.consultuscare.com**.

Country Cousins: **www.country-cousins.co.uk**.

Universal Aunts Ltd: **www.universalaunts.co.uk**.

The Lady magazine, published every Wednesday, has classified advertisements for domestic help.

Home helps and childminding

Local authorities sometimes have vacancies for home helps, to assist disabled or elderly people in their own home by giving a hand with the cleaning, light cooking and other chores. Ask your local social services department. If you already look after a grandchild during the day, you might consider caring for an additional couple of youngsters. You will need to be registered with the local social services department, which will explain all the requirements including details of any basic training – such as first aid – that you may first need to do.

Nursing

Qualified nurses are in great demand in most parts of the country and stand a good chance of finding work at their local hospital or through one of the many nursing agencies. Those with suitable experience, although not necessarily a formal nursing qualification, could apply to become a care support worker for the newly merged charity: Crossroads Care and The Princess Royal Trust for Carers have merged to form the leading carers' charity.

Carers Trust: **www.carers.org**.

Home sitting

Taking care of someone else's home while they are away on holiday or business trips is something mature, responsible people, usually non-smokers with no children or pets, can do. It is a bit like a paid holiday, depending on the responsibilities and on the size of the house or flat. Food and travelling expenses are normally also paid. It is useful to have your own car. Firms specializing in this type of work include:

Absentia: **www.home-and-pets.co.uk**.

Homesitters Ltd: **www.homesitters.co.uk**.

Rest Assured House Sitters: **www.restassuredhousesitters.co.uk**.

Universal Aunts Ltd: **www.universalaunts.co.uk**.

Cashing in on your home interests

Cooking, gardening, home decorating, dressmaking and DIY skills can all be turned into modest money-spinners.

Bed and breakfast

Tourist areas, in particular, offer scope for taking in B&B visitors. However, unless you want to make a regular business of it, it is advisable to limit the number of guests to a maximum of five. To be on the safe side, contact the local environmental health officer who will advise you of anything necessary you should do. You should also register with your local tourist information centre. See the section 'Letting rooms in your home' in Chapter 8, Your home (see also 'Paying guests or lodgers' in that chapter).

Cooking

Scope includes catering other people's dinner parties, selling home-made goodies to local shops and cooking for corporate lunches. Other than top-class culinary skills, requirements are a large deep freeze, a car (you will normally be required to do all the necessary shopping) and plenty of stamina. Notify your friends, advertise locally and set up a website.

Gardening

Small shopkeepers and florists sometimes purchase flowers or plants direct from local gardeners, in preference to going to the market. Alternatively, you might consider dried flower arrangements or herbs, for which there has been a growing demand. However, before spending any money, check around to find out what the sales possibilities are. If you are willing to tend someone else's garden, the likelihood is that you will be inundated with enquiries. Spread the word among friends and acquaintances as well as local advertising.

Dressmaking, upholstery and home decorating

If you are happy to do alterations, the chances are that you could be kept busy from dawn to dusk. Many shops are desperate for people who sew. Likewise, many individuals and families would love to know of someone who could alter clothes, as well as dress-make properly. Perhaps to a slightly lesser extent, the same goes for curtains, chair covers and other soft furnishings. Often a good move is to approach firms selling materials for the home, which might be only too glad to put work out to you. If you spread the word among neighbours that you are available, or put a card in the newsagent's window, you may be surprised at the response. Do your friends envy your ability to assemble flat-packed furniture, fix things that are broken or decorate your house? Why not start charging for DIY? You can make money from any hobby – but there's more about this in Chapter 10, Starting your own business.

Agencies and other useful organizations

Job-hunting through agencies is very much a question of luck but there is no need to be out of work for long if you are proactive. Work for the over-50s and -60s varies and if you are seeking challenging opportunities, it might be worth checking the following sites:

Executive Stand-By: **www.esbpeople.co.uk**.

Manpower UK: **www.candidate.manpower.com**.

Parity: **www.parity.net**.

Prime 50 Plus: **www.prime50plus.co.uk**.

Skilled People: **www.skilledpeople.com**.

Chapter Twelve
Voluntary work

You and your mother are always trying to help lame dogs over stiles – even if they're not lame and don't want to go.

NOEL COWARD: THE VORTEX

Did you know that one in five of the over 50s is a volunteer? This data recently released by the Office for National Statistics (ONS – **www.ons.gov.uk**) suggests that simple and cost-effective solutions provided by those who volunteer help tackle many problems. Volunteers are the often unsung heroes of their communities, but more importantly, those who do it have greater overall life satisfaction. It appears that older people benefit more from volunteering than younger ones, as it gives them a sense of purpose. The WRVS Chief Executive, David McCullough, was quoted in 2013 as saying: 'We know through our own research that older volunteers live happier and healthier lives and we see this every day. Over half of our volunteers are in this age group, with some still volunteering into their 90s and over the age of 100. However with an ageing population, this country needs more people to step up and volunteer to make life better for others. So we would encourage anyone thinking of volunteering to take the plunge and get involved!' (**www.maturetimes.co.uk**). How's that for a challenge?

A shining example for trying new things is 91-year-old, Margaret Leigh-Jones. This amazing lady hit the headlines last year when she began presenting at Hampshire nostalgia radio station, Angel FM, which made her possibly Britain's oldest DJ. The Havant-based great-grandmother began by answering the phones at the not-for-profit station, but was soon persuaded to take up a role co-hosting a two-hour show and this, she said, changed her life. For her the key to staying young is keeping active – she still cycles every day (**www.bbc.co.uk/news/magazine-22602801**).

So if you are under 100, and interested in volunteering, why not give it a go? The local WRVS centre might be a good first point of contact.

They can give advice on where the kind of help and assistance you can offer would best be placed. So much real value is given to communities by older people who have lived, experienced pain and survived the highs and lows of life. One way to define volunteering is to distinguish 'involvement' from 'commitment' and consider the difference between a chicken and a pig. While the chicken is involved in the production of an egg, the pig is committed to the making of bacon. And so with volunteers. While you were working and being paid a salary you were doubtless involved in your work. But once you begin volunteering you will join the army of people who are committed to the work they do to help others.

Should you require facts and figures in support of the value of volunteering, did you know that older people provide a range of formal and informal volunteering services worth over £10 billion per annum to the national economy? The value of this volunteering effort can be expected to grow to just under £15 billion by 2020. This report (*Golden Age Pensioners* published by the WRVS in 2011) also revealed the fact that pensioners' net contribution to the UK economy is between £30 billion and £40 billion a year because they pay tax, spend money that creates jobs, deliver billions of pounds of free care to others and contribute to charities and volunteering.

Top tips: Motivators if you are thinking of volunteering

- wanting to 'make a difference' to other people's lives;

- enjoying using your skills in new and valuable ways;

- feeling better both physically and mentally;

- supporting local activities and neighbourhood organizations;

- being a committed member of social and charitable projects;

- actively participating in democratic institutions – such as parish/community councils, boards of school governors, Neighbourhood Watch;

- finding opportunities to help in education, sport, culture, leisure, conservation and the environment.

It is vital we celebrate and maximize the contributions of older people. Someone who is starting to volunteer at the age of 60 or just over, could have 20 years or more of positive contribution to make. So if this appeals to you, why not give it some thought? Here are some suggestions as to what you might do.

Types of work

Clerical

Any active group is likely to need basic administrative help, from typing and stuffing envelopes to answering the telephone and organizing committees. This may involve a day or so a week or occasional assistance at peak times. Many smaller charities in particular would also greatly welcome hearing from individuals with IT expertise to assist with setting up databases and websites.

Fundraising

Every voluntary organization needs money, and when donations are static or falling, more creativity and ingenuity are required to help bring in funds. Events are many and varied, but anyone with energy and experience of organizing fundraising events would be welcomed with open arms as a volunteer.

Committee work

This can cover anything from very occasional help to a virtually full-time commitment as branch treasurer or secretary. People with business skills or financial or legal backgrounds are likely to be especially valuable, and those whose skills include minute-taking are always in demand.

Direct work

Driving, delivering 'meals on wheels', counselling, visiting the housebound, working in a charity shop, helping with a playgroup, respite care for carers: the list is endless and the value of the work incalculable. While certain qualifications and experience have particular value in some circumstances, there are many interesting and useful jobs for those without special training. As regards time commitment, do what you feel comfortable with. Whether one morning a month or a certain number of hours per week, it is far better to be reliable than to over-promise and have to cancel or let people down. Equally, as with a paid job, before you start you should be absolutely clear about all the terms and conditions:

- What sort of work is involved?
- Who will be working with you?
- What is expected?
- When will you be needed?
- Are expenses paid? What for? How much?

Once you have all this mapped out you will find that voluntary work is not only rewarding in its own right but also allows you to make a real contribution to the community.

Should you consider working with vulnerable people (young or old) you will need to have a full DBS (formerly CRB) check. This was covered in Chapter 11, Looking for paid work, and applies to many jobs these days, both paid and unpaid. For further information about this see the government website: **www.gov.uk** – Employing people (select the 'Recruiting and hiring' link).

Choosing the right voluntary work

Once you've decided that you might take on some volunteering, next you will need to find out where the opportunities are in your local area and what particular outlet would suit your talents. You may have friends or neighbours who are already involved in volunteering locally. Asking their advice would be a start, as they may well have some good suggestions or know which organizations are in need of extra pairs of hands. However, if you don't know where to start, the organizations listed here are arranged in broad categories of interest. As there are literally thousands of voluntary groups, national and local, that need help in some way or other, it is impossible to include them all or describe all their activities and volunteering opportunities. For a full list of charities, you could search **www.charitychoice.co.uk**. The following websites are general national volunteering organizations and can act as signposts to help you learn more about them and how you can get involved.

National Council for Voluntary Organisations (NCVO):
    www.ncvo-vol.org.uk.

REACH: **www.reachskills.org.uk**.

Volunteer Development Scotland: **www.vds.org.uk**.

Volunteering England: **www.volunteering.org.uk**.

Wales Council for Voluntary Action: **www.wcva.org.uk**.

General

The scope of the work of the following well-known charities is so broad that they almost justify a category to themselves:

British Red Cross: **www.redcross.org.uk**.

Citizens Advice Bureau: **www.citizensadvice.org.uk**.

Community Service Volunteers (CSV): **www.csv.org.uk**.

Lions Clubs International: **www.lionsmd105.org**.

Toc H: **www.toch-uk.org.uk**.

WRVS: **www.wrvs.org.uk**.

Animals

Animal charities exist to protect animals from harm. Some are dedicated to stopping animal cruelty and others provide care for animals that have been neglected or mistreated. Animal conservation charities work hard to save endangered animals from extinction, for example by protecting their natural habitat, or putting a stop to animal poaching and illegal trade. Some animal charities have sanctuaries or wildlife parks where they rehabilitate rescued animals for release back into the wild. There are over 20 animal charities in the UK, all of whom require volunteers, so you can choose the type of animal you want to help. Some suggested websites:

Blue Cross: **www.bluecross.org.uk**.

Cats Protection: **www.cats.org.uk**.

Cinnamon Trust: **www.cinnamon.org.uk**.

Dogs Trust: **www.dogstrust.org.uk**.

PDSA: **www.pdsa.org.uk**.

Pet Fostering Service Scotland: **www.pfss.org.uk**.

Pets As Therapy (PAT): **www.petsastherapy.org**.

RSPCA: **www.rspca.org.uk**.

Royal Society for the Protection of Birds (RSPB): **www.rspb.org.uk**.

World Society for the Protection of Animals (WSPA):
　www.wspa.org.uk.

Wildfowl & Wetlands Trust (WWT): **www.wwt.org.uk**.

Bereavement

There are a number of bereavement charities in the UK. To find specific charities, you could search **www.charitychoice.co.uk**, where you'll find such organizations as dedicated child bereavement charities and grief counselling organizations. Here are some suggestions:

Bereavement Counselling Charity: **www.bereavementcharity.org.uk**.

Cruse Bereavement Care: **www.cruse.org.uk**.

Winston's Wish: **www.winstonswish.org.uk**.

Children and young people

If helping children and young people is close to your heart, there are many UK-based charities involved with children and youths. By volunteering your time and skills, you can make a huge difference. The work done by this section of charities ranges from research, health and social care, disability, education, child protection, overseas aid to holidays and recreation. To see which ones exist, you could search **www.charitychoice.co.uk**. Here are just a few of them:

Action for Sick Children: **www.actionforsickchildren.org**.

Barnardo's: **www.barnardos.org.uk**.

Beanstalk (formerly Volunteer Reading Help):
　www.beanstalkcharity.org.uk.

Children's Society: **www.childrenssociety.org.uk**.

Children's Trust Tadworth: **www.thechildrenstrust.org.uk**.

NSPCC: **www.nspcc.org.uk**.

Save the Children: **www.savethechildren.org**.

Scout Association: **www.scouts.org.uk**.

Sea Cadet Corps: **www.ms-sc.org**.

Conservation

Should you be interested in promoting urban or rural conservation, there are several UK-based organizations listed concerned with the general issue of conservation. Others look at specific areas like urban conservation, architectural conservation or rural development. For a list of charities in this sector, see **www.charitychoice.co.uk**. Here are some for starters:

Architectural Heritage Society of Scotland: **www.ahss.org.uk**.

Campaign to Protect Rural England (CPRE): **www.cpre.org.uk**.

Friends of the Earth: **www.foe.co.uk**.

Greenpeace: **www.greenpeace.org.uk**.

Ramblers: **www.ramblers.org.uk**.

The Conservation Volunteers (TCV): **www.tcv.org.uk**.

The elderly

Are you interested in helping the elderly? The following charities cover assisted living, elderly care and welfare, independent living and will be happy to accept your assistance. If you want to help the aged by volunteering your time, search **www.charitychoice.co.uk**, or begin your research here:

Abbeyfield: **www.abbeyfield.com**.

Age UK: **www.ageuk.org.uk**.

Carers Trust: **www.carers.org**.

Carers UK: **www.carersuk.org**.

Contact the Elderly: **www.contact-the-elderly.org.uk**.

Independent Age: **www.independentage.org.uk**.

The family

There are a number of UK-based family support charities, each having a particular area of work. Perhaps there's an adoption and fostering, poverty charity, domestic violence charity or group offering financial support for families you'd like to find out more about. Search for charities in this sector on **www.charitychoice.co.uk**, or start with these websites:

British Association for Adoption & Fostering: **www.baaf.org.uk**.

Family Action: **www.family-action.org.uk**.

Marriage Care: **www.marriagecare.org.uk**.

Relate: **www.relate.org.uk**.

Shelter: **www.relate.org.uk**.

Standing Together Against Domestic Violence: **www.standingtogether.org.uk**.

Health and disability

If you are interested in health and wellbeing, there are many UK-based health charities. Is your interest in organizations supporting people with particular conditions – for example, obesity, heart disease, mental health or cancer charities? Or are you keen to support charities for disabled people? There are charities concerned with specific conditions, such as cerebral palsy or multiple sclerosis, and those providing care for the disabled. Whether you are looking for a specific charity, or wish to volunteer, search **www.charitychoice.co.uk**, or have a look at these websites:

Attend: **www.attend.org.uk**.

BackCare: **www.backcare.org.uk**.

British Deaf Association: **www.bda.org.uk**.

British Heart Foundation (BHF): **www.bhf.org.uk**.

Cancer Research UK: **www.cancerresearchuk.org**.

Diabetes UK: **www.diabetes.org.uk**.

Guide Dogs: **www.guidedogs.org.uk**.

Leonard Cheshire Disability: **www.lcdisability.org**.

Marie Curie Cancer Research: **www.mariecurie.org.uk**.

Mind (The National Association for Mental Health): **www.mind.org.uk**.

Parkinsons UK: **www.parkinsons.org.uk**.

RDA (Riding for the Disabled Association): **www.rda.org.uk**.

Royal National Institute of Blind People (RNIB): **www.rnib.org.uk**.

St John Ambulance: **www.sja.org.uk**.

Scope: **www.scope.org.uk**.

Thrive: **www.thrive.org.uk**.

Heritage and the arts

There are numerous opportunities if you wish to volunteer in the culture and heritage charity sector. Whether your interest is historic or new, there are many categories among the UK-based arts charities and national heritage organizations. Further information on charities in this sector can be found on **www.charitychoice.co.uk**, or have a look at these websites:

Ancient Monuments Society: **www.ancientmonumentssociety.org.uk**.

Architectural Heritage Fund: **www.ahfund.org.uk**.

Archaeology for All: **www.newarchaeologyuk.org**.

English Heritage: **www.english-heritage.org.uk**.

National Trust: **www.nationaltrust.org.uk**.

SPAB (Society for the Protection of Ancient Buildings): **www.spab.org.uk**.

The needy

There are many social welfare charities, all of whom will be delighted to receive your help. Whether you wish to volunteer with refugee charities, addiction charities or poverty charities, you can easily find the social welfare charity of greatest interest to you by searching on **www.charitychoice.co.uk**, or starting with these websites:

Alexandra Rose Charities: **www.alexandrarose.org.uk**.

Elizabeth Finn Care: **www.elizabethfinncare.org.uk**.

Oxfam: **www.oxfam.org.uk**.

Salvation Army: **www.salvationarmy.org.uk**.

Samaritans: **www.samaritans.org**.

Shelter: **www.shelter.org.uk**.

Offenders and the victims of crime

If you are interested in helping ex-offenders' rehabilitation and victim support, a number of charities in this sector can be found by searching on **www.charitychoice.co.uk**, or start here with these websites:

Nacro: **www.nacro.org.uk**.

New Bridge Foundation: **www.newbridgefoundation.org.uk**.

Supporting Others through Volunteer Action (SOVA):
   www.sova.org.uk.

Victim Support: **www.victimsupport.org.uk**.

Politics

You may not immediately think of political parties in the context of voluntary work, but all of them use vast numbers of volunteer helpers. Between elections the help is mostly required with fundraising, committee work and staffing the constituency offices. At election time, activity is obviously intense. See the major parties' websites for details:

Conservative Party: **www.conservatives.com**.

Green Party: **www.greenparty.org.uk**.

Labour Party: **www.labour.org.uk**.

Liberal Democrats: **www.libdems.org.uk**.

Plaid Cymru: **www.plaidcymru.org**.

Scottish National Party: **www.snp.org**.

Social Democratic and Labour Party (SDLP): **www.sdlp.ie**.

UKIP: **www.ukip.org.uk**.

Ulster Unionist Party: **www.uup.org**.

Service personnel and veterans

Want to support armed and ex-services charities? Whatever your interest, you'll find loads of UK-registered organizations offering support for soldiers, sailors and airmen and women in this sector on **www.charitychoice.co.uk**, or you could start with the following:

ABF The Soldiers' Charity: **www.soldierscharity.org**.

Blind Veterans UK: **www.blindveterans.org.uk**.

Combat Stress: **www.combatstress.org.uk**.

Help for Heroes: **www.helpforheroes.org.uk**.

Royal Air Force Benevolent Fund: **www.rbf.org**.

Royal Alfred Seafarers' Society: **www.royalalfredseafarers.com**.

Royal British Legion: **www.britishlegion.org.uk**.

SSAFA: **www.ssafa.org.uk**.

Work after work

Would you like to support organizations that are associated with commerce, trades and the professions? Or do you wish to get involved with employment charities, professional associations or groups concerned with apprenticeships? Search on **www.charitysearch.co.uk** to view the whole sector, or see below:

British Chambers of Commerce: **www.britishchambers.org.uk**.

National Federation of Enterprise Agencies: **www.nfea.com**.

Scottish Business in the Community: **www.sbcscot.com**.

Long-term volunteering

If you are thinking of a long-term, probably residential commitment there are a number of organizations both in the UK and abroad in need of voluntary help for a wide variety of projects. Some require specialist skills, such as engineering or medicine; others essentially need people with practical qualities, common sense and enthusiasm. Each organization has a minimum period of service. General conditions are similar for all of them; travel is paid, plus a living allowance or salary that is based on local levels rather than on expatriate rates. Couples without dependent children are welcome, as long as both have the necessary skills. National Insurance Contributions are provided, and a resettlement grant is paid on completion of the tour.

Overseas

There are four main organizations for overseas volunteering: Voluntary Service Overseas (VSO), Skillshare International, Progressio and International Service, details of which have already been provided in Chapter 11 (Looking for paid work: 'Working in developing countries').

Volunteering abroad for the over-50s is often referred to as 'golden gapping'. It is gaining popularity among many 50- to 75-year-olds. Thousands of mature people have enjoyed gap years recently and the number is growing. If a life-changing experience and doing some voluntary work abroad before or just after you retire appeal to you, **Gap Year Advice For All** should be able to help; see website: **www.gapadvice.org**. (This is further described in Chapter 14, Holidays.)

In the UK

Although the organizations in this section are primarily concerned with schemes requiring volunteer help for between two weeks and six months, they would also welcome shorter-term help.

Sue Ryder Care: **www.sueryder.org**.

Vitalise: **www.vitalise.org.uk**.

Chapter Thirteen
Health

> *The only way to keep your health is to eat what you don't want, drink what you don't like, and do what you'd rather not.*

MARK TWAIN

When filling in forms these days, have you noticed where you are invited to place a cross in the box that corresponds with your age, this is edging closer to the highest figures? Does this worry you? Is it galling to be bracketed as old? If you want to check how you rate, here's Raymond Brigg's 'Notes from the Sofa', which appeared in *The Oldie* (February 2013):

TEN CHARACTERISTICS OF OLD AGE:

1   Rigid in adhering to routines of daily life? *Can't answer that now – four minutes past five! Late for tea.*

2   Are your thoughts tinged with pessimism? *Don't know about 'tinged'...*

3   Difficulties with decision making? *Not sure whether to answer that or not...*

4   Unable to think of, or do, two things at once? *I thought I had a cup of tea somewhere... I did make it, didn't I?*

5   Blunting of feeling? Apathy, Indifference? *Who cares about the tea? Who cares the world is getting hotter? I'll be gone soon...*

6   Resistant to change? *Who wants change? Things can only get worse.*

7   Lack of spontaneity? *Yes, thank goodness. Lack of spontaneity has kept me out of all sorts of trouble.*

8   Greater caution? *Definitely. It's being cautious that stops that life-threatening spontaneity.*

9   Increased anxiety? *He who is not anxious has no imagination.*

10 Distrust of the unfamiliar? *Well, of course. You don't know where they've been.*

Whether or not you concur with the responses to these questions, it is never too late to do the best you can to stay healthy and fit during retirement. The choices you make about how well you are going to age don't just involve diet and exercise. Mind, emotions and sleep also play a big part. Learning simple healthy ageing secrets can add years to your life. You don't have to move to Okinawa in Japan, Sardinia or the Greek Island of Ikaria – though if you do happen to live in one of these places you are likely to live to beyond 100. According to Ikarians, you shouldn't eat processed food, smoke, get stressed or worry about death. Research has shown that a good healthy diet, sensible exercise, afternoon naps, frequent socializing with friends and family and drinking moderate amounts of wine are key. Although we are all likely to get ill at some stage, maintaining a good quality of life helps ward off diseases for a number of years.

So, if you are approaching retirement, or are in your early 60s, now's the time to assess your lifestyle strategy should you have one. Exercise is most important if you are to keep healthy, whatever age you are. You can exercise anywhere and there are a number of ways to keep fit even without realizing you are doing it: by walking, gardening and housework. It makes sense for all of us over-55s to look after ourselves and not take our health for granted.

Keep fit

There are limitless opportunities to take up every type of keep fit activity at any age, but it is particularly important for older people, including those with disabilities. Information on where you can find classes in your area is available online, in your local newspaper or library. The following organizations may also be able to help you:

Extend: **www.extend.org.uk**.

Fitness League: **www.thefitnessleague.com**.

Keep Fit Association: **www.keepfit.org.uk**.

Medau Movement: **www.medau.org.uk**.

Pilates

Pilates is an invigorating form of exercise for your mind and body that can improve your strength, flexibility and overall mobility. It helps restore your body to balance; as a result your posture will change and you will move more efficiently.

Pilates Foundation: **www.pilatesfoundation.com**.

Yoga

Yoga is popular with all ages and is a means of improving fitness and helping relaxation. Classes are available nationwide and there are a number of specialist organizations:

British Wheel of Yoga: **www.bwy.org.uk**.

Iyengar Yoga Institute: **www.iyi.org.uk**.

Yoga for Health and Education Trust (YHET):
    www.yoga-health-education.org.uk.

Yoga Village UK: **www.yogauk.com**.

Sensible eating

Most of us over-55s are aware of healthy eating guidelines, but often fail to put our knowledge into practice. A survey by the **Food Standards Agency** (FSA) found that almost a quarter of people in this age group agreed strongly with the statement that 'life's too short to worry about what I eat'.

And more than a third concurred wholeheartedly with the sentiment, 'I've always eaten this way and it's done me no harm.' The survey results were published at the same time as the FSA's new leaflet *The Good Life*, which gives practical advice to help the over-50s improve their diets and ward off heart disease, cancer and osteoporosis. To read, order or download a copy, see **www.food.gov.uk**; or **www.eatwell.gov.uk**.

Should you be considering a change in diet or eating habits, sometimes kick-starting your new regime is the way forward. Whether you get a health check from your GP, take out a subscription to a health magazine, join a slimming club or book a short stay at a spa, whatever you choose should help you towards a healthier lifestyle. One organization, whose balanced approach to weight loss, whatever your age, emphasizes the importance of making small, lifetime changes that can be maintained for the long term is Weight Watchers: **www.weightwatchers. co.uk**.

Keeping healthy in the heat

Despite prolonged winters and cold weather, the older we get the more conscious we should be of the effects of the sun (when it eventually starts shining). The NHS warns that anyone over the age of 65 is in the 'high-risk' category for heat-related illness. Too much sun or getting overheated can induce sunstroke and dehydration, while also exacerbating existing health problems, such as heart disease and high blood pressure. These guidelines should help you keep your cool:

- *Stay hydrated*. Dehydration is dangerous. The hotter months are definitely the time you should take in at least six to eight glasses of fluids a day. Keep a bottle of water with you, especially when on the road, as caffeine and alcohol actually dehydrate you.

- *Wear sunscreen*. The older we get the more susceptible to certain types of skin cancer we are. Find the right sunscreen for you and top up regularly for the best protection.

- *Protect your eyes*. Protecting eyes from the brightness and UV rays of the sun will promote better eyesight and prevent cataracts. Another useful item is a wide-brimmed hat that will shade your eyes while also protecting your ears, nose and head from sunburn.

- *Lower your temperature*. If you're feeling too hot, taking a cool shower is an effective way of maintaining a safe temperature. If you feel discomfort from the heat, aim to spend the warmest parts of the day in the shade or in air-conditioned areas.

- *Be prepared*. Keep a sunhat in the car, spare water bottles in your fridge and stock up on sunscreen. Our weather is unpredictable, and whether you are a sun worshipper or prefer the shade, it's best not to get caught out.

Food safety

Food poisoning can happen at any age but older people are more at risk because of associated health complications. Medication such as antibiotics taken by elderly people also increases the risk of food poisoning. People who have long-term chronic illnesses and health problems are also more susceptible. There are a few ways that food poisoning can occur; one of the most common is by consuming food that is past its use-by date. Elderly people who are afflicted by food poisoning will suffer much more severe symptoms than younger people. Dehydration can become a serious factor and can lead to decreased blood pressure. There are a number of precautions that should be taken to reduce the risk of food poisoning. These include:

- Not eating food products that are past their sell-by or use-by dates.
- Make sure food is stored in refrigerators set at the right temperature.
- Follow cooking instructions carefully.
- Do not eat raw or undercooked meat products or eggs.
- Wash hands and work surfaces that have been used to prepare meat, seafood and eggs.
- Always wash raw vegetables thoroughly, especially vegetables that are not going to be cooked.
- Ensure that frozen foods are completely thawed before cooking and never refreeze thawed foods.
- Never eat undercooked foods in restaurants. Always send undercooked food back to be cooked completely.
- Have two chopping boards: one for meat and one for everything else.
- Cover the food in your fridge with shrink-wrap; this includes leftovers.
- Never keep cooked and uncooked food together, as they can contaminate each other.
- Keep all parts of your kitchen clean.

● Do not reheat food more than once and don't keep cooked food longer than two days.

Drink

Retirement is no reason for giving up pleasures. In moderate quantities alcohol can be an effective nightcap and can also help to stimulate a sluggish appetite. However, bear in mind that alcoholism is the third greatest killer after heart disease and cancer. Whereas most people are sensible and can control the habit themselves, others may need help. The family doctor will be the first person to check with for medical advice. But additionally, for those who need moral support, the following self-help groups may be the answer:

Al-Anon Family Groups UK & Eire: **www.al-anonuk.org.uk**.

Alcohol Concern: **www.alcoholconcern.org.uk**.

Alcoholics Anonymous: **www.alcoholics-anonymous.org.uk**.

Smoking

If you are a smoker and would like to cut down or give up altogether, apart from willpower, the ban on smoking in restaurants, bars and pubs and other designated areas should have an impact. Any age is a good time to stop smoking, since smokers are 20 times more likely to contract lung cancer. They are also at more serious risk of suffering from heart disease, chronic bronchitis and other ailments. Dozens of organizations concerned with health have information on giving up smoking. The following are helpful:

NCSCT (National Centre for Smoking Cessation and Training): **www.ncsct.co.uk**.

Quit: **www.quit.org.uk**.

Smokefree: **www.smokefree.nhs.uk**.

Smokeline (Scotland only): **www.canstopsmoking.com**.

Stop Smoking UK: **www.stopsmokinguk.org**.

Accident prevention

One of the most common causes of mishap is an accident in the home. In particular this is due to falling and incidents involving faulty electrical wiring. The vast majority of these could be avoided by taking normal common-sense precautions, such as repairing or replacing worn carpets and installing better lighting near staircases. For a list of practical suggestions, see 'Safety in the home', in Chapter 8, Your home. **ROSPA** (Royal Society for the Prevention of Accidents) has some excellent advice on this subject: see **www.rospa.com/home safety**.

If you are unlucky enough to be injured in an accident, whether in the street or elsewhere, the Law Society offers a free service called the Accident Line to help you decide whether you can make a claim. You will be entitled to a free consultation with a local solicitor specializing in personal injury claims:

Accident Line: **www.accidentlinedirect.co.uk**.

National Accident Helpline: **www.national-accident-helpline.co.uk**.

Aches, pains and other abnormalities

Age itself has nothing to do with the vast majority of ailments. Many people ignore the warning signs when something is wrong, yet treatment when a condition is still in its infancy can often cure it altogether, or at least help to delay its advance. The following should always be investigated by a doctor:

- any pain that lasts more than a few days;
- lumps, however small;
- dizziness or fainting;
- chest pains, shortness of breath or palpitations;
- persistent cough or hoarseness;
- unusual bleeding from anywhere;
- unnatural tiredness or headaches;
- frequent indigestion;
- unexplained weight loss.

Health insurance

In a recent survey of 1,000 UK adults commissioned by Private Medical Insurance provider CS Healthcare, almost a fifth of over-55s are saving for medical provision, despite being one of the groups hit hardest by the recession. However, nearly 60 per cent admitted they were confused when buying health insurance cover due to the number and variety of health insurance products on offer. A fifth said they became so confused by the entire process they found it impossible to compare like for like. PMI can be a low cost route to peace of mind when it comes to medical treatment, but policy holders often get a nasty shock when they reach retirement age, when their premiums start to rocket – just at the point when their income has reduced. However, switching to a cheaper scheme gets more difficult as we get older. Pre-existing medical conditions, including associated complaints, will normally be excluded when you take out a new policy.

The NHS has, generally, an excellent record in dealing with urgent conditions and accidents. However, it sometimes has a lengthy waiting list for the less urgent and more routine operations. By using health insurance to pay for private medical care you will probably get faster treatment, as well as greater comfort and privacy in hospital. Here are some organizations that provide cover:

AXA PPP Healthcare: **www.axappphealthcare.co.uk**.

BUPA: **www.bupa.co.uk**.

Exeter Family Friendly Society: **www.exeterfamily.co.uk**.

Saga Services Ltd: **www.saga.co.uk**.

SimplyHealth: **www.simplyhealth.co.uk**.

Help with choosing a scheme

With so many plans on the market, selecting the one that best suits your needs can be quite a problem. An Independent Financial Adviser (IFA) or specialist insurance broker could advise you.

Association of Medical Insurance Intermediaries (AMII):
www.amii.org.uk.

Medibroker: **www.medibroker.co.uk**.

The Private Health Partnership: **www.php.co.uk**.

Private patients – without insurance cover

If you do not have private medical insurance but want to go into hospital in the UK as a private patient, there is nothing to stop you, provided your doctor is willing and you are able to pay the bills. The choice if you opt for self-pay lies between the private wings of NHS hospitals or hospitals run by charitable or non-profit-making organizations, such as:

BMI Healthcare: **www.bmihealthcare.co.uk**.

Nuffield Health: **www.nuffieldhealth.com**.

Medical tourism

A Medical Tourist is a person who travels abroad for specific medical treatment or alternative therapy to restore their health and at the same time experience local culture. This is often heralded as a new industry, but in fact is nothing of the kind, dating back to the ancient Greeks, who travelled to Epidauria for healing. It became popular in England in the 18th century when the spa towns sprang up, and people travelled across the country in search of healing mineral waters. The majority of people in the UK who choose medical tourism go abroad for dental treatment and cosmetic surgery. The avoidance of waiting times is the leading factor for doing so. More than 75,000 people last year sought faster or cheaper alternatives elsewhere. You can save over 50 per cent on the fees that you would pay for private treatment in the UK. Within the EU some treatments are available on the NHS, as long as you can prove that you are facing 'undue delay'. To find out more, here are a few websites:

Health Tourism Show: **www.healthtourismshow.com**.

Medical Tourist Company: **www.themedicaltouristcompany.com**.

Travel Health.Co.Uk: **www.travelhealth.co.uk**.

Treatment Abroad: **www.treatmentabroad.com**.

Long-term care insurance (LTCI)

Long-term care insurance covers the care and support you may need in later life due to frailty or disability. This care helps you carry out normal daily activities which you may have difficulty with such as helping you get out of bed, get dressed or go shopping. The government does provide some state support to help you with the costs of long-term care. However, this support is means-tested and you will be assessed on what personal savings, property and other assets you may own. Once this assessment is done, you will be told whether or not you qualify for state support. If you don't qualify for state support, the insurance industry offers a range of financial products and solutions to help you pay for your long-term care costs. You should discuss your options with a qualified adviser to get more information. A useful booklet *A Brief Guide to Long Term Care Insurance, Choosing the right option for you* is available from **Association of British Insurers (ABI): www.abi.org.uk**.

A possible alternative to a conventional long-term care policy is *critical illness insurance*, which pays a lump sum if you are unfortunate enough to suffer from cancer or have a stroke. Another option that has been growing in popularity is to buy a *care fee annuity* as and when the need arises. An advantage is that you buy a care plan only at the time it would actually be useful. If contemplating this option, it is wise to ask your IFA to recommend what would be your best choice. All LTCI products and services now come under the compulsory jurisdiction of the Financial Ombudsman Service and the Financial Services Compensation Scheme. If you choose to seek the advice of an IFA, refer to Chapter 6, Financial advisers, where there is more information.

Hospital care cash plans

These are inexpensive insurance policies that provide cover for everyday health-care costs. Claims are made after the customer has paid for the treatment and are reimbursed within a week. See **British Health Care Association: www.bhca.org.uk**.

Permanent health insurance (PHI)

PHI should not be confused with other types of health insurance. It is a replacement-of-earnings policy for people who are still in work and who, because of illness, are unable to continue with their normal occupation for a prolonged period and in consequence suffer loss of earnings. While highly recommended for the self-employed, many employees have some protection under an employer's policy. Either way, if you are close to retirement, PHI is unlikely to feature on your priority list.

Health screening

Health screening is a wise precaution. Most provident associations offer a diagnostic screening service to check general health and to provide advice on diet, drinking and smoking if these are problem areas. Screening services normally recommend a check-up every two years, and centres are usually available to members of insurance schemes and others alike.

BMI Healthcare: **www.bmihealthcare.co.uk**.

BUPA: **www.bupa.co.uk**.

National Health Service: **www.nhs.uk**.

National Health Service

Choosing a GP

If you move to a new area, the best way to choose your new GP is to ask for a recommendation. Otherwise your local primary care trust or strategic health authority can assist, or you can search the NHS website: **www.nhs.uk**.

Points you may want to consider are: how close the doctor is to your home; whether there is an appointments system; and whether it is a group practice and, if so, how this is organized. All GPs must have practice leaflets, available at their premises, with details about their service. Having selected a doctor, you should take your medical card to the receptionist to have your name registered. This is not automatic as there is a limit to the number of patients any one doctor can accept. Also, some doctors prefer to meet potential patients before accepting them on their list. If you do not have a medical card, you will need to fill in a simple form.

Changing your GP

If you want to change your GP, you go about it in exactly the same way. If you know of a doctor whose list you would like to be on, you can simply turn up at his or her surgery and ask to be registered; or you can ask your local primary care trust, or health board in Scotland, to give you a copy of its directory before making a choice. You do not need to give a reason for wanting to change, and you do not need to ask anyone's permission.

NHS Direct

If you need medical advice when you are on holiday or at some other time when it may not be possible to contact your doctor, NHS Direct offers a 24-hour free health advice service, staffed by trained nurses. See website: **www.nhsdirect.nhs.uk**.

An alternative to dialling 999

Last year trials of a three-digit telephone number for those needing non-emergency medical care were launched in North East England.

NHS County Durham and Darlington Primary Care Trusts piloted the free 111 number, to act as an alternative to 999, followed by Nottingham, Lincolnshire and Luton. This government service has not initially replaced NHS Direct, but may do so in the longer term if successful. If so, it will be available nationwide: **www.nhs.uk/NHSEngland/ AboutNHSservices/Emergencyandurgentcareservices/Pages/NHS-111. aspx**.

People calling 111 will be able to get health advice and also information about local services such as out-of-hours GPs, walk-in centres, emergency dentists and 24-hour pharmacies. It is hoped it will take the pressure off 999 calls, amid estimates suggesting that up to half of these calls do not need an emergency response. But anyone calling the number with an emergency will have an ambulance despatched without the need for the call to be transferred.

Help with NHS costs

If you or your partner are in receipt of Income Support, income-based Jobseeker's Allowance or the Pension Credit Guarantee Credit, you are both entitled to help with NHS costs. For full information and advice see NHS Choices: **www.nhs.uk/NHSE England/healthcosts**.

If you live in Scotland, see: **www.scotland.gov.uk/healthcosts**.

Prescriptions

Both men and women aged 60 and over are entitled to free NHS prescriptions. Certain other groups are also entitled to free prescriptions, including those on low income. If you are not sure if you qualify, you should pay for your prescription and ask the pharmacist for an NHS receipt form FP57, which tells you how to claim a refund. For further information, see leaflet HC11, 'Help with health costs', obtainable from some pharmacies and GP surgeries.

People who do not qualify but who require a lot of prescriptions could save money by purchasing a prescription prepayment certificate. A prepayment certificate will work out cheaper if you are likely to need more than four prescription items in three months, or more than 14 items in 12 months, as there is no further charge regardless of how many prescription items you require. See website: **www.nhsbsa.nhs.uk** or, if you live in Scotland, **www.scotland.gov.uk/healthcosts**.

Going into hospital

Many patients are unaware that they can ask their GP to refer them to a consultant at a different NHS trust or even, in certain cases, help make arrangements for them to be treated overseas. Before you can become a patient at another hospital, your GP will need to agree to your being referred. Those likely to need help on leaving hospital should speak to the hospital social worker, who will help make any necessary arrangements. Help is sometimes available to assist patients with their travel costs to and from hospital.

If you go into hospital you will continue to receive your pension as normal. Your pension – as well as Employment and Support Allowance, Severe Disablement Allowance, Income Support and Pension Credit Guarantee Credit – will continue to be paid in full, without any reductions, for the duration of your stay. For further information, see leaflet GL12, 'Going into hospital?', obtainable from your GP, social security or Jobcentre Plus offices and NHS hospitals.

Complaints

If you wish to make a complaint about an NHS organization, you should contact them directly first. If you're not sure where to start or how to get in touch with an NHS body or independent regulator, here are some suggestions. The first stage is known as *local resolution*. If you are not satisfied with this, you can ask the NHS trust or strategic health authority for an *independent review*. The complaints manager will be able to tell you whom to contact about arranging this. If you are still dissatisfied after the independent review, then the Health Service Ombudsman (formerly known as the Health Service Commissioner) may be able to help.

NHS Choices: **www.nhs.uk/choiceintheNHS/Rightsandpledges/ complaints**.

Parliamentary and Health Service Ombudsman for England: **www.ombudsman.org.uk**.

Public Services Ombudsman for Wales: **www.ombudsman-wales.org.uk**.

Scottish Public Services Ombudsman: **www.spso.org.uk**.

An alternative approach is to contact the independent advice centre that offers guidance to patients in the event of a problem with the health service:

Patients Association: **www.patients-association.com**.

Complementary and alternative medicine

Complementary and alternative medicine (CAM) includes a group of diverse medical and health-care systems, practices, and products that are not generally considered part of conventional medicine. Complementary medicine is generally regarded as a complementary treatment that is used alongside conventional medicine, whereas alternative medicine is regarded as a treatment used in place of conventional medicine. Here are some of the better known organizations:

British Acupuncture Council (BacC): **www.acupuncture.org.uk**.

British Chiropractic Association: **www.chiropractic-uk.co.uk**.

British Homeopathic Association: **www.trusthomeopathy.org**.

British Hypnotherapy Association: **www.hypnotherapy-association.org**.

General Osteopathic Council: **www.osteopathy.org.uk**.

International Nature Cure Society: **www.naturecuresociety.org**.

National Institute of Medical Herbalists: **www.nimh.org.uk**.

Eyes

It is advisable to have your eyes tested at least every two years. Regular sight tests can pick up many conditions and detect signs of other diseases, so it is a sensible precaution to do this. You will qualify for a free NHS sight test if you are aged 60 and over; you live in Scotland; you or your partner receive Income Support, Family Credit, income-based Jobseeker's Allowance, Pension Credit Guarantee Credit and are entitled to or named on a valid NHS Tax Credit exemption certificate or are named on a valid HC2 certificate. People with mobility problems who are unable to get to an optician can ask for a domiciliary visit to have their eyes examined at home. The going rate for private sight tests if you do have to pay is about £25. There is a voucher system for helping with the purchase of glasses or contact lenses for those on low incomes. People who are registered blind are entitled to a special tax allowance each year. For 2013/14 it is £2,160.

All the main banks will provide statements in Braille; several institutions offer large-print chequebooks or templates for chequebooks, as well as other facilities such as a taped version of their annual report. There is no extra charge for these services.

Here are some useful organizations for matters relating to sight:

Royal National Institute of Blind People (RNIB): **www.rnib.org.uk**.

International Glaucoma Association: **www.glaucoma-association.com**.

Partially Sighted Society: **www.partsight.org.uk**.

BT: **www.bt.com/includingyou**.

British Wireless for the Blind: **www.blind.org.uk**.

Calibre Audio Library: **www.calibre.org.uk**.

Feet

Many people forget about their feet until they begin to give trouble. Podiatry is available on the National Health Service without referral from a doctor being necessary, but facilities tend to be very oversubscribed, so in many areas it is only the very elderly or those with a real problem who can get appointments. The professional association for registered chiropodists and podiatrists has a list of over 10,000 private practitioners.

Society of Chiropodists and Podiatrists: **www.scpod.org**.

Hearing

In the UK alone there are 10 million people living with a hearing loss; and only 2 million of them are wearing hearing aids, even though many more could benefit from them. Being able to hear properly is important for a number of reasons: safety and awareness; conversation and interaction; enjoyment and entertainment. Because hearing works 'invisibly' it isn't always given as much attention as it should. Changes happen so gradually, hearing loss can often go undetected. Signs to look out for are:

- not hearing the doorbell or a telephone ring;
- turning up the television too loud for the comfort of others;
- failing to hear people come into the room;
- misunderstanding what has been said in conversation;
- not speaking clearly or speaking in a monotonous tone;
- uncertainty about where sounds are coming from;
- difficulty in hearing at a distance or in public gatherings.

If you have noticed any of these, talk to your GP, who may refer you to an audiologist or hearing care professional. Friends and family can do a great deal to help those who are deaf or hard of hearing. One of the essentials is not to shout but to speak slowly and distinctly. You should always face the person, so he or she can see your lips, and avoid speaking with your hand over your mouth or when smoking. Learning British Sign Language is another option. In case of real difficulty, write down your message. There are other specialist organizations that can give you a lot of help on hearing aids and on other matters:

Action on Hearing Loss: **www.actiononhearingloss.org.uk**.

British Deaf Association (BDA): **www.bda.org.uk**.

British Tinnitus Association (BTA): **www.tinnitus.org.uk**.

Hearing Link: **www.hearinglink.org**.

Teeth

People in their 50s, 60s and 70s look much younger these days thanks to advances in medicine and a healthier diet and lifestyle. But one thing that can let the older generation down is discoloured or misshapen teeth. Everyone knows the importance of having regular dental check-ups. Dentistry is one of the treatments for which you have to pay under the NHS, unless you are on a very low income. If you or your partner is in receipt of Income Support, income-based Jobseeker's Allowance or Pension Credit, you are entitled to free NHS dental treatment. You may also receive some help if you are in receipt of the Working Tax Credit; for details, see leaflet HC11. To avoid any nasty surprises when the bill comes along, it is important to confirm possible costs with your dentist before he or she treats you, and to check that you are being treated under the NHS. This also applies to the hygienist, should you need to see one. To find a dentist in your area, search **NHS Choices: www.nhs.uk**.

Prevention is always better than cure. If you want free, independent and impartial advice on all aspects of oral health and free literature on a wide range of topics, including patients' rights, finding a dentist and dental care for older people, see **British Dental Health Foundation: www.dentalhealth.org**.

For those who like to be able to budget ahead for any dental bills, best advice is to take out a dental health plan. One of the UK's leading dental payment plan specialist has over 6,500 member dentists and approximately 1.8 million patients across the UK – **Denplan: www.denplan.co.uk**.

Personal relationships

Retirement, for couples, involves a major lifestyle change, since one partner may be retiring earlier or later than the other. If they retire at the same time, couples will need to adjust to spending longer together. Sadly some people feel as the years have rolled by that they have less in common than they once had. However, statistics show that the over-hyped rise in 'silver-surfer' divorces is due to an increase in the age at which couples marry, not higher divorce rates. Should couples find it difficult to resolve differences once retired, there are a number of organizations that offer help and guidance:

Albany Trust: **www.albanytrust.org**.

Marriage Care: **www.marriagecare.org.uk**.

Scottish Marriage Care: **www.scottishmarriagecare.org**.

Relate: **www.relate.org.uk**.

Relationships Scotland: **www.relationships-scotland.org.uk**.

Help for grandparents

Regular contact with grandparents has been shown to be of great benefit to grandchildren from birth onwards. Sadly it is difficult for grandparents to maintain close contact with their grandchildren should adult children divorce. While some divorcing parents work hard to avoid this happening, others deny grandparents access and sometimes sever the relationship completely. There are a number of organizations that have experience of advising grandparents and offer practical help and support should this be of concern to you.

Grandparents' Association: **www.grandparents-association.org.uk**.

Grandparents Plus: **www.grandparentsplus.org.uk**.

Gransnet: **www.gransnet.com**.

Depression

Depression in later life is a widely under-recognized and under-treated medical condition. Up until recently many health professionals – including GPs – failed to identify depression, seeing it as an inevitable feature of ageing and so have not offered the treatments and support available to other age groups. Most forms of depression can be treated, regardless of the person's age, using medication, talking treatments or other interventions.

It is can be difficult to diagnose depression in older people because it often occurs alongside other mental and physical illnesses, such as dementia and chronic illnesses such as stroke, diabetes and cancer. In addition many older people do not seek help from their GP. It is important to seek help as early as possible. Here are some useful websites:

Depression Alliance: **www.depressionalliance.org**.

Mind: **www.mind.org.uk**.

Samaritans: **www.samaritans.org**.

Sane: **www.sane.org.uk**.

Some common disorders

The rest of this chapter deals with some of the more common disorders, such as back pain and heart disease. If you are unfortunate enough to be affected, or have a member of your family who is, here are some organizations that provide information and support.

Aphasia

This condition makes it hard to speak, read or understand language, and affects individuals who have suffered a stroke, a head injury or other neurological damage. The national charity that can help is: **Speakability**: **www.speakability.org.uk**.

Arthritis and rheumatism

Although arthritis is often thought of as an older person's complaint, it accounts for the loss of an estimated 70 million working days a year in Britain, and 10 million people suffer from it. You don't have to put up with the pain of arthritis as there are a number of organizations that can help:

Arthritic Association: **www.arthriticassociation.org.uk**.

Arthritis Care: **www.arthritiscare.org.uk**.

Arthritis Research UK: **www.arthritisresearchuk.org**.

Back pain

Four out of five people suffer from back pain at some stage of their lives. While there are many different causes, doctors agree that much of the trouble could be avoided through correct posture, care in lifting heavy articles, a firm mattress, and chairs that provide support in the right places.

For further information, see **BackCare**: **www.backcare.org.uk**.

Blood pressure

High blood pressure can be symptomless yet it is the leading cause of strokes in the UK and can lead to heart attack and heart failure. One in three adults has high blood pressure but a third of those will be completely unaware of it. Anyone over the age of 50 should keep a check on their blood pressure as it tends to rise with age. Post-menopausal women also see an increase in their blood pressure. The good news is that blood pressure can be successfully managed with medication and some simple lifestyle changes, such as:

- Watch your salt intake.
- Eat at least five portions of fruit and vegetables per day.
- Watch your weight.
- Cut down on alcohol.
- Take regular exercise.
- Laugh – watch a funny movie.
- Be sociable – lonely people often suffer from high blood pressure.

For further information see **The Blood Pressure Association: www. bloodpressureuk.org.**

Cancer

With continuing research and improved treatments more people suffering from cancer today can be expected to make a complete recovery. Early diagnosis can make a vital difference and if you are offered the opportunity for screening or testing it is advisable to take advantage of it. It also goes without saying that anyone with a lump or swelling, however small, should waste no time in having it investigated by a doctor.

There are now over 300 cancer charities in existence, each researching or focusing on a particular variant of the disease. Here are a few, but to find a list of all of them consult **www.charitychoice.co.uk:**

Bowel Cancer UK: **www.bowelcanceruk.org.uk.**

Breast Cancer Care: **www.breastcancercare.org.uk.**

Cancer Research UK: **www.cancerresearch.org.**

Macmillan Cancer Support: **www.macmillan.org.uk.**

Chest and heart diseases

The earlier sections on smoking, diet, drink and exercise list some of the most pertinent 'dos and don'ts' that can help prevent heart disease. Statistics reveal that UK death rates from coronary heart disease are among the highest in the world, killing almost 120,000 people a year, and coronary heart disease is responsible for one in five of all deaths. Although people tend to think of heart attacks as particularly affecting men, over four times as many women die from heart disease as from breast cancer. The following charity plays a leading role in the fight against diseases of the heart and circulation:

British Heart Foundation: **www.bhf.org.uk**.

Diabetes

Diabetes occurs when the amount of glucose in the blood is too high for the body to use properly. It can sometimes be treated by diet alone; sometimes pills or insulin may also be needed. Diabetes can be diagnosed at any age, although it is common in the elderly and especially among individuals who are overweight. For further information see:

Diabetes UK: **www.diabetes.org.uk**.

Independent Diabetes Trust: **www.iddtinternational.org**.

Migraine

Migraine affects over 10 million people in the UK. It can involve severe head pains, nausea, vomiting, visual disturbances and in some cases temporary paralysis. The leading UK charity that funds and promotes research, holds international symposia and runs an extensive support service is the Migraine Trust: **www.migrainetrust.org**.

Osteoporosis and menopause problems

Bone is a living tissue which needs to be kept healthy. It changes throughout our lifetime, with new bone constantly replacing old bone. From the age of 35 our bones begin to weaken gradually. This can lead to osteoporosis: a condition in which bones become so fragile that they can break very easily. The most common injuries from falls affect the spine, hip and wrist. One in two women (and one in five men) suffer from osteoporosis. Following the menopause, women's levels of the hormone oestrogen naturally decrease.

AgeUK compiled a list of ways to boost bone health:

- Weight-bearing exercise is important to help keep your bones strong. Walking, tennis, aerobics and dancing strengthen your bones.

- Enjoy a balanced diet. Milk, cheese, yoghurt, baked beans, lentils and dried apricots are great sources of calcium.

- Taking a stroll in the summer sun (just 10 minutes will help) is a great way of absorbing vitamin D, which keeps bones healthy.

- Avoid smoking. Smokers lose bone at a faster rate than non-smokers.

- Drink moderately.

The following websites may be useful:

Menopause Exchange: **www.menopause-exchange.co.uk**.

National Osteoporosis Society: **www.nos.org.uk**.

Women's Health Concern: **www.womens-health-concern.org**.

Stroke

A stroke is a brain injury caused by the sudden interruption of blood flow. Over 130,000 people suffer a stroke every year in England and Wales. It is unpredictable in its effects, which may include muscular paralysis or weakness on one side, loss of speech or loss of understanding or language, visual problems or incontinence. Prevention is similar to the prevention of heart disease. A stroke has a greater disability impact than any other medical condition. The Stroke Association is the only UK-wide charity solely concerned with combating stroke in people of all ages. See **Stroke Association: www.stroke.org.uk**.

Disability

Disability is covered in Chapter 15, Caring for Elderly Parents, so if you or someone in your family has a problem not mentioned here, you may find the answer you need there.

Chapter Fourteen
Holidays

> *There ain't no surer way to find out whether you like people or hate them than to travel with them.*

MARK TWAIN

Are you a keen traveller? Do you relish the thought of going on holiday as often as possible – while you have time, health and money? The over-50s are worth a vast amount to the travel industry, which is probably why there is an ever – increasing choice of holidays on offer to us pensioners. You can forget Sir Ranulph Fiennes: according to *The Oldie Magazine* (May 2013) the world's most intrepid traveller is not an ex-British Army officer who auditioned for the role of James Bond, but an 88-year-old widow called Mrs Cole. In expeditions to over 150 countries, she's faced stampeding Tanzanian elephants (from whom her husband and son fled), stared out six-feet long crocodiles in Venezuela and calmly warded off two silver-back gorillas in the Congo Basin. Her advice to other travellers is: 'If you're confronted by a wild animal, try not to run away. Stand still and remain calm. The chances are you will diffuse the situation.' Mrs Cole, a worldwide explorer and loyal customer of her tour company, has been praised by their management: 'Her knowledge of the world betters almost everyone; she is fearless. If she ever wanted to go back to work, she would make the best ever tour guide.'

Now whether you count yourself in this bracket or not, holidays should be exciting and full of treasured memories. In retirement, some of us enjoy reading travel articles, watching documentaries about far-flung places in our armchairs, while others carry out extensive research on possible destinations before making holiday plans. What is it about travel that people love and why do we do it? There are many reasons: the way it challenges us, gives us the opportunity to enjoy new experiences, discover new cultures and languages, to party, to have fun, see new sights and eat delicious food. This year perhaps you'll try something different that will provide unforgettable experiences.

The fact that you've retired makes very little difference to what you can do or where you can go. Lots of people combine holidays with a special interest, such as painting or music. There is ample opportunity for you to enrol for summer school, exchange homes with someone in another country or sign on for a working holiday, such as a voluntary conservation activity or home and pet sitting, for which you get paid. The choice is enormous. If you wish to go somewhere exotic, it is likely the prices will be high; but if your budget is limited, with a bit of research you will find some holidays that are extremely reasonable in cost. Whether you are fit and active or require special care, there are plenty of options. Retirement is a time for experimentation, so don't think about your age being an issue – there's plenty of opportunity to embrace new experiences.

Here are some *top tips* from travel experts to keep in mind before you book:

- Spend some time researching the best deals so you don't pay over the odds.

- Be sure to take out travel insurance – the cheapest is not always best – and do check the small print.

- If you are happy joining a group tour, find one that suits your age range and interests.

- If you're not tied down with commitments, late booking can yield great discounts.

- When looking for places to eat and drink at your destination, ask for recommendations for local or hidden gems.

- There are lots of opportunities for over-50s singles who enjoy travelling. A number of tour companies operate specific departures and don't charge hefty supplements.

- And, if you love travelling, have lots of holiday and travel experience, you could consider becoming a holiday rep. Did you know that over 20 per cent of all tour guides are 50 years old and over...

Since there are so many types of holidays to choose from, for ease of reference, entries are listed under subheadings. To avoid repetition, the majority are featured only once, in the most logical place. At the end of the chapter, there is a general information section with brief details about insurance, concessionary fares and other travel tips.

Art and cultural appreciation

Cultural holidays offer a combination of visits to places of artistic, historic, musical and architectural interest, with lectures given by professional academics, writers and curators. They are carefully researched and provide high standards of customer service including comfortable hotels and authentic restaurants. Here are a few to consider:

Abercrombie & Kent: **www.abercrombiekent.com**.

Ace Cultural Tours: **www.aceculturaltours.co.uk**.

Cox and Kings: **www.coxandkings.co.uk**.

Kirker Holidays: **www.kirkerholidays.com**.

Martin Randall Travel: **www.martinrandall.com**.

Opera Tours Italy: **www.operatoursitaly.com**.

Specialtours: **www.specialtours.co.uk**.

Ultimate Travel Company: **www.theultimatetravelcompany.co.uk**.

Festivals

There is a feast of music, drama and the arts to be found annually all over Britain and you will find a number of lists printed in the national press (*Guardian*, *Telegraph* and *Times*) giving information on the music, poetry, literary and arts festivals taking place throughout the year. To find out what is going on where, in your local area or any other part of the UK, contact the Arts Council or your regional Arts Council office. There are simply too many to list here, but the booklet *Go Away Britain – The Oldie's Guide to Britain through its Festivals* provides a comprehensive list: **www.theoldie.co.uk**.

Arts and crafts

In this section the focus is on taking courses on such subjects as crochet, knitting, painting, basket making and jewellery making, for those who want to discover new skills. Further suggestions are also given in Chapter 9, Leisure activities. There are plenty of good residential arts and crafts holidays offered by a number of organizations. See:

Field Studies Council: **www.field-studies-council.org**.

Marlborough College Summer School: **www.mcsummerschool.org.uk**.

The Crafts Council: www.craftscouncil.org.uk.

West Dean College: **www.westdean.org.uk**.

Coach holidays

Some coach companies organize holidays, as distinct from simply offering a mode of transport. Before embarking on a lengthy coach tour, try a few shorter excursions to see how you cope with the journey. A couple of good websites to get you started are:

Find A Coach Holiday: **www.findacoachholiday.com**.

National Express: **www.nationalexpress.com**.

Other websites which offer good choices of coach holidays include:

www.nationalholidays.com;

www.silvertraveladvisor.com;

www.shearings.com;

www.grandukholidays.com.

Historical holidays

Holidays with a particular focus on history are becoming increasingly popular. For those with a passion for historic locations there are a number of companies offering to 'keep the spirit alive' of what went on in times gone by. Memorable events need to be communicated to future generations and here are a few websites to whet your appetite.

Battlefield Tours: **www.battlefieldtours.co.uk**.

Commonwealth War Graves Commission: **www.cwgc.org**.

Holts Tours – Battlefields & History: **www.holts.co.uk**.

Military History Tours: **www.militaryhistorytours.co.uk**.

Poppy Travel: **www.poppytravel.org.uk**.

The Cultural Experience: **www.theculturalexperience.com**.

Language courses

If you are hoping to travel more when you retire, being able to speak the language when abroad will greatly add to your enjoyment. The quickest and easiest way to learn is undoubtedly in the country itself. Alternatively whether you wish to attend a course, classes or learn via computer, CDs or private tutor, with a bit of research you will find what you need. Here are some suggestions for learning Italian, German, French and Spanish:

British Institute of Florence: **www.britishinstitute.it**.

Goethe-Institut: **www.goethe.de**.

Institut-Français: **www.institut-francais.org.uk**.

Instituto Cervantes: **www.londres.cervantes.es**.

Other people's homes

Living in someone else's home for free is one of the cheapest ways of enjoying a holiday. There are two ways of doing this: exchange your home with another person in this country or abroad, or become a home sitter and mind someone else's property while they are away.

Home exchange

With home swap sites, you find a property you like, and if the owners also like yours, then you swap homes for a holiday. Some people even exchange their cars and pets. Here are some websites to look at:

Guardian Home Exchange: **www.guardianhomeexchange.co.uk**.

Happy Home Swap: **www.happyhomeswap.com**.

Home Base Holidays: **www.homebase-hols.com**.

Home Exchange: **www.homeexchange.com**.

Home Exchange Gold: **www.homeexchangegold.com**.

HomeLink: **www.homelink.org.uk**.

Simply Home Exchange: **www.simplyhomeexchange.com**.

Home and pet sitting

Retired people are generally considered ideal home sitters: you provide a caretaking service and get paid for doing so. Duties variously involve light housework, plant watering, care of pets and sometimes tending the garden. Careful vetting of applicants is essential, as are first-class references. See:

Absentia: **www.home-and-pets.co.uk**.

Animal Angels: **www.animalangels.co.uk**.

Boateng Homes: **www.boatenghomes.co.uk**.

Homesitters: **www.homesitters.co.uk**.

Trusted House Sitters: **www.trustedhousesitters.com**.

Overseas travel

Many big tour operators make a feature of offering special holidays designed for the over-55s. Also included here are companies that specialize in arranging cruises and packaged motoring holidays, and information on timesharing.

Easier.com: **www.easier.com/travel**.

Explore Worldwide: **www.explore.co.uk**.

Relais du Silence: **www.relaisdusilence.com**.

Saga Holidays: **www.saga.co.uk/travel**.

Silver Travel Advisor: **www.silvertraveladvisor.com**.

Telegraph Travel: **www.telegraph.co.uk/traveladvice**.

Travelsphere: **www.travelsphere.co.uk**.

Cruises

Some 2 million people in the UK take a cruise holiday every year and that figure is rising. Finding a cruise that suits you has never been easier.

Certain destinations, such as Alaska, lend themselves to a seafaring experience; others can be reached only by ship. And it's hard to beat a cruise if you want a first taste of the islands of the Caribbean. If you are interested in finding our more, visit

The Cruise Show: www.cruisingshow.com.

Here are some *top tips* for cruising:

- *Avoid an inside cabin.* It will be cheaper because there is no natural light, but it plays havoc with your body clock.

- *Don't pay the brochure price.* Protect yourself by booking your cruise through an ABTA agent.

- *Remember that prices usually include extras.* If you think the cost is high, remember that food and non-alcoholic drinks are included.

- *Watch out for on-board credit offers.* Cruise lines tempt customers with on-board credit that can only be spent on the ship.

From among the mass of companies offering cruise travel advice and tours, here are just a few websites to look at. Start with:

Alastair MacKenzie's Travel Lists: **www.travel-lists.co.uk.**

Avalon Waterways: **www.avaloncruises.co.uk.**

Blue Water Holidays: **www.cruisingholidays.co.uk.**

Celebrity Cruises: **www.celebritycruises.co.uk.**

Cunard: **www.cunard.co.uk.**

Fred Olsen Cruise Lines: **www.fredolsencruises.com.**

Hebridean Island Cruises: **www.hebridean.co.uk.**

Hurtigruten Norwegian Cruises: **www.hurtigruten.co.uk.**

NCL (Norwegian Cruise Line): **www.ncl.co.uk.**

Noble Caledonian: **www.noble-caledonian.co.uk.**

P&O Cruises: **www.pocruises.com**.

Princess Cruises: **www.princess.com**.

Royal Caribbean International: **www.royalcaribbean.co.uk**.

SeaDream Yacht Club: **www.seadream.com**.

Silversea: **www.silversea.com**.

Six Star Cruises: **www.sixstarcruises.co.uk**.

Titan River Cruises: **www.titantravel.co.uk/rivercruises**.

Viking River Cruises: **www.vikingrivercruises.co.uk**.

Voyages of Discovery: **www.voyagesofdiscovery.co.uk**.

Voyages to Antiquity: **www.voyagestoantiquity.com**.

Windstar Cruises: **www.windstarcruises.com**.

Cargo ship cruises

If price is one of the main considerations, travelling via cargo ship could be the solution. Accommodation and facilities (there is often a swimming pool) vary according to the size and type of vessel.

Cargo Ship Voyages: **www.cargoshipvoyages.com**.

Strand Voyages: **www.strandtravelltd.co.uk**.

Possibly the most unusual cruise in the world is on board one of the few Royal Mail ships still working. **RMS St Helena** is equipped to provide a relaxing cruise experience to the island of St Helena, which is just a speck in the Atlantic ocean, south of the equator. The ship sails there from the UK and South Africa, calling at various islands along the way. See website: **www.rms-st-helena.com**.

Motoring holidays abroad

A number of organizations, including in particular some ferry operators, offer packages for the motorist that include ferry crossings, accommodation and insurance. While these often provide very good value, some people prefer to make all their own arrangements in order to get exactly what they want. Here are some of the major operators:

AA: **www.theaa.com**.

Brittany Ferries: **www.brittany-ferries.co.uk**.

RAC: **www.rac.co.uk**.

Here are some *top tips* when motoring abroad, if taking your own vehicle:

- Have your car thoroughly serviced before you go.

- Make sure your GB sticker is clearly visible.

- Check with the FCO for travel advice via their website.

- Have headlight converters if driving in Europe.

- Get insured for medical and travel purposes for the countries you are visiting.

- Invest in a good guide book on your destination that advises on local customs and laws.

- Check whether you require a green card for the countries you are visiting.

- Make sure your passport is valid and you have necessary visas.

- Find out about speed limits and if you require any specific equipment.

- Does your breakdown cover provide roadside assistance while abroad?

- Make sure all documentation is easily available, should you need it.

- Take the following with you: a tool kit, the manual for your car, a rented spares kit, a fuel can, a mechanic's light that plugs into the cigarette lighter socket, at least one extra set of keys, and any extras required by local laws such as a reflective tabard and warning triangles.

- Always lock your car and park it in a secure place overnight (nearly 75 per cent of luggage thefts abroad are from cars).

Other sources of advice and services are:

Association of British Insurers: **www.abi.org.uk**.

Aria Assistance: **www.aria-assistance.co.uk**.

Green Flag: **www.greenflag.com**.

If instead of taking your own car you plan to hire a vehicle overseas, you will probably have to buy special insurance at the time of hiring the vehicle. Make sure that this is properly comprehensive (check for any excesses or exclusions) or, at the very least, it gives you adequate third-party cover. If in doubt, seek advice from the local motoring organization regarding essential requirements, and do not sign any documents unless you understand them.

How is your driving?

If you've recently travelled in a car and been frightened by a friend's driving, or you think you might be starting to scare others with your driving skills, it is simple enough to get yourself checked. The Institute of Advanced Motorists offers to assess anyone over 55 on their driving skills: it is sensible to take advantage of this exercise every few years or so to maintain confidence and be safe on the road.

IAM Driving Road Safety: **www.iam.org.uk**.

Short breaks

Many organizations offer short-break holidays all year round, with special bargain prices in spring and autumn. British hotels have winter breaks from November to April, and overseas travel operators slash prices during the off-peak seasons. Here are just a few websites to look at:

City Break Holidays: **www.citiesdirect.co.uk**.

Responsible Travel: **www.responsibletravel.com**.

Shortbreaks.com: **www.short-breaks.com**.

Shortbreak.UK.com: **www.shortbreak.uk.com**.

Superbreak: **www.superbreak.com**.

Travel 55: **www.travel55.co.uk**.

Timesharing

Timesharing is an investment in long-term holidays. The idea is that you buy the use of a property for a specific number of days each year, either for an agreed term or in perpetuity. Most timeshare schemes allow you to swap your week(s) for time in other developments throughout the world for your annual holiday, via one of the exchange companies.

A week's timeshare will vary in price depending on the location, the size of the property, the time of year and the facilities of the resort. There are maintenance charges on top and you should always check that these are linked to some form of cost-of-living index such as the RPI. Another useful point to check is that there is an owners' association linked to the property. There are still stories about unscrupulous operators, so to avoid getting caught out you should be wary of such enticing promotional gifts as a 'free' holiday flight to visit the property. These websites provide information and safeguards:

RCI Europe: **www.rci.com**.

Interval International: **www.intervalworld.com**.

Resort Development Organisation: **www.rdo.org**.

Existing owners wishing to sell their property should be on their guard against unknown resale agents contacting them and offering, in exchange for a registration fee, to act on their behalf. A telephone call to the RDO will establish whether the company is a member body. If not, leave well alone.

Holiday Property Bond

Although it has been in existence for more than 25 years, this remains one of the best-kept secrets in the holiday industry. It is a uniquely flexible alternative to fixed-week timeshare and villa ownership. By securing a financial interest in HPB's entire portfolio of villas, cottages and apartments, bondholders and their family and friends are entitled to use any bond property at any time – rent free. (It is a privilege that can be passed on, without charge, to holders' children and grandchildren too.)

Holiday Property Bond: **www.hpb.co.uk**.

Rail holidays

You don't have to be a rail enthusiast to enjoy a holiday by train. Whether you wish to explore the world, or simply parts of the UK, there are many wonderful routes to travel and here are some useful websites to research:

www.diamondrailholidays.co.uk;

www.discoverytrains.net;

www.greatrail.com;

www.orient-express.com;

www.railholidays.com;

www.seat61.com;

www.planetrail.co.uk.

Retreats

If peace and quiet is what you seek when you are on holiday, a retreat might be the answer. This organization has retreat centres all over Britain and Ireland:

The Retreat Association: **www.retreats.org.uk**.

Self-catering and low-budget holidays

Should you be interested in self-catering or budget holidays, you may be surprised at the variety and choice available. Camping, caravanning or renting very simple accommodation with friends may suit you, or you might prefer the luxury end of the scale.

Camping and Caravanning Club:
    www.campingandcaravanningclub.co.uk.

English Country Cottages: **www.english-country-cottages.co.uk**.

Farm Stay UK Ltd: **www.farmstayuk.co.uk**.

Scottish Country Cottages: **www.scottish-country-cottages.co.uk**.

Landmark Trust: **www.landmarktrust.org.uk**.

National Trust Holiday Cottages: **www.nationaltrustcottages.co.uk**.

National Trust for Scotland: **www.nts.org.uk/holidays**.

Venuemasters: **www.venuemasters.co.uk**.

YHA (England and Wales) Ltd: **www.yha.org.uk**.

Special interest holidays

This section includes weekend courses and more formal summer schools, between them offering a huge variety of subjects. It also includes holidays in the more conventional sense, both in Britain and abroad, but with the accent on a hobby.

Centre for Alternative Technology: **www.cat.org.uk**.

Denman College: **www.denmancollege.org.uk**.

Field Studies Council (FSC): **www.field-studies-council.org**.

HF Holidays Ltd: **www.hfholidays.co.uk**.

Painting and Cooking in Italy: **www.paintinginitaly.com**.

Peak District National Park: **www.peakdistrict.gov.uk**.

Vegi Ventures: **www.vegiventures.com**.

Sport

Holidays with on-site or nearby sporting facilities exist all over the country. The list that follows is limited to organizations that can advise you about organized residential courses or can offer facilities. For wider information, see Chapter 9, Leisure activities, which lists some of the national sports associations.

Boating

The beauty of life aboard a boat is you're not on a set holiday itinerary. There's no rushing to the next destination, unless you want to. Whether you choose to holiday abroad or in Britain, you have loads of choice. If you're new to boating, it's akin to travelling in a cosy floating villa, with all the comforts of home and each day you wake up in a beautiful new destination.

Beautiful Boating Holidays: **www.leboat.co.uk**.

Blakes: **www.blakes.co.uk**.

Hoseasons Boating Holidays: **www.hoseasons.co.uk**.

Royal Yachting Association (RYA): **www.rya.org.uk**.

Waterways Holidays: **www.waterwaysholidays.com**.

Cycling

Cycling holidays are a great way to explore stunning countryside. If you wish to take to two wheels for your holiday, you can enjoy bike touring in many parts of the world. Depending on age, health and fitness it is advisable to choose suitable terrain for your level of expertise.

CTC Cycling Holidays: **www.cyclingholidays.org**.

Cycle Breaks: **www.cyclebreaks.com**.

Cycling for Softies: **www.cycling-for-softies.co.uk**.

Saddle Skedaddle: **www.skedaddle.co.uk**.

UK Cycling Holidays: **www.ukcyclingholidays.co.uk**.

Wheely Wonderful Cycling: **www.wheelywonderfulcycling.co.uk**.

Golf

There are some amazing holiday destinations for golf players. Whether you wish to travel abroad, or play on a UK course, there is a destination or vacation to suit you, including special golfing weekends and short-break holidays.

Golf Escapes: **www.golf-escapes.com**.

Golf Holidays.Com: **www.golfholidays.com**.

Supertravel: **www.supertravel.co.uk**.

Your Golf Travel: **www.yourgolftravel.com**.

Rambling

Rambling features on many special interest and other programmes as one of the options on offer. The organizations that specialize in rambling holidays are:

ATG Oxford: **www.atg-oxford.co.uk**.

Exodus: **www.exodus.co.uk**.

Rambling Tours: **www.ramblingtours.co.uk**.

Ramblers Worldwide Holidays: **www.ramblersholidays.co.uk**.

Skiing

Why do people love skiing? Some reasons given: the speed is exhilarating; it is exercise without feeling it; the views in the mountains are amazing; you get plenty of fresh air as well as physical and mental challenges. Whether you are a skier or snowboarder there are lots of organizations, tour operators and destinations to choose from:

Ski Club of Great Britain: **www.skiclub.co.uk**.

CrystalSki: **www.crystalski.co.uk**.

Disability Snowsport UK: **www.disabilitysnowsport.org.uk**.

Powder White: **www.powderwhite.com**.

Tennis

The key ingredients of a good tennis holiday are: good weather, a great tennis venue and exceptional accommodation. There are a number of companies who offer tennis holidays to suit your needs, whether you are a single traveller, a family or a group of friends.

ActiveAway: **www.activeaway.com**.

Discovery Tennis: **www.discoverytennistours.com**.

Lawn Tennis Association (LTA): **www.lta.org.uk**.

Roger Walker Travel: **www.tennisholidays.co.uk**.

Wine tasting

The combination of an enjoyable holiday with great wine-tasting experiences is something that appeals to many people. Tours offer plenty of variety with visits, talks, convivial meals, free time for exploring as well as memorable tastings.

Arblaster & Clarke Wine Tours: **www.winetours.co.uk**.

Grape Escapes: **www.grapeescapes.net**.

Smooth Red: **www.smoothred.co.uk**.

Winetasting France: **www.winetastingfrance.com**.

Working holidays

There is scope for volunteers who would like to engage in a worthwhile project during their holidays. Activities vary from helping run play schemes to conservation work. A few are listed here but most are mentioned in Chapter 12, Voluntary work:

British Trust for Conservation Volunteers (BTCV): **www.btcv.org.uk**.

National Trust Working Holidays: **www.nationaltrust.org.uk**.

Toc H: **www.toch-uk.org.uk**.

Wwoof France: **www.wwoof.fr**.

Golden gappers

The number of older people taking time out of their normal working life and escaping on a gap year has increased dramatically over the last few years. But so has the number of over-50s and retirees (often referred to as 'Grey' or 'Golden Gappers') increased as these established individuals can afford to take time out. This group has the time, resources and energy to enjoy doing something completely different, many of them inspired by their children who have already flown the nest. Rather than sit at home, they take the long haul trips not always possible previously. Top 10 destinations for the over-50s are: Australia, Canada, New Zealand, United States, Caribbean, Italy, Seychelles, Ireland, Florida and the Maldives.

If you think escaping on a gap year could be fun and want the latest information and advice, see:

Gapadvice: **www.gapadvice.org**.

DIY Holidays: **www.diydoctorholidays.co.uk**.

Holidays for singles

Many people travel on their own, some may be single, others not. These people, for whatever reason, choose to (or have to) travel alone. If you are single, widowed, divorced or simply having to travel without your partner – you're probably looking for the opportunity to meet other, like-minded people to share the holiday experience with. If you enjoy holidays but don't enjoy travelling alone, there are a number of companies which specialize in organising trips for solo holidaymakers.

Exodus: **www.exodus.co.uk**.

Friendship Travel: **www.friendshiptravel.com**.

Just You: **www.justyou.co.uk**.

One Traveller: **www.onetraveller.co.uk**.

Solitaire: **www.solitairhols.co.uk**.

Solos: **www.solosholidays.co.uk**.

Travel One: **www.travelone.co.uk**.

Holidays for those needing special care

A good holiday is one of life's greatest pleasures and a vital tonic to body, mind and spirit. The great news is that affordable, accessible and enjoyable holidays for the disabled are on the increase. More airlines, hotels and resorts are providing people with disabilities or mobility issues the opportunities to travel, enjoy holidays and see the world. Specially designed self-catering units are more plentiful and of a higher standard. Also, an increasing number of trains and coaches are installing accessible loos.

Travel and other information

If you need help getting on and off a train or plane, inform your travel agent in advance. Arrangements can be made to have staff and a wheelchair available to help you at both departure and arrival points. If you are travelling independently, you should ring the airline and/or local station and explain what assistance you require, together with details of your journey, so that facilities can be arranged at any interim points, should you need to change trains. Organizations that can help you include:

Age UK: **www.ageuk.org.uk**.

Accessible Travel & Leisure: **www.accessibletravel.co.uk**.

Can Do Holidays: **www.candoholidays.com**.

Choice Care Assisted Holidays: **www.choicecareservices.co.uk**.

Disabled Access Holidays: **www.disabledaccessholidays.com**.

Enable Holidays: **www.enableholidays.com**.

Holidays for the Disabled: **www.holidaysforthedisabled.com**.

Tourism for All/Vitalise: **www.tourismforall.org.uk**.

Virgin Holidays: **www.virginholidays.co.uk**.

Another source to contact is your local social services department. Some local authorities arrange holidays or give financial help to those in real need.

Touring in the UK

If you plan to holiday within the UK and are looking for hotels and accommodation in Britain, or are simply after UK travel, attractions or event information, you will find everything you need to know at:

Discovering Britain: **www.discoveringbritain.org**.

Discover Northern Ireland: **www.discovernorthernireland.com**.

UK Tourist Attractions: **www.uktouristattractions.co.uk**.

Visit Britain: **www.visitbritain.com**.

Visit London: **www.visitlondon.com**.

Visit Scotland: **www.visitscotland.com**.

Visit Wales: **www.visitwales.co.uk**.

Long-haul travel

The specialist organizations listed below can offer a great deal of practical information and help, as well as assist in obtaining low-cost fares, if you are planning to travel independently. Round-the-world air tickets are an excellent buy. Travel agents may also achieve savings by putting together routes using various carriers. Most airlines offer seasonal discounts that sometimes include a couple of nights' concessionary hotel stay, if you want to break your journey or visit another country at minimum extra travel cost.

Hays Travel: **www.haystravel.co.uk**.

Trailfinders Travel Centre: **www.trailfinders.com**.

Voyages Jules Verne: **www.vjv.com**.

WEXAS: **www.wexas.com**.

Visa and passport requirements and health and safety advice

It is vital that you check passport and visa requirements as well as any immunization guidelines for the countries you are travelling to (and through) as early as possible as processing necessary documentation can take some time. As a starting point, you should ensure your passport has at least six months validity beyond your length of stay as this is now a mandatory requirement for many countries around the world. The best website for up-to-the-minute travel advice for your destination and guidance on everything from health and immunization to passport and visa requirements is the **Foreign & Commonwealth Office: www. gov.uk/foreign-travel-advice**.

For information on tax and duty free reliefs when bringing goods into the UK, see **HM Revenue & Customs: www.hmrc.gov.uk/customs**.

Insurance

With people living longer and travelling more than ever before, age should be no barrier to travel. However, there are many pensioners who come up against an upper age limit for travel insurance. Once you are over 65, not only is it more difficult to obtain but also tends to be considerably more expensive. However, were you unfortunate enough to fall ill or experience some other mishap, it would almost certainly cost you very much more than paying a bit extra for decent insurance. With travel insurance you will need to disclose any pre-existing medical conditions fully before you can get a quote. If you are travelling independently, it is even more important to be properly insured. Under these circumstances you will not be protected by the normal compensation that the reputable tour operators provide for claims for which they could be held liable in the event of a mishap.

To check your options and find out more, have a look at the following websites:

Age UK: **www.ageuk.org.uk**.

American Express: **www.americanexpress.com**.

Insurance Choice: **www.insurancechoice.co.uk**.

Laterlife Travel Insurance: **www.laterlife.com**.

Motability: **www.motability.co.uk**.

Onestop4:Insurance: **www.onestop4.co.uk**.

Saga: **www.saga.co.uk**.

Here are some *top tips* when buying holiday insurance. Your policy should cover you for:

- *medical expenses*, including hospital treatment and the cost of an ambulance, an air ambulance and emergency dental treatment, plus expenses for a companion who may have to remain overseas with you should you become ill;

- *personal liability cover*, should you cause injury to another person or property;

- *personal accident* leading to injury or death (check the small print, as some policies have reduced cover for older travellers);

- *additional hotel and repatriation costs* resulting from injury or illness;

- *loss of deposit or cancellation* (check what emergencies or contingencies this covers);

- *the cost of having to curtail your holiday*, including extra travel expenses, because of serious illness in the family;

- *compensation for inconvenience* caused by flight cancellations or other travel delays;

- *cover for baggage and personal effects* and for emergency purchases should your baggage be delayed;

- *cover for loss of personal money* and documents.

Before purchasing new insurance, check whether any of the above items are already covered under an existing policy. This might well apply to your personal possessions and to medical insurance. Even if the policy is not sufficiently comprehensive for travel purposes, it will be better and cheaper in the long run to pay a small supplement to give you the extra cover you need than to buy a holiday insurance package from a tour operator. A cost-effective plan may be to extend any existing medical insurance to cover you while abroad. Then take out a separate policy (without medical insurance) to cover you for the rest of your travel needs. Two websites that provide good advice regarding the amount of cover you should be looking for in your travel insurance policy are:

The Association of British Insurers: **www.abi.org.uk**.

The Association of British Travel Agents (ABTA): **www.abta.com**.

Compensation for lost baggage

If the airline on which you are travelling loses or damages your baggage, you should be able to claim compensation up to a maximum value of about £850. (The figure may vary slightly up or down, depending on currency fluctuations.)

Cancelled or overbooked flights

Denied Boarding Regulations apply to passengers departing from an airport within the EU, whatever the airline is. The Regulations also apply to passengers departing from an airport outside the EU for an airport within the EU, if the operating air carrier is a Community carrier. Despite the title of the Regulation, its impact is wider than denied boarding, as it also covers cancellation and delay. Where a carrier expects to have to deny boarding, it must first call for volunteers, in exchange for benefits. If there are not enough volunteers, then the carrier can deny boarding to passengers against their will, but must then pay compensation and give assistance. For full details and information on this subject, see:

Air Travel Advisory Bureau (ATAB): **www.atab.org.uk**.

Aviation Consumer Advocacy Panel: **www.caa.co.uk**.

Medical insurance

This is one area where you should never skimp on insurance. Although many countries now have reciprocal arrangements with the UK for emergency medical treatment, these vary greatly in both quality and generosity. Some treatments are free, as they are on the National Health Service; others, even in some EU countries, may be charged for as if you were a private patient.

The Department of Health has advice for travellers. In particular you should get a European Health Insurance Card (EHIC). This card entitles the holder to free or discounted medical treatment at state-run hospitals and GPs in any EEA (European Economic Area) country plus Iceland, Liechtenstein, Norway and Switzerland. But it is not insurance and will not, for instance, arrange for repatriation, nor pay for a hotel room if you have to extend your stay to look after a sick relative. See **European Health Insurance Card: www.ehic.org.uk**.

However, even the very best reciprocal arrangements may not be adequate in the event of a real emergency. In the United States the cost of medical treatment is astronomical. For peace of mind, experts recommend cover of £1 million for most of the world and up to £2 million for the United States. Some policies offer higher or even unlimited cover. Although theoretically there is no upper age limit if you want to take out medical insurance, some insurance companies are very difficult about insuring older travellers. Many request a note from a qualified medical practitioner stating that you are fit to travel if you are over 75, or require you to confirm that you are not travelling against medical advice.

Book through a reputable operator

It is essential that holidaymakers check to ensure that their travel agent or tour operator is affiliated to an association with strict regulations that its member companies must follow. No one can guarantee you against every mishap, but a recognized travel company plus adequate insurance should go a long way towards giving you at least some measure of protection. See **Air Travel Advisory Bureau (ATAB): www.atab.org.uk**.

Travel and other concessions

Buses, coaches, some airline companies and especially the railways offer valuable concessions to people of retirement age.

Trains

Some of the best-value savings that are available to anyone aged 60 and over are provided by train companies. These include:

Disabled Persons Railcard: **www.disabledpersons-railcard.co.uk**.

Family Friends Railcard: **www.familyandfriends-railcard.co.uk**.

Network Railcard: **www.railcard.co.uk**.

Senior Railcard: **www.senior-railcard.co.uk**.

Buses and coaches

Over 11 million people over 60 in the UK use buses for free travel around the country. Make the most of this while you can: it is reported that the government has plans to raise the eligible age gradually to 65. Bus passes are usually issued free by local authorities. For further information see GOV.UK: **www.gov.uk/apply-for-elderly-person-bus-pass**.

Airlines

Several of the airlines offer attractive discounts to older travellers. The terms and conditions vary, with some carriers offering across-the-board savings and others limiting them to selected destinations. Likewise, in some cases the qualifying age is 60; in others, it is a couple of years older. A particular bonus is that concessions are often extended to include a companion travelling at the same time. Ask your travel agent or the airline at the time of booking what special discounts, if any, are offered.

Overseas

Many countries offer travel and other reductions to retired holidaymakers including, for example, discounts for entry to museums and galleries, day excursions, sporting events and other entertainment. As in Britain, provisions are liable to change, and for up-to-date information probably the best source to contact is the national tourist office of the country to which you are travelling. All EEA countries – as well as most lines in Switzerland – give 25 per cent reductions on international rail fares. These are available to holders of a Railplus Card who are purchasing international rail travel tickets and are applicable to both first- and second-class travel.

Airport meet-and-greet services

With the number of 'Meet and Greet' parking services at UK airports on the increase, it can be hard to make a confident choice. While you do leave your vehicle at an airport at your own risk, The British Parking Association provides a few handy hints to follow when selecting a service:

- Is the member of staff that greets you wearing a uniform – and carrying an ID badge? If so, check the badge – does it match up with the company you think you're dealing with, in the location you're at?

- Are you doing business in a designated location – such as a stand at the airport or a kiosk in the vicinity of the airport? Not having premises is a surefire indication that something might not be right.

- Check where the company will be storing your car. Can they point out their storage facility? If it is off-site, which they usually are, can they tell you where it is, or show you a picture? Does the company own the storage facility?

- Ask whether the car park in which your car will be stored has the 'Park Mark'. The Park Mark® is given to car parking facilities that have undergone an annual police assessment. See:

  British Parking Association: **www.britishparking.co.uk**.

  Park Mark Safer Parking: **www.parkmark.co.uk**.

Tips for safe travelling

Remember to pack any regular medicines you require: even familiar branded products can be difficult to obtain in some countries. In addition, take a mini first-aid kit with you.

If you are going to any developing country, consult your doctor as to what pills (and any special precautions) you should take.

An overdose of sun can be painful. In some countries it really burns, so take it easy, wear a hat and apply plenty of protective lotion.

Be careful of the water you drink. Beware the water, ice, salads, seafood, ice cream and any fruit that you do not peel yourself. Always wash your hands before eating or handling food, particularly if you are camping or caravanning.

Have any inoculations or vaccinations well in advance of your departure date. When flying, wear loose clothes and above all comfortable shoes, as feet and ankles tend to swell in the air.

To avoid risk of deep vein thrombosis, which can be fatal, medical advice is to do foot exercises and walk around the plane from time to time. For long-haul travel especially, wear compression stockings and, another tip, unless advised otherwise by your doctor, take an aspirin before flying.

For more information and advice, see **Safe Travel: www.safetravel.co.uk.**

Chapter Fifteen
Caring for elderly parents

'You are old, Father William,' the young man said, 'and your hair has become very white; And yet you incessantly stand on your head – Do you think, at your age, it is right?'

LEWIS CARROLL

How fit and active are you? Do you play badminton and go to the gym every week? And when did you last skydive for charity? One remarkable 90-year-old from Eastbourne in Sussex, does all of the above. She is one of the growing band of 'old old', or the fourth generation, as they are now called. Another example is an amazing lady in Bangor who has just turned 106. She says the key to her long and healthy life is not worrying about anything. She lived independently in her own home well into her late 90s. She remains sharp, walks unaided and entertains other residents in her nursing home with piano playing. With more than 1.5 million over-85s in the UK, and this number set to double by 2030, the demography of this country is changing dramatically. But it is wrong to assume that the ageing population are all likely to become a burden. Many of the elderly, given a bit of support in the community, stand a good chance of remaining independent for a long time. Old age may bring its challenges, but it does not necessarily spell a downward spiral to infirmity. The majority of people in their late 80s rate their health and quality of life as good, but there are two key factors: remaining active and maintaining friendships (Source: **www.bbc.co.uk/news/health-21757212**).

With such an overwhelming amount of information available these days on how to live well and what to do to ensure a safe, healthy and happy old age, is growing old getting easier? Much of the advice is based on sound evidence, but there is a lot that is confusing and contradictory:

what seems good for people one day can all too often be reported as being bad for them the next. If you are one of the many recently retireds who cares about, or actively cares for, ageing parents, working out how best to help them enjoy their final years can be a daunting task. There is a wealth of suggestions, active campaigns, products, training and research being carried out, making it almost impossible to keep track. One of the more recent projects is by Age UK's Research into Ageing Fund (RiAF). Here scientists are working to help alleviate memory loss, restore speech after a stroke, improve muscle strength to prevent falls and much more. Their excellent booklet, *Improving Later Life*, is well worth reading. For more information and to obtain a copy, see Age UK's website: **www.ageuk.org.uk/improvinglaterlifebook**.

The most often expressed wish by elderly people is that they remain independent and able to live in their own home for as long as possible. With a bit of support from friends, relatives or local care organizations, many should be able to do this. Should you become responsible for looking after elderly, frail or disabled relatives, you are not alone. There are more than 6.4 million carers in the UK, with 2 million taking up the role every year. Carers save the economy a staggering £119 billion each year, an average of £18,473 each (source: Carers UK: **www.carersuk.org**). One thing that is vital as people get older is remaining positive about their physical health, because it is good for their mental health as well. According to recent research, genetics accounts only for about a quarter of what determines the length of life. This means that three-quarters of how well people age is dictated by factors that are within each individual's control, such as nutrition and lifestyle. If you are keen to help your parent, relative or friend remain well and happy for as long as possible, read on:

Ten top tips for healthy ageing (from RiAF):

- Looking on the brighter side of life is really important.

- Think ahead: stay curious and stay fit.

- Try to maintain a healthy immune system in older age.

- Be sociable: social isolation causes stress, which lowers immunity.

- Look after the eyes: good vision underpins independent living.

- Get regular health checks for risk factors of stroke and heart disease.

- Protect the skin you're in. Avoid excessive exposure to the sun.

- Use it or lose it. It's never too late to start strengthening muscles.

- To sleep or not to sleep? Managing sleep is vital to healthy ageing.

- Report any problems to your GP at an early stage: better late than never.

The main focus of this chapter is on helping the elderly remain as independent as possible, for as long as possible, until a care home or nursing home becomes necessary. Knowing what facilities are available and what precautions your parents can take against a mishap occurring is an important factor. Being aware of whom they can turn to in an emergency can make all the difference. There is now much greater awareness of the needs of the elderly, mostly in regard to the financial implications of funding older people's care. In line with this, many provisions for the elderly have improved enormously. It is possible to find out from your local authority what programmes operate in your area that can help. Ask your parents' GP where to start, such as obtaining an assessment from Adult Social Services.

It is well worth investing a bit of time finding out where help and support can be accessed and familiarizing yourself (on your parents' behalf) with how to source funding or access equipment and personal aids. A bit of time spent improving their home to make it easier to cope as they get older, and fine-tuning their social and support network, should make all the difference and help them maintain their independence for longer. Here's one interesting and simple example: for the last 12 years a successful campaign, Spring Online, delivered by Digital Unite, has helped older people combat the effects of 'digital exclusion'. More than 7 million people in the UK have never used the internet – 6.3 million of them aged over 55. There have been many success stories, including a 100-year-old woman who asked for a laptop for her birthday present, and a recovering stroke victim who learned to access online banking and shopping, making a huge difference to his quality of life. (For more information see: **www.digitalunite**.)

Many families face the difficult choice between moving parents in with them or allowing them to continue to live on their own. While the decision will depend on individual circumstances, if safe to do so 'staying put' is usually preferable. In order to avoid moving, the best solution for most elderly people is to adapt their home to make it safer and more convenient.

Ways of adapting a home

Many elderly people will not require anything more complicated than a few general improvements. These could include better lighting, especially near staircases, a non-slip mat and grab rails in the bathroom, and safer heating arrangements. For some, a practical improvement might be to lower kitchen and other units, to place them within easy reach to make cooking less hazardous. Another fairly simple option is to convert a downstairs room into a bedroom and en suite bath or shower, should managing the stairs be proving difficult. These and other common-sense measures are covered in more detail in Chapter 8, Your home. Should such arrangements not really be sufficient, in the case of a physically handicapped or disabled person, more radical changes will usually be needed. This involves accessing help from the GP and local authority.

Local authority help

The state system is designed to support the elderly in their own home for as long as possible. Local authorities have a legal duty to help people with disabilities and, depending on what is required and the individual's ability to pay, may assist with the cost. Best advice is to approach their GP or contact the social services department direct. A sympathetic doctor will be crucial support at this stage, particularly if he or she has known them for some years and is familiar with their circumstances. The GP will be able to advise what is needed and supply any prescriptions, such as for a medical hoist, and will also be able to suggest which unit or department to approach, and make a recommendation to the housing department, should re-housing be desirable. If your parents can afford it, they will have to pay for the services they need themselves. If their income and savings are low, the council may pay part or all of the cost.

Local authority services

Social services departments (*social work departments* in Scotland) provide many of the services that people with disabilities may need, including:

- practical help in the home, perhaps with the support of a home help;
- adaptations to the home, such as a ramp for a wheelchair or other special equipment for your safety;
- meals on wheels;
- provision of day centres, clubs and similar;
- the issue of badges for cars driven or used by people with a disability (in some authorities this is handled by the works department or by the residents' parking department);
- advice about other transport services or concessions that may be available locally.

In most instances, you should speak to the social worker allocated to look after your elderly relatives, who will either be able to make the arrangements or point you in the right direction. He or she will also be able to tell you of any special facilities or other help provided by the authority.

Health care and specialist services

Local authorities employ a number of specialist helpers, variously based in the social services department or health centre, who are there to assist:

- *Social workers* are normally the first people to contact if your parents need a home help or meals on wheels, or have a housing difficulty or other query. Contact the local social services department or, in Scotland, the social work department.
- *Occupational therapists* have a wide knowledge of disability and can assist individuals via training, exercise or access to aids, equipment or adaptations to the home. Contact the local social services department.
- *Health visitors* are qualified nurses with a broad knowledge of health matters and other available services. Rather like social workers, health visitors can put your parents in touch with whatever specialized facilities are required. Contact is through the local health centre.
- *District nurses* are fully qualified nurses who will visit a patient in the home, change dressings, attend to other routine nursing matters, monitor progress and help with the arrangements if more specialized care is required. Contact is through the health centre.

- *Physiotherapists* use exercise and massage to help improve mobility and strengthen muscles, for example after an operation or to alleviate a crippling condition. They are normally available at both hospitals and health centres.
- *Medical social workers* (MSWs) (previously known as almoners) are available to consult if patients have any problems – whether practical or emotional – on leaving hospital. MSWs can advise on coping with a disablement, as well as such practical matters as transport, after-care and other immediate arrangements. They work in hospitals, and an appointment should be made before the patient is discharged.

Council tax

If an elderly relative has a disability, they may be able to claim a reduction on their council tax. If they have a blue badge on their car, they may get a rebate for a garage. They should apply to the housing benefits officer, but different councils employ different officers to deal with this; see website: **www.gov.uk – Disabled People**.

Help with home repair and adaptations

Disabled facilities grant

This is a local council grant to help towards the cost of adapting a home to enable a disabled or elderly person to live there. It can cover a wide range of improvements to help the occupants manage more independently. This includes work to facilitate access either to the property itself or to the main rooms, the installation of ramps or a lift; the provision of suitable bathroom or kitchen facilities; and various other works which would make a home safe for a disabled person. Provided the applicant is eligible, currently a mandatory grant of up to £30,000 in England, £25,000 in Northern Ireland and £36,000 in Wales may be available. See website: **www.gov.uk – Disabled People**.

Home Improvement Agencies (HIAs)

Home Improvement Agencies assist vulnerable homeowners and private sector tenants who are older, disabled or on a low income to repair, improve, maintain or adapt their homes. They are local, not-for-profit organizations. There are approximately 200 home improvement agencies in England and around 85 per cent of residents in England have access to a home improvement agency. They are sometimes known as Care & Repair or Staying Put schemes. For HIAs in the UK, see:

Foundations: **www.foundations.uk.com.**

Care and Repair Cymru: **www.careandrepair.org.uk.**

Care and Repair Scotland: **www.careandrepairscotland.co.uk.**

Other organizations which can help include:

Age UK: **www.ageuk.org.uk.**

British Red Cross: **www.redcross.org.uk.**

Assist UK: **www.assist-uk.org.**

CAE (Centre for Accessible Environments): **www.cae.org.uk.**

DEMAND (Design & Manufacture for Disability):
www.demand.org.uk.

Disability Wales/Anabledd Cymru: **www.disabilitywales.org.**

Disabled Living Foundation (DLF): **www.dlf.org.uk.**

Hearing and Mobility: **www.hearingandmobility.co.uk.**

REMAP: **www.remap.org.uk.**

Alarm systems

Alarm systems for the elderly are many and varied, but the knowledge that help can be summoned quickly in the event of an emergency is reassuring in its own right to many elderly or disabled people. Having a personal alarm can enable many people to remain independent far longer than would otherwise be sensible. Some alarm systems allow people living in their own homes to be linked to a central control, or have a telephone link, enabling personal contact to be made. Others simply signal that something is wrong. Sometimes a relative or friend who has been nominated will be alerted. Your parents' local authority social services department will have information. See website: **www.gov.uk.**

A number of organizations offer alarm systems, medical alerts and other devices. Some useful websites include:

DLF (Disabled Living Foundation): **www.dlf.org.uk.**

Contact4me: **www.contact4me.com.**

Helpline Limited: **www.helpline.co.uk**.

MedicAlertUK: **www.medicalert.org.uk**.

Community alarms

Telephone alarm systems operated on the public telephone network can be used by anyone with a direct telephone line. The systems link into a 24-hour monitoring centre and the individual has a pendant that enables help to be called even when the owner is some distance from the telephone. Grants may be available in some cases to meet the costs.

Age UK Personal Alarm Service: **www.ageuk.org.uk**.

SeniorLinkEldercare: **www.seniorlinkeldercare.com**.

Main local authority services

Quite apart from any assistance with housing, local authorities supply a number of services that can prove invaluable to elderly people. The two most important are meals on wheels and home helps. Additionally, there are social workers and various specialists concerned with aspects of health care (already mentioned above). Since the introduction of Community Care, local authority social services departments have taken over all responsibility for helping to assess and coordinate the best arrangements for individuals according to their particular requirements. Other organizations which may offer home help include the British Red Cross and Age UK (websites already listed above).

Meals on wheels

The meals on wheels service is sometimes run by local authorities direct and sometimes by voluntary organizations, such as WRVS, acting as their agents. The purpose is to deliver ready-made meals to individuals in their own homes. Different arrangements apply in different areas, and schemes variously operate from two to seven days a week, or possibly less frequently if frozen meals are supplied. For further information, contact the local social services department or see website: **www.gov.uk** – Meals at home services. The other organization which delivers over 6 million meals a year to people who have difficulty with shopping, carrying food home or cooking for themselves is **WRVS**: **www.wrvs.org.uk**.

Home helps

Local authorities have a legal obligation to run a home-help service to help frail and housebound elderly people with such basic household chores as shopping, tidying up, a little light cooking and so on. In many areas the service is badly overstretched, so the amount of help actually available varies considerably, as does the method of charging. A health and social care assessment with the social services department of your local council is often the first step towards getting the help and support your parents need. See website: **www.gov.uk** – Disabled people.

Good neighbour schemes

A number of areas of the country have an organized system of good neighbour schemes. In essence, these consist of volunteers agreeing to act as good neighbours to one or several elderly people living close by. Depending on what is required, they may simply pop in on a daily basis to check that everything is all right, or they may give more sustained assistance such as providing help with dressing, bathing, shopping or preparing a light meal. To find out whether such a scheme exists locally, ask the local authority, social services, your parents' health centre, or the Citizens Advice Bureau.

Key voluntary organizations

Voluntary organizations complement the services provided by statutory health and social services in making life easier for elderly people living at home. The range of provision varies from area to area but can include:

- lunch clubs;
- holidays and short-term placements;
- day centres and clubs;
- friendly visiting;
- aids such as wheelchairs;
- transport;
- odd jobs and decorating;
- gardening;

- good neighbour schemes;
- prescription collection;
- advice and information;
- family support schemes.

The particular organization providing these services depends on where your parents live, but the best place to get advice is the local Citizens Advice Bureau. These are the key agencies:

Age UK: **www.ageuk.org.uk**.

Age Scotland: **www.ageuk.org.uk/scotland**.

Age Wales: **www.ageuk.org.uk/cymru**.

Age Northern Ireland: **www.ageuk.org.uk/northern-ireland**.

Disability Wales: **www.disabilitywales.org**.

Update (Scotland's disability information service): **www.update.org.uk**.

Care Information Scotland: **www.careinfoscotland.co.uk**.

Centre for Individual Living, Northern Ireland: **www.cilbelfast.org**.

British Red Cross: **www.redcross.org.uk**.

St John Ambulance: **www.sja.org.uk**.

WRVS: **www.wrvs.org.uk**.

Other sources of help and advice include:

Civil Service Retirement Fellowship: **www.csrf.org.uk**.

Disability Rights UK: **www.disabilityrightsuk.org**.

Jewish Care: **www.jewishcare.org**.

National Brokerage Network: **www.nationalbrokeragenetwork.org.uk**.

Transport

Difficulty in getting around is often a major problem for elderly and disabled people. In addition to the facilities run by voluntary organizations already mentioned, there are several other very useful services:

Forum of Mobility Centres: **www.mobility-centres.org.uk**.

London Taxicard: **www.londoncouncils.gov.uk/services/taxicard**.

Motability: **www.motability.co.uk**.

Driving licence renewal at age 70

All drivers aged 70 are sent a licence renewal form to have their driving licence renewed. The entitlement to drive will need to be renewed by the **DVLA**; the new licence will normally be valid for three years. See website: **www.gov.uk** – Driving, Transport and Travel.

Holidays

Many people in their late 70s and older travel across the world, go on activity holidays and see the great sights in the UK and abroad without any more difficulty than anyone else. They will find plenty of choice in Chapter 14, Holidays, including information about how to obtain assistance at airports and railway stations. However, some elderly people need special facilities if a stay away from home is to be possible. A number of organizations can help:

Able Travel: **www.able-travel.com**.

Accessible Travel and Leisure: **www.accessibletravel.co.uk**.

Can be done: **www.canbedone.co.uk**.

Chalfont Line: **www.chalfont-line.co.uk**.

Disability Holidays Guide.com: **www.disabilityholidaysguide.com**.

Enable holidays: **www.enableholidays.com**.

Tourism for All: **www.tourismforall.org.uk**.

Voluntary organizations

A number of the specialist voluntary organizations run holiday centres or provide specially adapted self-catering accommodation. In some cases, outings and entertainment are offered; in others, individuals plan their own activities and amusement. Guests requiring assistance usually need to be accompanied by a companion, although in a few instances care arrangements are inclusive. Most of the organizations can advise about the possibility of obtaining a grant or other financial assistance.

Holidays for all: **www.holidaysforall.org.uk**.

Holiday with Help: **www.holidayswithhelp.org.uk**.

Leonard Cheshire: **www.leonard-cheshire.org**.

Vitalise: **www.vitalise.org.uk**.

The *Disabled Travellers' Guide*, published by the AA, lists a wide choice of holiday venues where disabled travellers can go in the normal way but with the advantage of having special facilities provided. Downloadable in pdf format, it gives information on holiday accommodation suitable for disabled individuals and their families, together with advice on travelling in Europe. See website: **www.theaa.com**.

Power of Attorney

Giving another person Power of Attorney authorizes someone else to take business and other financial decisions on the donor's behalf. A Lasting Power of Attorney continues, regardless of any decline, throughout the individual's life. To protect the donor and the nominated attorney, the law clearly lays down certain principles that must be observed, with both sides signing a declaration that they understand the various rights and duties involved. The law furthermore calls for the power to be formally registered with the Public Trust Office in the event of the donor being, or becoming, mentally incapable.

A Lasting Power of Attorney permits someone to be appointed to make decisions on behalf of another. It is normally used when someone is unable to make their own decision. There are two types: health and welfare; and property and financial affairs. One type of Lasting Power of Attorney can be made at a time, or it is possible to do both together.

The right time to arrange a Power of Attorney is while an individual is in full command of his or her faculties, so that potential situations that would require decisions can be properly discussed and the donor's wishes made clear. For the Lasting Power of Attorney to be valid, the donor must in any event be capable of understanding what he or she is agreeing to at the time of making the power. If an elderly person you care about is considering setting up an LPA, it is advisable that they consult their GP and the family solicitor.

For further information see: **www.gov.uk/power-of-attorney/** or **www.justice.gov.uk/forms**.

Living-in help

Temporary

Elderly people living alone can be more vulnerable to flu and other winter ailments; they may have a fall; or, for no apparent reason, they may go through a period of being forgetful and neglecting themselves. Equally, as they become older, they may not be able to cope as well with managing their homes or caring for themselves. In the event of an emergency or if you have reason for concern – perhaps because you are going on holiday and will not be around to keep a watchful eye on them – engaging living-in help can be a godsend. Most agencies tend inevitably to be on the expensive side, although in the event of a real problem they often represent excellent value for money. A more unusual and interesting longer-term possibility is to recruit the help of a Community Service Volunteer.

Community Service Volunteers (CSVs)

CSV is the UK's leading training and volunteering charity, training over 12,000 young people and adults each year. They provide practical assistance in the home and also offer companionship. Usually a care scheme is set up through a social worker, who supervises how the arrangement is working out. Volunteers are placed on a one-month trial basis. For more information contact your parents' local social services department, or see **CSV: www.csv.org.uk**.

Agencies

The agencies listed specialize in providing temporary help, rather than permanent staff. Fees are normally paid by private funding, but depending on individual circumstances, public financial assistance may be available.

Bunbury Care Agency: **www.bunburyagency.com**.

Consultus Care & Nursing Agency Ltd: **www.consultuscare.com**.

Country Cousins: **www.country-cousins.co.uk**.

Live-In Support: **www.live-insupport.co.uk**.

The Care Agency: **www.thecareagency.co.uk**.

For a further list of agencies, see *The Lady* magazine, or search the internet under the heading 'Nursing agencies' or 'Care agencies'.

Nursing care

If one of your parents needs regular nursing care, the GP may be able to arrange for a community or district nurse to visit him or her at home. This will not be a sleeping-in arrangement but simply involves a qualified nurse calling round when necessary. If they need more concentrated home nursing you will have to go through a private agency. Some of those listed above can sometimes supply trained nurses. Additionally, there are many specialist agencies that can arrange hourly, daily or live-in nurses on a temporary or longer-term basis.

Fees and services vary considerably. Costs vary throughout the country, with London inevitably being most expensive. Private health insurance can sometimes be claimed against part of the cost, but this is generally only in respect of qualified nurses. Your local health centre or social services department should be able to give you names and addresses of local agencies, or search the internet under the heading 'Nursing agencies'.

Permanent

There may come a time when you feel that it is no longer safe to allow one of your parents to live entirely on his or her own. One possibility is to engage a companion or housekeeper on a permanent basis. However, if you want to investigate the idea further, many domestic agencies supply housekeeper-companions. Alternatively, you could advertise in the most widely read publication for these kinds of posts. See **The Lady Magazine: www.lady.co.uk**.

Permanent help can also sometimes be provided by agencies, which will supply continuous four-weekly placements. This is an expensive option, and the lack of continuity can at times be distressing for elderly people, particularly at the changeover point. The agencies listed above may be worth contacting.

Au pairs are cheaper but a drawback is that most au pairs speak inadequate English (at least when they first arrive). As they are technically students living *en famille*, they must by law be given plenty of free time to attend school and study. For more information see: **www.gov.uk/au-pairs-employment-law**.

Flexible care arrangements

One of the problems for many elderly people is that the amount of care they need is liable to vary according to the state of their health. There are other relevant factors including, for example, the availability of neighbours and family. Whereas after an operation the requirement may be for someone with basic nursing skills, a few weeks later the only need may be for someone to act as a companion. Under normal circumstances it may be as little as simply popping in for the odd hour during the day to cook a hot meal and check all is well. Here are a few agencies that offer a flexible service:

Anchor Care: **www.anchor.org.uk**.

Christies Care: **www.christiescare.com**.

Cura Domi – Care at Home: **www.curadomi.co.uk**.

Miracle Workers: **www.miracle-workers.co.uk**.

UKHCA (United Kingdom Home Care Association): **www.ukhca.co.uk**.

Although any of these suggestions can work extremely well for a while, with many families it may sooner or later come down to a choice between residential care and inviting a parent to live with you. Sometimes, particularly in the case of an unmarried son or daughter or other relative, it is more practical to move into the parent's (or relative's) home if the accommodation is more suitable.

Emergency care for pets

For many elderly people a pet is a very important part of their lives. It provides companionship and fun as well as stimulating them into taking regular outdoor exercise. Because pets usually have shorter life spans than us, some may have planned for this event. But what if your elderly loved ones become ill or incapacitated, or dies first? To ensure that their beloved pet will continue to receive care should something unexpected happen, it is vital to plan ahead. The following organizations will be able to help under these circumstances:

Blue Cross: **www.bluecross.org.uk**.

Cats Protection: **www.cats.org.uk**.

Cinnamon Trust: **www.cinnamon.org.uk**.

Dogs Trust: **www.dogstrust.org.uk**.

National Animal Welfare Trust: **www.natw.org.uk**.

Pet Fostering Service Scotland: **www.pfss.org.uk**.

Practical help for carers

If your elderly relative is still fairly active – visits friends, does his or her own shopping, or enjoys some hobby that gets him or her out and about – the strains and difficulties involved in caring for them may be fairly minimal. This applies particularly if your parent is moving in with you and your home lends itself to creating a granny flat, so everyone can retain some privacy and your parent can continue to enjoy maximum independence. However, this is not always possible, and in the case of an ill or very frail person far more intensive care may be required. It is important to know what help is available and how to obtain it. The many services provided by local authorities and voluntary agencies, described earlier in the chapter, apply as much to an elderly person living with a family as to one living alone. If there is nothing there that solves a particular problem you may have, it could be that one of the following organizations could help:

Age UK: **www.ageuk.org.uk**.

British Red Cross: **www.redcross.org.uk**.

Carers Trust: **www.carers.org**.

Independent Age: **www.independentage.org**.

WRVS: **www.wrvs.org.uk**.

Most areas have respite care facilities to enable carers to take a break from their dependants from time to time. Depending on the circumstances, this could be for just the odd day or possibly for a week or two to enable carers who need it to have a real rest. A particularly welcome aspect of respite care is that many schemes specially cater for, among others, elderly people with dementia.

Holiday breaks for carers

There are various schemes to enable those with an elderly relative to go on holiday alone or simply to enjoy a respite from their caring responsibilities. A number of local authorities run *fostering schemes*, on similar lines to child fostering. There may be a charge, or the service may be run on a voluntary basis (or be paid for by the local authority). Some voluntary organizations arrange *holidays for older people* to give relatives a break. Different charities take responsibility according to the area where you live: the Citizens Advice Bureau, volunteer centre or social services department should know whom you should approach.

Another solution is a *short-stay home*, which is residential accommodation variously run by local authorities, voluntary organizations or private individuals, catering specifically for elderly people. The different types of home are described under the heading 'Residential care homes' further on in this chapter. For information about local authority provision, ask the social services department. If, as opposed to general care, proper medical attention is necessary, you should consult your parent's GP. Many *hospitals and nursing homes* offer short-stay care arrangements as a means of relieving relatives, and a doctor should be able to help organize this for you.

Benefits and allowances

There are benefits and allowances available to those with responsibility for the care of an elderly person and/or to elderly people themselves. If you are caring for someone, **Gov.uk** is the place to turn to for the latest and widest range of online public information. It is the gateway for government advice. There is a section for carers covering support services and assessments, carer's rights, working and caring, carer's allowance and much more, and includes information for disabled people. See website: **www.gov.uk** – Disabled people.

Entitlements for carers

Home Responsibilities Protection

This is a means of protecting your state pension if you are unable to work because of the need to care for an elderly person. For further details, see under 'The state pension' at the start of Chapter 3, or look at the following websites: **www.gov.uk; www.hmrc.gov.uk; www.nidirect.gov.uk.**

Carer's Allowance

If you spend at least 35 hours a week caring for someone who is getting attendance allowance or the middle or highest rate of the Disability Living Allowance care component, you may be able to claim Carer's Allowance. You cannot get this if you are already getting the state pension or work and earn over £100 per week. See: **www.gov.uk/carers-allowance**.

Entitlements for elderly or disabled people

Attendance Allowance

This is paid to people aged 65 or over who are severely disabled, either mentally or physically, and have needed almost constant care for at least six months. (They may be able to get the allowance even if no one has actually given them that help.) An exception to the six months' qualifying period is made in the case of those who are terminally ill, who can receive the allowance without having to wait. There are two rates of allowance: £53.00 or £79.15 per week. See: **www.gov.uk/attendance-allowance**.

Personal Independence Payment

From April 2013 a new benefit called Personal Independence Payment (PIP) began replacing Disability Living Allowance (DLA) for disabled people aged 16 to 64. As with DLA, Personal Independence Payment is designed to help disabled people live more independently and support those with the greatest need. It is made up of two parts, a Daily Living component and a Mobility component. There are two rates – standard and enhanced. For more information on the changes, and eligibility criteria, see: **www.gov.uk/pip**.

Cold Weather Payment

If your elderly relative is in receipt of certain benefits, he/she may be eligible for Cold Weather Payment. These are made when the local temperature is either recorded as, or forecast to be, an average of zero degrees Celsius or below over seven consecutive days. The amount paid is £25.00. Those eligible should receive it without having to claim. For more information, see website: **www.gov.uk/cold-weather-payment**.

Winter Fuel Payment

This is a special annual tax-free payment of between £100 and £300 given to all households with a resident aged 60 and over. See: **www.gov.uk/winter-fuel-payment**.

Free off-peak bus travel

People over the age of 60 and also disabled people can travel free on any bus service in the country. See Chapter 14, section on 'Travel and other concessions'.

Free TV licence

Anyone aged 75 or over is eligible for a free TV Licence for their main address. There are currently almost 4 million free TV Licences in force – and with some 4.9 million adults over the age of 75 living in the UK, TV Licensing is encouraging those able to claim the concession to apply online: **www.tvlicensing.co.uk**.

Financial assistance

A number of charities give financial assistance to elderly people in need. Some of these may have been listed in earlier sections but are also relevant here:

Counsel and Care: **www.counselandcare.org.uk**.

Elizabeth Finn Care: **www.elizabethfinncare.org.uk**.

Guild of Aid for Gentlepeople: **www.turn2us.org.uk**.

Independent Age: **www.independentage.org.uk**.

Independent Living Fund (ILF): **www.ilf.org.uk**.

Motability: **www.motability.co.uk**.

RABI (Royal Agricultural Benevolent Institution): **www.rabi.org.uk**.

SSAFA Forces Help: **www.ssafa.org.uk**.

For many people, one of the main barriers to getting help is knowing which of the many thousands of charities to approach. Free services which help older people in genuine financial need receive the support that may be available to them from a variety of charitable sources are provided by:

Charity Search: **www.charitysearch.org.uk**.

Turn2Us, part of Elizabeth Finn Care: **www.turn2us.org.uk**.

Useful reading

For other sources of financial help, ask at your library, or search online for *A Guide to Grants for Individuals in Need*, published by the Directory of Social Change (**www.grantsforindividuals.org.uk**).

Independent Age is a support community for thousands of older people across the UK and the Republic of Ireland. Their helpful publication, *Wise Guide – Life-improving advice for the over-65s*, is the practical elderly person's handbook. See: **www.independentage.org**.

Age UK Guides and factsheets are aimed at keeping elderly people up-to-date with home and care information. Guides are short and easy to digest giving a comprehensive overview of a subject. Factsheets are longer, more detailed and aimed at professionals. See: **www.ageuk.org.uk/publications**.

Special accommodation

Elderly parents who no longer feel able to maintain a family home may decide that the time has come to move into accommodation that is smaller, easier and more economic to maintain. Some people refer to this point in their lives as 'Managing the End Game'. Moving into purpose-designed retirement housing, with a high degree of independence and with the option to have a range of support resources as and when required, is a solution that suits increasing numbers of people. There is a wide choice available to meet individual requirements, budgets and tastes. Should their health deteriorate, they may need care in their new home, or at least the chance to call for more support if needed in the future.

Retirement living accommodation offers elderly parents the ability to maintain as much of their independence as possible, and a degree of flexibility should their needs change at any time in the future. Retirement villages are gaining in popularity and there is the added luxury of having a ready-made social network for your parents outside their front door, of people of their own age who may have similar interests. The real value of these places lies not in their facilities and activities, however attractive, but in the people who live there. Choosing the right accommodation for elderly parents is critically important, as it can make all the difference to independence, lifestyle and general wellbeing. It can also, of course, lift a great burden off families' shoulders to know that their parents are happy and comfortable, in safe surroundings, among congenial people with the added benefit of on-the-spot help, should this be necessary.

Just to sound a note of warning: there have been recent revelations in the press about bad practice in retirement and sheltered housing management, which are little short of disgraceful (for example, adding VAT to electricity bills which already contain VAT, and paying an 'exit fee' to the freeholder if the property is sold, which can be as much as 5 per cent of the sale price). One suggested solution is for flat owners to club together and take over the management. Advice on this can be obtained from the Campaign Against Residential Leasehold Exploitation (**www.carlex.org.uk**) and the Right to Manage Federation (**www.rtmf.org.uk**).

Sheltered housing

There are many different types of sheltered housing schemes. Some will have a scheme manager (a warden) who lives onsite or offsite, and all should provide 24-hour emergency help through an alarm system. Each scheme usually has between 20 and 40 self-contained flats or bungalows, but there will often be communal areas. If residents require more support, extra-care sheltered housing may be available.

Sheltered housing for sale

Good developments are always sought after and can require you to join a waiting list. There are many companies offering sheltered housing for sale, with standards and facilities varying enormously. Some also provide personal care services as an adjunct to their retirement home schemes. Flats and houses are usually sold on long leases (99 years or more) for a capital sum, with a weekly or monthly service charge to cover maintenance and resident support services. Should a resident decide to move, the property can usually be sold on the open market, either through an estate agent or through the developer, provided the prospective buyer is over 55 years of age. Although the rights of sheltered housing residents have been strengthened over the years, you would nevertheless be strongly recommended to get any contract or agreement vetted by a solicitor before proceeding.

The range of prices is very wide, depending on size, location and type of property. Weekly service charges vary widely too. Additionally, there is usually an annual ground rental – and council tax is normally excluded. A particular point to watch is that the service charge tends to rise annually, sometimes well above the inflation level. Owners of sheltered accommodation have the same rights as other leaseholders, and charges can therefore be challenged by appeal to a leasehold valuation tribunal.

For further information see:

Elderly Accommodation Counsel: **www.eac.org.uk**.

Retirement Homesearch: **www.retirementhomesearch.co.uk**.

New developments are constantly under construction. Properties tend to be sold quickly soon after completion, so it pays to find out about future developments and to get on any waiting lists well in advance of a prospective purchase. Firms specializing in this type of property can be found on:

Retirement Housing Group: **www.retirementhousinggroup.com**.

Housing associations build sheltered housing for sale and also manage sheltered housing developments on behalf of private construction companies; see:

Anchor: **www.anchor.org.uk**.

National Housing Federation: **www.housing.org.uk**.

Rented sheltered housing

This is normally provided by local authorities, housing associations and certain benevolent societies. As with accommodation to buy, quality varies.

Local authority housing is usually only available to people who have resided in the area for some time. There is often an upper and lower age limit for admission, and prospective tenants may have to undergo a medical examination, since as a rule only those who are physically fit are accepted. Should a resident become infirm or frail, alternative accommodation will be found. Apply to the local housing or social services department or via a housing advice centre.

Housing associations supply much of the newly built sheltered housing. Both rent and service charges vary around the country. In case of need, Income Support or Housing Benefit may be obtained to help with the cost. Citizens Advice Bureau and housing departments often keep a list of local housing associations. There are hundreds to choose from; here are just a few:

Abbeyfield: **www.abbeyfield.com**.

Anchor: **www.anchor.org.uk**.

Girlings: **www.girlings.co.uk**.

Habinteg Housing Association: **www.habinteg.org.uk**.

Hanover: **www.hanover.org.uk**.

Jewish Community Housing Association Ltd: **www.jcha.org.uk**.

Southern Housing Group: **www.shgroup.org.uk**.

Benevolent societies

These are charitable organizations which help a particular group of people in need. Here are just a few:

Housing 21: **www.housing21.co.uk**.

Royal Alfred Seafarers' Society: **www.royalalfredseafarers.com**.

Royal British Legion: **www.ritishlegion.org.uk**.

SSAFA Forces Help: **www.ssafa.org.uk**.

Alternative ways of buying sheltered accommodation

For those who cannot afford to buy into sheltered housing either outright or through a mortgage, there are a variety of alternative payment methods.

Shared ownership and 'Sundowner' schemes

Part-ownership schemes are now offered by a number of developers. Would-be residents, who must be over 55 years, part-buy or part-rent with the amount of rent varying according to the size of the initial lump sum. Residents can sell at any time, but they only recoup that percentage of the sale price that is proportionate to their original capital investment, with no allowance for any rental payments made over the intervening period.

'Investment' and gifted housing schemes

Some charities and housing associations operate these schemes, for which a capital sum is required, to obtain sheltered accommodation. *Investment* schemes work as follows. The buyer puts in the larger share of the capital, usually 50 to 80 per cent, and the housing association puts in the remainder. The buyer pays rent on the housing association's share of the accommodation and also service charges for the communal facilities.

Gifted housing schemes differ in that an individual donates his or her property to a registered charity, in return for being housed and cared for in his or her own home. The attraction is that the owner can remain in his or her own property with none of the burden of its upkeep. However, it is advisable to consult a solicitor before signing anything, because such schemes have the big negative of reducing the value of the owner's estate, with consequent loss for any beneficiaries. See:

Age UK: **www.ageuk.org.uk/giftedhousing**.

Almshouses

Most almshouses are endowed by a charity for the benefit of older people of reduced means who live locally or have a connection with a particular trade. There are now over 2,000 groups of almshouses, providing about 35,000 dwellings. Although many are of considerable age, most of them have been modernized and new ones are being built. Rents are not charged, but there will be a maintenance contribution towards upkeep and heating.

Almshouses do not provide the same security of tenure as some other tenancies, so it is advisable to check with a lawyer exactly what the beneficiary's rights are. There is no standard way to apply for an almshouse, since each charity has its own qualifications for residence. For more information see:

Almshouse Association: **www.almshouse.org**.

Salvation Army homes

There are 17 care homes for elderly people in various parts of the UK, offering residential care for men and women unable to manage in their own homes, owned and operated by the **Salvation Army: www.saha.org.uk**.

Granny flats

A granny flat or annexe is a self-contained unit attached to a family house. A large house can be converted or extended for this purpose, but planning permission is needed. Enquire at your local authority planning department. Some councils, particularly new towns, have houses to rent with granny flats.

Extra-care schemes

A number of organizations that provide sheltered accommodation also have extra-care sheltered housing, designed for those who can no longer look after themselves without assistance. Although expensive, it is cheaper than most private care homes and often more appropriate than full-scale nursing care. A possible problem is that tenants of some of these schemes do not have security of tenure and, should they become frail, could be asked to leave if more intensive care were required. Among the housing associations that provide these facilities are Housing 21, Hanover Housing Association, Anchor and Abbeyfield (see the details listed earlier in this chapter).

Homesharing – a new idea

Homesharing is a new concept in the UK offering an alternative to residential or live-in care. It is similar to taking in a lodger, but with a focus for those in later life to be able to do this safely and maximizing the benefits for both parties. Where an elderly person has a spare room in their house, renting that room to a young person will bring them companionship, income through rent and a situation where they benefit from help around the house. For more information see My Ageing Parent: **www.myageingparent.com/home-sharing**.

Community Care

The much-awaited reform of the long-term care system will be brought forward by a year to 2016 and the cap on payments is to be set at £72,000. From 2016 this will be the amount people must pay towards their long-term care needs, with the state stepping in to pay the rest. This will not prevent people having to sell their homes to meet the cost of their own care, experts warn, as the cap will cover only nursing, not residential costs and food. Individuals will still have to find the money for residence fees.

It is anticipated that nearly 70 per cent of men and some 85 per cent of women over the age of 65 will need care at some time. Frailty in old age is quite different from actual illness, where elderly people are entitled to receive free treatment under the National Health Service. While some older people can afford to retire in comfort and others are confident and optimistic about how they will end their days, it is very sad when relatives have to sell their loved ones' property so that they can afford to pay for their growing care needs in their later years.

Care homes

If your parents need to move into a care home, the state may help with the cost. The rules are complex and only a brief outline is given here. For more information, the local council is the point of contact. If moving into a nursing home is a continuation of NHS treatment that your parents have been having for an illness – for example he or she is discharged from hospital direct to a home – this should be paid for by the NHS. However, this is a grey area and you may have to be persistent to get their costs met in this way.

If they do not qualify for NHS continuing care, they may still qualify for some state help with care home fees, provided their needs assessment found this was the best option for them and their means are low. If their capital (savings and other assets) are above a set threshold, they will have to pay for themselves. If their capital is less, their local council may pay part or, if their capital is below the lower threshold, the full amount. Moving into a care home is a big decision, whether you are doing it yourself or for a loved one. Here are some suggestions before taking the decision:

- Is a care home really needed? Get advice on the housing options.
- What type of care home is wanted? Some offer accommodation and help with personal care; other care homes offer nursing care as well as the basic help.
- How to find a care home? Think of it like buying a house: you need to get a feel for what is out there before making a decision. Personal recommendations are important.
- How much will it cost? There is a lot of difference in care home fees. If the local council is paying, it will set a maximum cost that

it will contribute. If the costs are higher, a relative or friend will need to top up that amount. If your parents are self-funding, make sure they can afford the fees.

Residential care homes (care homes registered to provide personal care)

There may come a time when it is no longer possible for an elderly person to manage without being in proper residential care. In a residential care home, sometimes known as a 'rest home', the accommodation usually consists of a bedroom plus communal dining rooms, lounges and gardens. All meals are provided, rooms are cleaned, and staff are at hand to give whatever help is needed. Homes are run by private individuals (or companies), voluntary organizations and local authorities. All homes must be registered with the Commission for Social Care Inspection to ensure minimum standards. *An unregistered home should not be considered.* It is very important that the individual should have a proper chance to visit it and ask any questions. Before reaching a final decision, it is a good idea to arrange a short stay to see whether the facilities are suitable and pleasant.

Moving to a new care home can be a highly distressing experience for an elderly person who has become attached to the staff and made friends among the other residents, so making an enquiry about long-term plans for the home is prudent. Though a move can never be totally ruled out, awareness of whether the home is likely to remain a going concern could be a deciding factor when making a choice.

Private homes

Private care homes are often converted houses, taking up to about 30 people. As more companies move into the market, the homes can be purpose-built accommodation and may include a heated swimming pool and luxury facilities. The degree of care varies. If a resident becomes increasingly infirm, a care home will normally continue to look after him or her if possible. It may, however, become necessary at some point to arrange transfer to a nursing home or hospital. Fees vary enormously.

Voluntary care homes

These are run by charities, religious bodies or other voluntary organizations. Eligibility may be determined by age, background or occupation, depending on the criteria of the managing organization. Income may be a factor, as may general fitness, and individuals may be invited to a personal interview before acceptance onto the waiting list. Priority tends to be given to those in greatest need. Homes are often in large converted houses, fees vary depending on locality.

Local authority homes

These are sometimes referred to as 'Part III accommodation', and admission will invariably be arranged by the social services department. If someone does not like the particular accommodation suggested, he or she can turn it down and ask the department what other offers might be available. Weekly charges vary around the country. In practice, individuals are charged only according to their means.

Nursing homes (care homes registered to provide nursing care)

Nursing homes provide medical supervision and fully qualified nurses, 24 hours a day. Most are privately run, with the remainder being supported by voluntary organizations. All nursing homes in England must be registered with the Commission for Social Care Inspection, which keeps a list of what homes are available in the area. In Wales, the inspectorate is called the Care Standards Inspectorate for Wales, and in Scotland it is called the Scottish Commission for the Regulation of Care.

Private

These homes normally accommodate between 15 and 100 patients. Depending on the part of the country, charges vary. Some fees rise depending on how much nursing is required. For information about nursing homes in the UK, contact the following:

Elderly Accommodation Counsel: **www.eac.org.uk**.

RNHA (Registered Nursing Home Association): **www.rnha.co.uk**.

UKHCA (United Kingdom Home Care Association Ltd): **www.ukhca.co.uk**.

Voluntary organizations

These normally have very long waiting lists, and beds are often reserved for those who have been in the charity's care home. Voluntary organizations that run care homes include:

Careways Trust: **www.carewaystrust.org.uk**.

Friends of the Elderly: **www.fote.org.uk**.

IndependentAge: **www.independentage.org.uk**.

Jewish Care: **www.jewishcare.org**.

Costs of care

Free nursing care

Since October 2001, the nursing costs of being in a home have been made free to all patients. This does not include the personal care costs (eg help with bathing, dressing or eating), nor the accommodation costs; individuals will continue to be assessed for both of these under the rules described below. In Scotland, exceptionally, the personal care costs are also free. The provision of free nursing care may make only a fairly limited contribution to the cost of being in a home. Patients are assessed according to their needs and the amount of actual nursing care they require.

Financial assistance for residential and nursing home care

Under the Community Care arrangements, people needing to go into a residential or nursing home may receive help from their local authority social services department. As explained earlier, the department will make the arrangements direct with the home following its assessment procedure and will seek reimbursement from the person towards the cost, according to set means-testing rules. For further information:

Citizens Advice Bureau: **www.citizensadvice.org.uk**.

Elderly Accommodation Counsel: **www.eac.org.uk**.

Funding care

A major worry for many elderly people going into residential care is the requirement to sell their own home to cover the costs. While this may still eventually be necessary, the rules have been made slightly more flexible to allow a short breathing space for making decisions. Planning for care is essential now that we are all living longer, and there are different types of care to consider: in the home, in residential care and then in nursing care. The funding aspect is complex. The starting point is to see what the local authority can provide. Beyond that, careful planning is required so that best use is made of your parents' income and assets. Some organizations offer advice and information for carers; see:

Care & Quality Commission: **www.cqc.org.uk**.

Home Instead Senior Care: **www.homeinstead.co.uk**.

Solicitors for the Elderly: **www.solicitorsfortheelderly.com**.

Further information

Key sources of information about voluntary and private homes are: the *Charities Digest* (available in libraries, housing aid centres and Citizens Advice Bureaux) and the *Directory of Independent Hospitals and Health Services* (available in libraries). The *Charities Digest* also includes information about hospices. Here are some other sources of advice not previously listed:

Action on Elder Abuse: **www.elderabuse.org.uk**.

R&RA (Relatives & Residents Association): **www.relres.org**.

Some special problems

A minority of people, as they become older, suffer from special problems that can cause great distress. Because families do not like to talk about these problems, they may be unaware of what services are available and so may be missing out on practical help and sometimes also on financial assistance.

Hypothermia

Elderly people tend to be more vulnerable to the cold. If the body drops below a certain temperature, this can be dangerous, because one of the symptoms of hypothermia is that sufferers no longer actually feel cold. Instead, they may lose their appetite and vitality and may become mentally confused. British Gas, electricity companies and the Solid Fuel Association are all willing to give advice on how heating systems can be used more efficiently and economically. It also is worth checking that elderly parents are on the correct tariff when it comes to utility bills. Some utility providers have reduced charges for elderly, vulnerable people who are in receipt of certain benefits.

Elderly and disabled people in receipt of Income Support may receive a Cold Weather Payment to help with heating costs during a particularly cold spell. Those eligible should receive the money automatically. In the event of any problem, ask at your social security office. In an emergency, such as a power cut, contact the Citizens Advice Bureau or Age UK. Every household with someone aged 60 or older will get an annual tax-free Winter Fuel Payment of between £200–£400. See website: **www.gov.uk** – Winter Fuel Payment.

Incontinence

Bladder or bowel problems can cause deep embarrassment to sufferers as well as inconvenience to relatives. The problem can occur in an elderly person for all sorts of reasons, and a doctor should always be consulted, as it can often be cured or at least alleviated by proper treatment. To assist with the practical problems, some local authorities operate a laundry service that collects soiled linen, sometimes several times a week. Talk to the health visitor or district nurse (at their local health centre), who will be able to advise about this and other facilities. For more information, see:

B&BF (Bladder and Bowel Foundation):
www.bladderandbowelfoundation.org.

Dementia

Sometimes an elderly person can become confused or forgetful, suffer severe loss of memory or have violent mood swings and at times be abnormally aggressive. It is important to consult a doctor as soon as possible. If dementia is diagnosed, there is ongoing research into finding a cure and there are some treatments that can delay the progression of some forms of dementia.

The most common type of dementia is Alzheimer's disease, which is usually found in people aged over 65. Approximately 24 million people worldwide have dementia, of which the majority of cases (over 60 per cent) are due to Alzheimer's. Clinical signs are characterized by progressive cognitive deterioration, together with a decline in the ability to carry out common daily tasks, and behavioural changes. The first readily identifiable symptoms of Alzheimer's disease are usually short-term memory loss and visual-spatial confusion. This advances to loss of familiar and well-known skills, such as recognition of objects and people.

It is important to consult your doctor as soon as you have concerns. It is also a good idea to talk to the health visitor, as he or she will know about any helpful facilities that may be available locally. The health visitor is also able to arrange appointments with other professionals, such as the community psychiatric nurse and the occupational therapist. People with dementia are still people and the Alzheimer's Society recommends the following tips: Always treat the person with respect and dignity; be a good listener and communicator; remember that little things mean a lot.

Sources of help and support for people with dementia and their carers are:

Alzheimer Scotland: **www.alzscot.org**.

Alzheimer's Society: **www.alzheimers.org.uk**.

Mind: **www.mind.org.uk**.

Chapter Sixteen
No one is immortal

Rooster today, feather duster tomorrow.

PROVERB, QUOTED IN THE *DAILY TELEGRAPH*

What are you doing to prepare yourself for the end of life? How do you think you will cope with old, old age? Baroness Trumpington (born in 1922) is an outstanding example of a nonagenarian. Aged 91, she is the oldest guest ever to have appeared on *Have I Got News for You*. In a recent interview she was reported as saying that one good thing about growing older is that you can get away with more, like saying things you would not have dared when younger. The bad thing, she admits, is not being able to do what you used to: play tennis, dance, sew needlepoint. When asked by her interviewer if she felt age made her wiser, she replied, 'No, but with age you gain a certain clarity. However, there is always the worry about how long before senility sets in.' Her reply to the question, Do you believe in the Pearly Gates, was 'I rather hope not. There are a hell of a lot of people I don't want to see again...'

Facing up to the end of our life is not easy. We know it's inevitable but many people find talking about death difficult, which can make it hard for loved ones to prepare for it, ascertain our wishes and how we would like to be treated. For a number of people approaching the end involves big questions, such as 'Why am I here? What's the real purpose of my life? What happens when I die?' Talking openly to trusted friends, family, health care professionals or spiritual advisers can be helpful in finding answers to some of these big questions. Doing so can help the psychological wellbeing, which in turn can often affect the physical state. Anxious people tense up. Relief from that can lessen physical pain as well as give peace of mind. End of Life Care (EOLC) is the phrase used in the NHS to describe the last year or two of someone's life, before the 'terminal' stage of an illness. Good End of Life Care means that the conditions have been created for people to face the end of their life in comfort and dignity, with the right people nearby. It starts with good communication.

Top tips: Five things you can do to die well:

- Make a will.

- Record your funeral preferences.

- Plan your future care and support.

- Register as an organ donor.

- Tell your loved ones your wishes.

Talking through options and deciding on practical details is so important. It is essentially a matter of making sure everyone who needs to know does, and that the right plan is in place. This could involve a legal document, such as a living will or an advance directive about medical treatment. We all know that we should write a will, but it is one of those things that many of us never seem to get around to. It is estimated that 53 per cent of people die intestate. Not writing a will could mean chaos and money problems for your family or dependants after you've gone. A great deal of heartbreak and real financial worry could be avoided if people are brave enough to broach the subject of dying before it is too late. At the earliest and most appropriate moment, if you can bring yourself and your relatives to have an honest and open discussion about mortality, it could potentially save huge amounts of trouble later on.

Wills

Planning what happens to your money and possessions after your death helps ensure your survivors are financially secure and that the people you want to inherit from you do so. When you retire, there are big changes to your finances as well as to the rest of your life. It is important then to review how your survivors would manage financially if you were to die. Would, in fact, your money and possessions (your 'estate') be passed on as you would wish? (Your estate is everything you own at the time you die, including your share of any joint possessions, less everything you owe.)

Three out of 10 people aged 65 and over die without having made a will. This is called dying 'intestate'. A will is, in its simplest form, a set of instructions about how your estate should be passed on. If you don't have a will, the law makes these decisions for you. This could mean that the wrong people inherit, your home might have to be sold to split the proceeds and your survivors could have extra work and stress. There are five rules of will making:

- The person making the will must be of sound mind.
- The will must be properly executed.
- The will must be correctly witnessed.
- Be clear about what or how much you want to leave and to whom.
- Remember to update your will as your life circumstances change.

Having a will is especially important if you live with an unmarried partner, have remarried, need to provide for someone with a disability, own a business, own property abroad, or your estate is large (ie over the inheritance tax threshold). A will is a legal document that sets out your wishes clearly and unambiguously. Although you can write your own will, it is safer to get a solicitor to do it.

Laws of intestacy

Under the intestacy laws:

- your husband, wife or civil partner and your own children are favoured; this includes a former partner if you are only separated rather than divorced;
- an unmarried partner and stepchildren have no rights;
- your husband, wife or civil partner does not automatically get the whole of your estate;
- possessions, including your home, may have to be sold to split the proceeds between your heirs;
- if you have no partner or children, more distant relatives inherit;
- if you have no relatives, the state gets the lot.

Making a will

You have three choices: you can do it yourself, you can ask your bank to help you, or you can use a solicitor or a specialist will-writing practitioner.

Doing it yourself

Home-made wills are not generally recommended, but provided your affairs are simple, it is possible to do so. You need to set out: who you want to benefit from your will; who should look after any children under 18; who is going to sort out your estate and carry out your wishes after death (your executor); what happens if the people you want to benefit die before you. Two witnesses are needed, and beneficiaries cannot witness a will, nor can the spouses of any beneficiaries. If making your own will, it is sensible to have it checked by a solicitor or by a legal expert from the Citizens Advice Bureau. (You should get legal advice if your will is not straightforward.)

For individuals with sight problems, **RNIB** has some helpful advice. See: **www.rnib.org.uk**.

Banks

Advice on wills and the administration of estates is given by the trustee companies of most of the major high street banks. In particular, the services they offer are to provide general guidance, to act as executor and to administer the estate. They will also introduce clients to a solicitor and keep a copy of the will – plus other important documents – in their safe, to avoid the risk of them being mislaid. Additionally, banks (as solicitors) can give tax planning and other financial guidance, including advice on inheritance tax. Some banks will draw up a will for you.

Solicitors and will-writing specialists

Solicitors may offer to draw up a will, act as executors and administer the estate. Like banks, they will also retain a copy of your will in safe-keeping (most will not charge for storing a will). If you do not have a solicitor, your friends may be able to recommend one, or ask at the Citizens Advice Bureau. The **Law Society** can also provide you with names and addresses, see: **www.lawsociety.org.uk**.

Alternatively, if you simply want help in writing a will, you could consult a specialist will-writing practitioner. The best approach is to contact one of the following organizations:

The Society of Will Writers: **www.willwriters.com**.

Trust Inheritance Limited: **www.trustinheritance.com**.

The Will Bureau: **www.twb.org.uk**.

Charges

A basic will costs around £150 or just under. However, if your affairs are complicated, it could be considerably more. Always ask for an estimate before proceeding. Remember that professional fees normally carry VAT. Many solicitors will give you a fixed-fee estimate for a will. The fees for will-writing practitioners are broadly in line with those of solicitors.

Community Legal Service funding (Legal Aid)

Financial assistance for legal help and advice is available to certain groups of people for making a will. These include people aged over 70, disabled people, and a parent of a disabled person whom the parent wishes to provide for in his or her will. Additionally, to qualify, the people will need to satisfy the financial eligibility criteria. For further information enquire at your Citizens Advice Bureau or other advice centre.

Age UK can help with information on locally based wills and legacy advisers who provide confidential, impartial advice to older people in their own homes about all aspects of making or revising a will. The advice service is available free of charge to anyone of retirement age: **www.ageuk.org**.

Executors

The person who sorts out your property when you die and carries out the instructions in your will is your executor. You can choose whoever you like to do this, but it's important to get the right person and it must be someone over the age of 18. Many people choose their spouse, civil partner or one of their children to be their executor. It is wise to choose two executors: one family member and one professional, such as a solicitor or accountant. It must be someone you trust, and someone who is good at dealing with paperwork. The duties of an executor are many. They might have to deal with the sale of your property so that the people who inherit the proceeds get the most money. They must ensure that the correct amount of Inheritance Tax or Capital Gains Tax gets paid. Family disagreements over how the assets of the deceased are distributed can be commonplace. The executor should have the capability to stay calm when dealing with disgruntled family members over the contents of a will.

When choosing an executor of a will, the following points are worth bearing in mind:

- A spouse as a sole executor is not the best choice, especially if both husband and wife are elderly.

- It is advisable not to appoint benefactors as an executor in case others claim there is a conflict of interests.

- The chosen person should be informed of the decision in order to agree to the role.

- Legally, the executor must be over 18, of sound mind and not in prison when the executor decision is made.

- If conflicts within the family are likely to be a factor, it may be worthwhile appointing more than one executor, or even hiring a professional executor.

- If a family member is chosen, he or she should have the time to carry out all the duties. This can be difficult if the executor does not live in the same part of the country.

Other points

Wills should always be kept in a safe place – and their whereabouts known. You must tell your executor where it is. The most sensible arrangement is for the solicitor to keep the original, and for you and your bank to have a copy each. A helpful initiative devised by the Law Society is a mini-form, known as a personal assets log. This is for individuals drawing up a will to give to their executor or close relatives. It is, quite simply, a four-sided leaflet with space to record essential information: name and address of solicitor; where the will and other important documents, for example share certificates and insurance policies, are kept; the date of any codicils and so on. Logs are obtainable from most solicitors.

Wills may need updating in the event of an important change of circumstances, for example a divorce, a remarriage or the birth of a grandchild. An existing will normally becomes invalid in the event of marriage or remarriage and should be replaced. Any changes must be by codicil (for minor alterations) or by a new will, and must be properly witnessed. The inheritance tax threshold is £325,000 for the 2013/14 tax year – frozen until 2015. If your estate is likely to exceed this amount, it is wise to review your will regularly. Partners who wish to leave all their possessions to each other should consider including a 'survivorship clause' in their wills, as an insurance against the intestacy rules being applied were they both, for example, involved in the same fatal accident. Legal advice is strongly recommended here.

If you have views about your funeral, it is sensible to write a letter to your executors explaining your wishes and to lodge it with your will. If you have any pets, you may equally wish to leave a letter filed with your will explaining what arrangements you have made for their immediate and long-term welfare. Over the years there has been increased interest in advance decision making. For those who would like more information on this matter, there are a number of organizations who can help.

Dignity in Dying: **www.dignityindying.org.uk**.

Dying Matters: **www.dyingmatters.org**.

Say It Once: **www.sayitonce.info**.

If you would be willing to donate an organ that might help save someone else's life, you could indicate this in your will or alternatively obtain an organ donor card. These are available from most hospitals, GP surgeries and chemists.

Inheritance tax points

Inheritance tax (IHT) is a tax on money or possessions you leave behind when you die, and on some gifts you make during your lifetime (see Chapter Four, Tax). There are two main aims to planning inheritance: to make sure your estate is divided as you wish; and to minimize the amount of tax paid on the estate. The particular inheritance planning strategies you adopt will depend largely on your personal intentions and circumstances.

Some ways of reducing IHT include: making tax-free gifts in your will. Bequests to charity and whatever you leave to your spouse or civil partner are tax free. Nearly 75 per cent of people give to charity during their lifetime, but only 7 per cent include a charitable legacy in their will. The government has changed the tax law reducing the inheritance tax payable on estates that give at least 10 per cent to charity. It is called Legacy 10, and anyone who does this will have the remainder of their estate taxed at 36 per cent instead of the usual 40 per cent IHT tax rate.

Charities have welcomed the move, as have many will-writers. Existing wills can be amended by codicil to include the 10 per cent provision providing the wording is precise enough to make the donor's wishes clear, yet not mention exact amounts because they won't know the size of their eventual estate. There is, however, no advantage to people with estates below the inheritance tax threshold.

Examples of IHT-free gifts:

1 Gifts you make during your lifetime:

   ● up to £3,000 a year of any gifts (or £6,000 if you did not use last year's allowance);

   ● £250 a year to any number of people;

   ● gifts on marriage up to £5,000 if you are a parent of the bride or groom and smaller sums for anyone else;

   ● gifts that form a regular pattern of spending from your income;

   ● gifts for the maintenance of your family;

   ● gifts to any person, provided you survive for seven years after making the gift.

2 Gifts you make during your lifetime or on death:

   ● gifts to your husband, wife or civil partner (in most cases);

   ● gifts to charities.

Useful reading

Will Information Pack, from Age UK; see: **www.ageuk.org.uk**. *How to Write Your Will* (the complete guide to structuring your will, inheritance tax planning, probate and administering an estate), by Marlene Garsia, published by Kogan Page; see: **www.koganpage.com**.

Provision for dependent adult children

A particular concern for parents with a physically or mentally dependent son or daughter is what plans they can make to ensure his or her care when they are no longer in a position to manage. There is no easy answer, as each case varies according to the severity of the disability or illness, the range of helpful voluntary or statutory facilities locally, and the extent to which they, as parents, can provide for their child's financial security long term. While social services may be able to advise, parents thinking ahead might do better to consult a specialist organization experienced in helping carers in this situation to explore the possible options available to them. Useful addresses are:

Carers UK: **www.carersuk.org**.

Carers Trust: **www.carers.org**.

Parents concerned about financial matters such as setting up a trust or making alternative provision in their will would also be advised to consult a solicitor or accountant.

Money and other worries – and how to minimize them

Many people say that the first time they really think about death, in terms of what would happen to their nearest and dearest, is after the birth of their first baby. As children grow up, requirements change, but key points that anyone with a family should consider – and review from time to time – include life insurance and mortgage protection. Both husbands and wives should have life insurance cover. If either were to die, not only would the partner lose the financial benefit of the other's earnings, but the partner would also lose immeasurably in other ways. Most banks and building societies urge homeowners to take out mortgage protection schemes. If you die, the loan is paid off automatically and the family home will not be repossessed. Banks also offer insurance to cover any personal or other loans. This could be a vital safeguard to avoid leaving the family with debts.

Funeral plans

Many people worry about funeral costs. They can be expensive, costing several thousands of pounds. To avoid worrying about not having enough money to cover your funeral costs, a funeral plan is a way of paying for a future funeral today. How they work: you pay either a lump sum or instalments to the plan provider, or to a funeral director. The money is invested either into a trust fund with trustees, or in an insurance policy, the money being used to pay for the funeral whenever that is. The aim is to safeguard your money until it's needed, and ensure it is used to pay for the funeral you've paid for.

Because trust funds and insurance policies are already regulated, the money you pay into these funds is protected by compensation arrangements.

Plan providers can register with the Funeral Planning Authority (FPA) if they agree to meet its rules and code of conduct. You can find a list of registered plan providers from **The Funeral Planning Authority: www.funeralplanningauthority.com**.

If you take out a funeral plan, make sure you have a written record of the arrangements and keep it safe. You should receive a plan confirmation. Make sure your next of kin knows you have already paid for your funeral and what the details are. Check to see that the plan provider has a clear complaints procedure and is a member of the FPA. Members must follow its standards when dealing with you and when considering any complaints.

The following organizations offer funeral plans:

Age UK: **www.ageuk.org.uk**.

Co-operative Funeralcare: **www.co-operative.coop/Funeralcare/**.

Dignity Caring Funeral Services: **www.dignityfuneralplans.co.uk**.

Golden Charter: **www.golden-charter.co.uk**.

Perfect Choice Funeral Plans: **www.perfectchoicefunerals.com**.

Those in receipt of Income Support, Pension Credit, Housing Benefit or Council Tax Benefit may qualify for a payment from the Social Fund to help with funeral costs. For details of eligibility and how you claim, see website: **www.gov.uk** – Bereavement benefits.

Dealing with a death

A very real crisis for some families is the need for immediate money while waiting for the estate to be settled. At least part of the problem can be overcome by couples having a joint bank account, with both partners having drawing rights without the signature of the other being required. Sole-name bank accounts and joint accounts requiring both signatures are frozen. For the same reason, it may also be a good idea for any savings or investments to be held in the joint name of the couple. Additionally, any financial and other important documents should be discussed together and understood by both parties. Both partners need to know where important papers are kept.

When someone dies, the bank manager should be notified as soon as possible so he or she can assist with the problems of unpaid bills and help work out a solution until the estate is settled. The same goes for the suppliers of essential services: gas, electricity, telephone and so on. Unless they know the situation, there is a risk of services being cut off if there is a delay in paying the bill. Add, too, any credit card companies, where if bills lie neglected the additional interest could mount up alarmingly.

Normally, you must register the death within the first five days (eight in Scotland). Your local registrar can be found on the government website: **www.gov.uk**. You will need to take to the registrar's office the medical certificate issued by the doctor who attended the death, and if possible, the deceased's medical card, birth certificate and any marriage or civil partnership certificate. The registrar will give you:

- a certificate allowing cremation or burial to go ahead; give this to the funeral director you appoint;

- a certificate to give to the Jobcentre Plus or the Pension Service, if the deceased had been getting state benefits or pensions;

- a leaflet with details of bereavement benefits you may be able to claim;

- one or more death certificates, for which there is a fee. You normally need to send a death certificate to each provider of pensions, life insurance, savings and investments that the deceased had. It is cheaper to buy extra certificates straight away than later.

For more information on what to do after a death, see the government website: **www.gov.uk**.

Registering a death is upsetting, and dealing with a death involves more paperwork and phone calls than a family wants to deal with at such a time. A new scheme, the **Tell Us Once** service, means people need make just one appointment with their local registrar, who can then advise 28 different services of the changed circumstances, including all state pensions and benefits through the Department for Work and Pensions, and HMRC, passports, driving licences, council tax, local library, Blue Badge and social services. See: **www.gov.uk/tell-us-once**.

Another organization that may be able to help you after a loved one has died has one aim: to reduce the amount of direct mail to those who are deceased. Originally launched in the UK in 2000, this service has since expanded into France and Canada. Coming to terms with the loss of a loved one takes time; receiving direct mail bearing the name of the deceased is often painful and unnecessary. For more information see:

The Bereavement Register: **www.the-bereavement-register.org.uk**.

Useful reading

What to Do after a Death, a free booklet, from any social security office, and *Planning for a Funeral*, a free fact sheet from Age UK, website: **www.ageuk.org.uk**.

State benefits and tax

Several extra financial benefits are given to widowed people. Most take the form of a cash payment. However, there are one or two tax and other points that it may be useful to know.

Benefits paid in cash form

There are three important cash benefits to which widowed people may be entitled: Bereavement Benefit, Bereavement Allowance and Widowed Parent's Allowance. These have replaced the former widow's benefits, as all benefits are now payable on equal terms to men and women alike. To find out more information see website: **www.gov.uk** – Bereavement benefits. You will be given a questionnaire (BD8) by the registrar when you register the death. It is important that you complete this, as it acts as a trigger to speed up payment of your benefits.

Bereavement Benefit

This is a tax-free lump sum of £2,000, paid as soon as people are widowed, provided that: the widowed person's spouse had paid sufficient NI Contributions; the widowed person is under state retirement age; or if over state retirement age, the widowed person's husband or wife had not been entitled to retirement pension.

Bereavement Allowance

Bereavement Allowance is for those aged between 45 and state pension age who do not receive Widowed Parent's Allowance. It is payable for

52 weeks and, as with widow's pension before, there are various levels of payment: the full rate and age-related allowance. Receipt in all cases is dependent on sufficient NI Contributions having been paid.

Full-rate Bereavement Allowance is paid to widowed people between the ages of 55 and 59 inclusive. Age-related Bereavement Allowance is for younger widows or widowers who do not qualify for the full rate. Bereavement Allowance is normally paid automatically once you have sent off your completed form BB1, so if for any reason you do not receive it you should enquire at your social security office. In the event of your being ineligible, owing to insufficient NICs having been paid, you may still be entitled to receive Income Support, Housing Benefit or a grant or loan from the Social Fund. See website: **www.gov.uk** – Bereavement benefits.

Widowed Parent's Allowance

This is paid to widowed parents with at least one child for whom they receive Child Benefit. The allowance is usually paid automatically. If for some reason, although eligible, you do not receive the money, you should inform your social security office.

Retirement pension

Once a widowed person reaches state retirement age, he or she should receive a state pension in the normal way. An important point to re-member is that a widow or widower may be able to use the late spouse's NICs to boost the amount he or she receives. See leaflet RM1, *Retirement – A Guide to Benefits for People Who Are Retiring or Have Retired.*

Problems

Both pension payments and bereavement benefits are dependent on sufficient NICs having been paid. Your social security office will inform you if you are not eligible. If this should turn out to be the case, you may still be entitled to receive Income Support, Housing Benefit, Council Tax Benefit or a grant or loan from the Social Fund. If you are unsure of your position or have difficulties, ask at your Citizens Advice Bureau, which will at least be able to help you work out the sums and inform you of your rights. See website: **www.citizensadvice.org.uk**.

Particular points to note

Most widowed people's benefits are taxable. However, the £2,000 Bereavement Benefit is tax free, as are pensions paid to the widows or widowers of armed forces personnel. Widowed people will normally be able to inherit their spouse's additional pension rights if they contributed to SERPS (see the note below) and/or the Second State Pension (S2P), or at least half their guaranteed minimum pension, if their spouse was in a contracted-out scheme. Additionally, where applicable, all widowed people are entitled on retirement to half the graduated pension earned by their husband or wife.

NB: SERPS benefits paid to surviving spouses are due to be halved over the coming years. Anyone over state pension age before 6 October 2002 is exempt from any cuts and will keep the right to pass on his or her SERPS pension in full to a bereaved spouse. Equally, any younger widower or widow who inherited his or her late spouse's SERPS entitlement before 6 October 2002 will not be affected and will continue to receive the full amount.

Women in receipt of widow's pension who remarry, or live with a man as his wife, lose their entitlement to the payment unless the cohabitation ends, in which case they can claim it again. If a woman is aged over 60, the fact that she is living with a man will not affect her entitlement to a retirement pension based on her late husband's contribution record. Widows and widowers of armed forces personnel whose deaths were a direct result of their service are now entitled to keep their armed forces attributable pension for life, regardless of whether they remarry or cohabit.

Tax allowances

Widows and widowers receive the normal single person's tax allowance of £9,440 and, if in receipt of Married Couple's Allowance, are also entitled to any unused portion of the allowance in the year of their partner's death.

Advice

Many people have difficulty in working out exactly what they are entitled to and how to claim it. The Citizens Advice Bureau is always very helpful. Additionally, Cruse and the National Association of Widows (see below) can assist you.

Organizations that can help

People deal with bereavement in various ways. For some, money problems seem to dominate everything. For others the hardest thing to bear is the loneliness of returning to an empty house. For older people who have been part of a couple for decades, widowhood creates a great gulf where for a while there is no real sense of purpose. Many widowed men and women go through a spell of feeling enraged against their partner for dying. Talking to other people who know the difficulties from their own experience can be a tremendous help. The following organizations not only offer opportunities for companionship but also provide an advisory and support service:

Cruse Bereavement Care: **www.cruse.org.uk**.

The National Association of Widows: **www.widows.uk.net**.

Many professional and other groups offer a range of services for widows and widowers associated with them. These include:

The Civil Service Retirement Fellowship: **www.csrf.org.uk**.

The War Widows Association of Great Britain: **www.warwidows.org.uk**.

Many local Age UK groups offer a counselling service. Trade unions are often particularly supportive, as are Rotary Clubs, all the armed forces organizations and most benevolent societies.

Directory of useful organizations and contacts

Benefits advice

Age UK, Tavis House, 1–6 Tavistock Square, London WC1H 9NA, tel: 0800 169 6565, website: **www.ageuk.org.uk**.

Citizens Advice Bureau (England, Wales and Northern Ireland), **www.citizensadvice.org.uk**; **www.adviceguide.org.uk**.

Citizens Advice Scotland, website: **www.cas.org.uk**.

Money Advice Scotland, tel: 0141 572 0237, website: **www.moneyadvicescotland.org.uk**.

Advice NI (Northern Ireland), tel: 028 9064 5919, website: **www.adviceni.net**.

Government benefits adviser, website: **www.gov.uk/benefits-adviser**.

Turn2us, to identify potential sources of funding for those facing financial difficulty, website: **www.turn2us.org.uk**.

Debt

Citizens Advice Bureau, free independent debt advice in England, Wales and Northern Ireland, website: **www.citizensadvice.org.uk**.

Citizens Advice Scotland, website: **www.cas.org.uk**.

Money Advice Scotland, tel: 0141 572 0237, website: **www.moneyadvicescotland.org.uk**.

National Debtline, tel: 0808 808 4000, website: **www.nationaldebtline.co.uk**.

National Debtline NI (Northern Ireland), tel: 0808 808 4000, website: **www.nationaldebtline.co.uk/northern-ireland/php**.

National Debtline Scotland, tel: 0808 808 4000, website: **www.nationaldebtline.co.uk/scotland/**.

Step Change Debt Charity: tel: 0800 138 1111, website: **www.stepchange.org**.

Debt Test, Money Advice Service: tel: 0300 500 5000 **www.moneyadviceservice.org.uk**.

Pay Plan, tel: 0800 280 2816, website: **www.payplan.com**.

Disabilities

Age UK, tel: 0800 169 6565, website: **www.ageuk.org.uk**.

Attendance Allowance and Disability Living Allowance, Disability Benefits Helpline tel: 08457 123 456.

Benefit Enquiry Line (for general enquiries and claim forms for disability and carer benefits), tel: 0800 882 200 (textphone 0800 243 355).

Carer's Allowance Unit, tel: 0845 608 4321 (textphone 0845 604 5312).

Free Tax Disc, tel: 0300 123 4321, website: **www.gov.uk/tax-disc**.

Pensions, Disability and Carers Service for Disability Living Allowance and Attendance Allowance (existing claims), tel: 08457 123 456.

Pension Credit, tel: 0800 99 1234, website: **www.gov.uk/pension-credit**.

Social Fund grants and loans, Jobcentre Plus (Great Britain), tel: 0800 055 6688, website: **www.gov.uk/contact-jobcentre-plus**.

Winter Fuel Payment Helpline, tel: 08459 15 15 15, website: **www.gov.uk/winter-fuel-payment-helpline**.

Energy-saving advice and grants

ACT ON CO_2 Advice Line, tel: 0800 512 012.

Energy Saving Trust, tel: 0300 123 1234, website: **www.energysavingtrust.org.uk**.

Warm Front (England), tel: 0800 316 2805, website: **www.gov.uk/warm-front-scheme**.

Warm Zone, website: **www.warmzones.co.uk**.

NEST (Wales Fuel Poverty Scheme), tel: 0808 808 2244, website: **www.nestwales.org.uk**.

Scotland – Energy Assistance Packages, tel: 0800 512 012, website: **www.scotland.gov.uk** – Home Energy Efficiency Programmes for Scotland.

Warm Homes Scheme (Northern Ireland), tel: 0800 988 0559, website: **www.warm-homes.com**.

To compare fuel deals, tel: 08454 04 05 06, website: **www.consumerfutures.org.uk**; or **www.cheapestoil.co.uk**.

Funeral and inheritance tax planning

Bereavement Register, tel: 0800 082 1230, website: **www.the-bereavement-register.com**.

Funeral Planning Authority Ltd, Knellstone House, Udimore, Rye, East Sussex TN31 6AR, tel: 0845 601 9619, website: **www.funeralplanningauthority.com**.

HMRC Probate and Inheritance Tax Helpline: tel: 0845 302 0900; website: **www.hmrc.gov.uk/inheritancetax/**.

For inheritance tax advice

Society of Trust and Estate Practitioners (STEP), Artillery House (South), 11–19 Artillery Road, London SW1P 1RT, tel: 020 7340 0500, website: **www.step.org**.

To register a death

General Register Office (England and Wales), website: **www.gro.gov.uk**; Scotland: **www.gro-scotland.gov.uk**; Northern Ireland: **www.nidirect.gov.uk/general-register-office-for-northern-ireland**.

To obtain a copy of the government booklet: 'What to do after a death': England and Wales: website: **www.gov.uk** – Death and bereavement; Scotland: **www.scotland.gov.uk**; Northern Ireland: **www.nidirect.gov.uk**.

Health and health care

Free prescriptions and other health benefits in UK, free booklet: HC11 'Help with Health Costs' from your GP or pharmacies, website: **www.nhs.uk/NHSEngland/Healthcosts/**.

For Scotland: free booklet HCS2 'Help with health costs', website: **www.scotland.gov.uk** – Publications.

Prescription pre-payment certificates (England), tel: 0845 850 0030; website: **www.nhsbsa.nhs.uk/1127.aspx**; Scotland: **www.psd.scot.nhs.uk/doctors/prepayment-certificates.html**.

In Northern Ireland and Wales prescriptions are free.

Holidays

To apply for a European Health Insurance Card (EHIC) Pick up a form at the Post Office or tel: 0300 3301 350, website: **www.nhs.uk/NHSEngland/Healthcareabroad/EHIC**.

House and home

For details about local Domestic Energy Assessors see EPC Register; website: **www.epcregister.com**.

For a free and impartial home energy check visit Energy Saving Trust; tel: 0300 123 1234, website: **www.energysavingtrust.org.uk**.

To find an independent surveyor/valuer

Royal Institute of Chartered Surveyors, tel: 0870 333 1600, website: **www.rics.org/uk**.

For help with property

The National Association of Estate Agents (NAEA) runs a service called 'PropertyLive', a network of estate agents providing access to a professional, friendly property service. See website: **www.Propertylive.co.uk**.

For protection

The Property Ombudsman scheme provides an independent review service for buyers or sellers of UK residential property in the event of a complaint. See website: **www.tpos.co.uk**.

Help for the elderly

Elderly Accommodation Counsel, Third Floor, 89 Albert Embankment, London SE1 7TP, tel: 0800 377 7070, website: **www.eac.org.uk; www.firststopadvice.org.uk; www.housingcare.org.uk**.

Independent Age, 6 Avonmore Road, London W14 8RL. tel: 0845 262 1863, website: **www.eac.org.uk; www.independentage.org**.

The Telephone Preference Service (TPS): You can register your phone number with the telephone preference service by calling 0845 070 0707 or you can do this online at **www.tpsonline.org.uk**.

Home improvement agencies

England – Foundations, tel: 0845 864 5201, website: **www.foundations.uk.com**.

Wales – Care & Repair Cymru, tel: 029 2067 4830, website: **www.careandrepair.org.uk**.

Scotland – Care & Repair Forum Scotland, tel: 0141 221 9879, website: **www.careandrepairscotland.co.uk**.

Northern Ireland – Fold Housing Association, tel: 028 9042 8314, website: **www.foldgroup.co.uk**.

Help for tenants

Association of Retirement Housing Managers (ARHM): c/o EAC, 3rd Floor, 89 Albert Embankment, London SE1 7TP. Tel: 020 7463 0660. Website: **www.arhm.org**.

Leasehold Advisory Service; tel: 0207 383 9800, website: **www.lease-advice.org**.

Landmark Leasehold Advisory Services Ltd specializes in providing legal services to residential leaseholders of England and Wales; see website: **www.landmarklease.com**.

Department for Communities and Local Government for advice on leasehold legislation and policy, tel: 0303 444 0000, website: **www.gov.uk/governemnt/organisations/department-for-communities-and-local-government**.

Independent financial advice

To find an Independent Financial Adviser

IFA Promotion/Unbiased.co.uk, website: **www.unbiased.co.uk**.

Institute of Financial Planning, One Redcliff Street, Bristol, BS1 6NP. Website: **www.financialplanning.org.uk**.

Personal Finance Society (PFS), website: **www.findanadviser.org**.

Financial Conduct Authority (formerly the FSA), 25 The North Colonnade, London E14 5HS, tel: 0800 111 6768, website: **www.fca.org.uk**.

Financial Ombudsman Service, South Quay Plaza, 183 Marsh Wall, London E14 9SR, tel: 0300 123 9123 or 0800 0234 567, website: **www.financial-ombudsman.org.uk**.

Financial Services Compensation Scheme, 10th Floor, Beaufort House, 15 St Botolph Street, London EC3A 7QU. tel: 0800 678 1100, website: **www.fscs.org.uk**.

Ethical Investment Research Service (EIRIS Foundation) Website: **www.yourethicalmoney.org**. Information about product providers and other sources that provide ethical investments.

MyLocalAdviser: **www.mylocaladviser.co.uk**. For financial advisers in your area.

Society of Later Life Advisers tel: 0845 303 2902; website: **www.societyoflaterlifeadvisers.co.uk**.

To find a stockbroker

See London Stock Exchange website: **www.londonstockexchange.com**, or the Association of Private Client Investment Managers and Stockbrokers (APCIMS) website: **www.apcims.co.uk**.

To find equity release providers

Equity Release Council incorporating SHIP standards:
   3rd Floor, Bush House, North West Wing, Aldwych, London WC2B
   4PJ, tel: 0844 669 7085. Website: **www.equityreleasecouncil.com**.

To find a tax adviser

Chartered Institute of Taxation, 1st Floor, Artillery House, 11–19
   Artillery Row, London SW1P 1RT. tel: 0844 579 6700,
   website: **www.tax.org.uk**.

Insurance

Association of British Insurers, 51 Gresham Street, London EC2V
   7HQ. Tel: 020 7600 3333 for advice and information on insurance:
   website: **www.abi.org.uk**.

Association of Medical Insurance Intermediaries (AMII), Suites 21–24,
   The North Colchester Business Centre, 340 The Crescent, Colchester
   CO4 9AD, tel: 01206 848 443. Website: **www.amii.org.uk**.

To check whether you have enough buildings insurance: The Building
   Cost Information Service of the RICS, Parliament Square, London
   SW1P 3AD. Tel: 020 7695 1500, website: **www.bcis.co.uk**.

To check a car's insurance group, **www.carpages.co.uk**;
   www.checkthatcar.com.

British Insurance Brokers Association (BIBA), to find an insurance broker,
   Consumer Helpline: 0870 950 1790, website: **www.biba.org.uk**.

Legal

To find a solicitor

Law Society, 113 Chancery Lane, London WC2A 1PL,
   tel: 0870 606 2555, website: **www.lawsociety.org.uk**.

Law Society of Scotland, 26 Drumsheugh Gardens, Edinburgh EH3
   7YR, tel: 0131 226 7411, website: **www.lawscot.org.uk**.

Law Society of Northern Ireland, 96 Victoria Street, Belfast BT1 3GN, tel: 028 9023 1614, website: **www.lawsoc-ni.org**.

Community Legal Advice (CLA). People living on a low income or benefits may be eligible for legal aid to get free specialist advice from qualified legal advisers. Tel: 0845 345 4345. See website: **www.justice.gov.uk/legal-aid/**.

Solicitors for Independent Financial Advice (SIFA), is the trade body for solicitor financial advisers. Its membership now also includes accountancy IFAs as members; see website: **www.sifa.co.uk**.

For Complaints about a legal services adviser: see Legal Services Ombudsman. Tel: 0300 555 0300. See Website: **www.legalombudsman.org.uk**.

Making a will

Institute of Professional Willwriters, Trinity Point, New Road, Halesowen, West Midlands, B63 3HY, tel: 0345 257 2570, website: **www.ipw.org.uk**.

Power of Attorney

Office of the Public Guardian, England and Wales, PO Box 16185, Birmingham B2 2WH. Tel: 0300 456 0300, website: **www.justice.gov.uk** – Office of the Public Guardian.

Office of the Public Guardian, Scotland, tel: 01324 678 300, website: **www.publicguardian-scotland.gov.uk**.

Office of Care and Protection, Northern Ireland, tel: 028 9032 8594, website: **www.courtsni.gov.uk**.

Leisure

Free digital TV channels

Freeview, website: **www.ukfree.tv/allchannels**; **www.freeview.co.uk**.

Freesat, PO Box 6296, London W1A 3FF. Tel: 0845 313 0051, website: **www.freesat.co.uk**.

Free bus travel

England and Wales, your local council or website:
www.gov.uk/apply-for-elderly-person-bus-pass.

Scotland, your local council or website: **www.transportscotland.gov.uk/
public-transport/concessionary-travel**.

Northern Ireland, your local council or website:
www.nidirect.gov.uk/free-bus-travel-and-concessions.

Cheap rail and coach travel

Rail travel in the UK, buy a Senior Railcard in UK from rail stations
or some travel agents, or tel: 0844 871 4036, website:
www.senior-railcard.co.uk.

Rail travel in Europe: Rail Europe Ltd, tel: 0844 48 4078,
website: **www.raileurope.co.uk**.

For cheap coach travel: National Express, tel: 0871 781 8178,
website: **www.nationalexpress.com**.

Money

For information and advice on money matters: Money Advice Service:
0300 500 5000, website: **www.moneyadviceservice.org.uk**.

To trace lost savings: Get a claim form from any bank or building
society, library or Citizens Advice, or see website:
www.mylostaccount.org.uk.

To trace lost investments: Unclaimed Assets Register, tel: 0844 481 81
80, website: **www.uar.co.uk**.

Internet comparison sites: **www.comparethemarket.com;
www.confused.com; www.moneyfacts.com;
www.moneysupermarket.com; www.which.co.uk/switch;
www.uswitch.com**.

Pensions

State Pension Forecasting website:
www.gov.uk/state-pension-statement.

The Pension Service for any query regarding State Pension, if you live in the UK, tel: 0845 606 0265. If you are within four months of your State Pension age and have not received your claim pack and you live in the UK: tel: 0800 731 7898

If you live abroad, The International Pension Centre, Tyneview Park, Whitley Road, Newcastle upon Tyne NE98 1BA, tel: 0191 218 7777, website: **www.gov.uk** – State pension.

To check your State Pension age: website: **www.gov.uk** – State pension.

Pension Tracing Service, Tyneview Park, Whitley Road, Newcastle upon Tyne NE98 1BA, tel: 0845 600 2537, website: **www.gov.uk** – Workplace and personal pensions.

Pensions Advisory Service for any help understanding your pension rights, tel: 0845 601 2923, website: **www.pensionsadvisoryservice.org.uk**.

Pensions Ombudsman website: **www.pensions-ombudsman.org.uk**.

Pension Protection Fund (PPF), Knollys House, 7 Addiscombe Road, Croydon, Surrey, tel: 0845 600 2541; website: **www.pensionprotectionfund.org.uk**.

Money Advice Service has comparison tables, if you wish to shop around for an annuity, website: **www.moneyadviceservice.org.uk/tables**.

Service Personnel & Veterans Agency Service to claim a war widow or widower's pension, tel: 0800 169 2277, website: **www.veterans-uk.info**.

Society of Later Life Advisers, tel: 0845 303 2909, website: **www.societyoflaterlifeadvisers.co.uk**.

Age UK Annuity Service, tel: 0800 023 2748, website: **www.ageuk.org.uk**.

Savings and investments

To find a credit union

Association of British Credit Unions Ltd (ABCUL), tel: 0161 832 3694, website: **www.abcul.org**.

Ace Credit Union Services, tel: 0191 276 3737, website: **www.aceus.org**.

Scottish League of Credit Unions, tel: 0141 774 5020, website: **www.scottishcu.org**.

UK Credit Unions, tel: 01706 214 322, website: **www.ukcu.co.uk**.

To compare savings accounts

Money Advice Service, tel: 0300 500 5000, website:
www.moneyadviceservice.org.uk/tables.

To find out about investment funds

Unit trusts and open-ended investment companies: Investment
Management Association (IMA), tel: 020 7831 0898, website:
www.investmentfunds.org.uk.

Investment trusts: Association of Investment Companies,
tel: 0207 282 5555, website: www.theaic.co.uk.

Life insurance funds: Association of British Insurers, website:
www.abi.org.uk.

Ethical investments: Ethical Investment Research Service, website:
www.eiris.org.

To report suspected investment scams

If you spot a scam or have been scammed, report it and get help.
Contact the Police's Action Fraud team on 0300 123 2040 or online
at www.actionfraud.police.uk or the Police in your area.

Tax

Free help with tax problems if your income is low

Tax Aid, website: www.taxaid.org.uk.

Tax Help for Older People, Unit 10, Pineapple Business Park, Salway
Ash, Bridport, Dorset DT6 5DB, tel: 0845 601 3321, or
0130 848 8066, website: www.taxvol.org.uk.

For tax help and advice

Association of Taxation Technicians, 1st Floor, Artillery House,
11–19 Artillery Row, London SW1P 1RT, tel: 0207 340 0551,
website: www.att.org.uk.

Chartered Institute of Taxation, 1st Floor, Artillery House, 11–19 Artillery Row, London SW1P 1RT. tel: 0844 579 6700, website: **www.tax.org.uk.**

Association of Chartered Certified Accountants, 29 Lincoln's Inn Fields, London WC2A 3EE, tel: 020 7059 5000, website: **www.acca.co.uk.**

Institute of Chartered Accountants in England and Wales, PO Box 433, Chartered Accountants' Hall, Moorgate Place, London EC2R 6EA, tel: 020 7920 8100, website: **www.icaew.co.uk.**

Institute of Chartered Accountants in Ireland, Chartered Accountants House, 47–49 Pearse Street, Dublin 2, Republic of Ireland, tel: 00353 1 637 7200, website: **www.icae.ie.**

Institute of Chartered Accountants of Scotland, CA House, 21 Haymarket Yards, Edinburgh EH12 5BH, tel: 0131 347 0100, website: **www.icas.org.uk.**

HM Revenue & Customs for local enquiry centres, see website **www.hmrc.gov.uk.** For your local tax office, see your tax return, other tax correspondence or check with your employer or scheme paying you a pension.

Contact the Adjudicator's Office for information about referring a complaint. The Adjudicator acts as a fair and unbiased referee looking into complaints about HMRC, including the Tax Credit Office, the Valuation Office and the Office of the Public Guardian and the Insolvency Service. The Adjudicator's Office, PO Box 10280, Nottingham, NG2 9PF. Tel: 0300 057 1111. See website: **www.adjudicatorsoffice.gov.uk.**

If you have received a HMRC related phishing/bogus e-mail, please forward it to the following e-mail address and then delete it: **phishing@hmrc.gsi.gov.uk.**

HMRC Helplines

Claiming back tax on savings income: tel: 0845 366 7850.

Registering for gross interest on savings: tel: 0845 980 0645.

Self-assessment: tel: 0845 900 0444.

Tax Credit Helpline: tel: 0845 300 3900.

Volunteering

To find out about how to volunteering across UK

REACH: **www.reachskills.org.uk**.

Volunteer Development Scotland: **www.vds.org.uk**.

Volunteering England: **www.volunteering.org.uk**.

Wales Council for Voluntary Action: **www.wcva.org.uk**.

Leading volunteering organizations

British Red Cross: **www.redcross.org.uk**.

Citizens Advice Bureau: **www.citizensadvice.org.uk**.

Community Service Volunteers (CSV): **www.csv.org.uk**.

Lions Clubs International: **www.lionsmd105.org**.

Toc H: **www.toch-uk.org.uk**.

WRVS: **www.wrvs.org.uk**.

Checks for volunteering

Disclosure and Barring Service (formerly Criminal Records Bureau):
Tel: 0870 909 0811. Website: **www.gov.uk/disclosure-barring-service**.

Work

To find out about rights at work

Advisory, Conciliation and Arbitration Service (ACAS) Great Britain,
tel: 0845 747 4747, website: **www.acas.org.uk**.

Labour Relations Service (Northern Ireland), tel: 028 9032 1442,
website: **www.lra.org.uk**.

Jobcentre Plus (Great Britain), website: **www.gov.uk/jobsearch**.

Local Jobs and Benefits Office (Northern Ireland), tel: 0800 353 530,
website: **www.nidirect.gov.uk/jobs-and-benefits-offices**.

Careers Advice Service (UK), tel: 0800 100 900,
https://nationalcareersservice.direct.gov.uk.

Skills Development Scotland, tel: 0800 917 8000, website:
www.skillsdevelopmentscotland.co.uk.

Careers Wales, tel: 0800 100 900, website: **www.careerswales.com**.

LearnDirect UK (except Scotland), tel: 0800 101 901, website:
www.learndirect.co.uk.

Professional Contractors Group (PCG): **www.pcg.org.uk**.

Recruitment and Employment Confederation, tel: 020 7009 2100,
website: **www.rec.uk.com**.

To register a new business

HM Revenue & Customs (HMRC), Newly Self-employed Helpline,
tel: 0845 915 4515, website: **www.hmrc.gov.uk**.

Companies House, tel: 0303 1234 500, website:
www.companieshouse.gov.uk.

HMRC Business Education & Support Team provides free training
events aimed at start-up businesses and on how to run a payroll:
www.hmrc.gov.uk/bst/index.htm.

Organizations providing free or subsidized help

Government resources

www.gov.uk contains the government's online resource for businesses.

Regional or country-specific support is also available at:

Regional help – **www.nationalenterprisenetwork.org**.

Northern Ireland – at **www.nibusinessinfo.co.uk**.

Scotland – at **www.business.scotland.gov.uk**.

Wales – at **www.business.wales.gov.uk**.

Start up Britain has been set up by the government to help you find
information about starting a business and contains offers and
discounts available to new business start-ups: **www.startupbritain.org**.

PRIME (The Prince's Initiative for Mature Enterprise) helps people over
the age of 50 set up in business for themselves: **www.prime.org.uk**.

Index

NB: page numbers in *italic* indicate figures or tables

Also available from **Kogan Page**

Find out more; visit **www.koganpage.com** and
sign up for offers and regular e-newsletters.

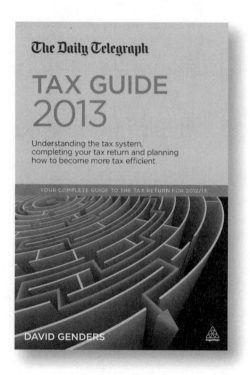